POWWOWING AMONG THE PENNSYLVANIA DUTCH

The Pennsylvania State University Press
University Park, Pennsylvania

POWWOWING AMONG THE Pennsylvania Dutch

A TRADITIONAL MEDICAL PRACTICE IN THE MODERN WORLD

David W. Kriebel

LIBRARY OF CONGRESS/CATALOGING-IN-PUBLICATION DATA

Kriebel, David W., 1961–
Powwowing among the Pennsylvania Dutch : a traditional medical practice in the modern world / David W. Kriebel.
p. cm.—(Pennsylvania German history and culture series ; no. 8)
(Publications of the Pennsylvania German Society ; v. 41)
Includes bibliographical references (p.) and index.
ISBN 9780271032139 (cloth : alk. paper)
1. German Americans—Pennsylvania—Folklore.
2. German Americans—Pennsylvania—Rites and ceremonies.
3. German Americans—Pennsylvania—Medicine.
4. Traditional medicine—Pennsylvania.
I. Title.

GR111.G47K75 2007
398.0893′1—dc22
2007026361

Printed in the United States of America
Published by
The Pennsylvania State University Press,
University Park, PA 16802–1003

The Pennsylvania State University Press
is a member of the
Association of American University Presses.

It is the policy of
The Pennsylvania State University Press
to use acid-free paper. This book is printed on Natures Natural,
containing 50% post-consumer
waste, and meets the minimum requirements of American
National Standard for Information Sciences—Permanence
of Paper for Printed Library Material,
ANSI Z39.48–1992.

CONTENTS

PREFACE

This is a book about an old practice that many people, including scholars, had believed to be extinct but that is still alive in the farmlands and hills of Pennsylvania Dutch country. My work concerns the area of southeastern and south-central Pennsylvania, but powwowing—*Brauche* or *Braucherei*, in the Pennsylvania Dutch dialect—is probably still being practiced in other areas of the United States and Canada where Pennsylvania Dutch people have settled.

It is important to distinguish Pennsylvania Dutch powwowing from the "powwows" of the various indigenous peoples known as American Indians or Native Americans. There may be some etymological connection—perhaps settlers who were not Pennsylvania Dutch observed these practices and saw them as similar to those of the indigenous people—but the origin of the term "powwow" as applied to *Brauche* remains obscure. In this book I have chosen to refer to the practice as "powwowing" rather than as *Brauche*, because "powwow" will be more familiar to many readers. Because my interviews were conducted in English, that was also the way most of my consultants referred to the practice, although sometimes I had to clarify what I meant by using the dialect term.

My use of the term "consultant" requires some clarification. The bulk of my work is based on ethnographic fieldwork, with the data deriving from observation and interaction with real people. The traditional term used by anthropologists and others conducting such fieldwork is "informant," but because many of my readers may be unfamiliar with this usage, I wanted to avoid any jarring initial associations with police informants. I considered the term "tradition-bearer," but rejected it because many of the people I spoke with cannot be considered to carry on a tradition associated with powwowing yet provided useful leads or background information. I settled on the term "consultant," a term used by some folklorists, because it better conveys my own relationship with the people who were kind enough to help me with this project. They are the real experts, and I am their grateful student.

I have chosen to use the term "Pennsylvania Dutch" rather than the more accurate "Pennsylvania German" when referring to the people and their subculture and dialect. The reason for this is twofold: nearly all my consultants used that term when referring to themselves, and I want to distinguish the people whom I have studied from those descended from later arrivals from German-speaking parts of Europe. However, readers unfamiliar with the term should note that "Dutch" is really an anglicization of the dialect term *Deitsch* (*Deutsch* in High German) and that the "Pennsylvania Dutch" are descendants of German-speaking immigrants from the seventeenth though early nineteenth centuries.

In the course of my research, I interviewed many people. I have included passages from my taped transcripts wherever a verbatim account would add clarification or interest. About half my consultants requested that I use pseudonyms, and I have honored their wishes. Whenever the name of a consultant is a pseudonym, I have pointed that out in a footnote the first time that pseudonym is used.

This work is aimed as much as possible at people interested in healing, tradition, and the Pennsylvania Dutch. Social scientists and others with an interest in theory may want to consult Appendix 1 for a more detailed theoretical background.

A note on statistics: A great deal of social science research relies on the statistical testing of samples drawn from the population being studied in order to reject or sustain hypotheses about that population. In such work, a random, or probability, sample is needed to ensure that the sample data are representative of the population from which it was drawn. Because of the nature of my field research and the secrecy surrounding powwowing today, it was impossible to obtain a truly random sample of consultants or survey respondents. Therefore, it would be inappropriate to apply statistical tests to such data and expect them to result in confirmation of hypotheses. However, such tests can be used in an exploratory study to suggest fruitful areas for future research. That is what I did in my initial research. Here, to avoid confusion, I have decided to eliminate any reference to quantitative measures of association and significance.

In any case, the chief value of this work is qualitative: to provide an appreciation for the powwower's art and practice and for the nuances of Pennsylvania Dutch culture and identity today. My scholarship, like much scholarship performed on powwowing in the past, has therefore been predominantly folkloristic and humanistic. What distinguishes my work from most is that it is a contemporary ethnography. I have tried to show that powwowing is a living, evolving practice and not some relic from a bygone past. It makes sense within the cultural models of the Pennsylvania Dutch and is believed in by people who are as rational and modern as anyone else.

Despite a number of articles on powwowing, including the groundbreaking work published by folklorist Don Yoder, before my own work there have been only book-length studies devoted to the subject.[1] These are folklorist Barbara L. Reimensnyder's *Powwowing in Union County: A Study of Pennsylvania Dutch Folk Medicine in Context* (1982) and anthropologist James Nyce's 1987 doctoral dissertation "Convention, Power, and the Self in German Mennonite Magic." Reimensnyder's work, which I have found quite useful, discusses powwowing as a healing practice in one central Pennsylvania county, whereas Nyce's focuses on the life and activities of a single powwow practitioner in an area of Canada settled by Mennonites. Although I found the scholarly literature to be faithful to the powwowing tradition, the general scholarly view when I began my work appeared to be that powwowing is a lost art, something that was once an important part of Pennsylvania Dutch culture but that has, to all intents and purposes, died out. Following publication of my dissertation (2001), however, that view appears to be changing. For instance, Erik Fasick, a young folklorist one of whose field photographs appears in this volume, has described powwowing as a living, contemporary healing practice (2006).

The most prominent books are nonscholarly and aimed at a curious public. A. Monroe Aurand's *The "Pow-Wow" Book* (1929) and Arthur Lewis's *Hex* (1969) focus on a 1920s murder case in York, Pennsylvania, that involved powwowing. While both contain a good deal of factual case material, both (and especially Aurand's work) also contain a heavy dose of sensationalism, and often scorn, for those who believe in or practice powwowing. More contemporary works are popular folklore writer Dennis Boyer's *Once Upon a Hex* (2004), a collection of folktales and lore relating

1. Yoder and Alfred Shoemaker published a number of articles on powwowing in *The Pennsylvania Dutchman* and *Pennsylvania Folklife*, including much primary-source material in the forms of communications with consultants and contributors. Most useful to me have been a letter from Yoder's consultant, powwower "Aunt" Sophia Bailer of Tremont (Yoder 1952), Yoder's articles "Twenty Questions on Powwowing" (1967), and "Hohman and Romanus: Origins and Diffusion of the Pennsylvania Dutch Powwow Manual" (1976). The latter appeared in Hand 1976, 235–48.

to powwowing and hexing (witchcraft), and Lehigh chemistry professor Ned D. Heindel's *Hexenkopf: History, Healing, and Hexerei* (2005), a historical account of powwowing and hex-related activity near a region of Northampton County, with special focus on the Saylor family of powwowers. These more recent books take the practice more seriously and contain useful material for further research, some of which Boyer has already performed. Powwowing has even made it into Wikipedia, that popular resource for undergraduate research papers).

Other works are mainly aimed not at documenting and explaining the practice but at providing instruction on how to become a powwower. These include Silver RavenWolf's 1997 *HexCraft: Dutch Country Magick* (now reissued under the title *American Folk Magick*), which interprets powwowing in light of the author's neo-paganism, and Karl Herr's more traditional *Hex and Spellwork: The Magical Practices of the Pennsylvania Dutch* (2002). Finally, there is the privately published *Powwow Power* (1998) by the late James D. Beissel, which mixes family history, the charm book *Secrets of Sympathy*, and an interview with a now-deceased powwower.

My work makes a unique contribution to the field by combining a fieldwork-based description of the practice of powwowing with analysis using the tools of social science. It demonstrates that powwowing is not a dead relic but a living and changing practice that is still important to a number of people. Having said that, I explain why it persists and why many believe it does not—or should not. I look at powwowing not only as a healing practice and a magico-religious ritual but also as custom and symbol. It is especially significant and contentious in concerns for the survival of Pennsylvania Dutch identity in the twenty-first century in the face of mass culture and assimilation. In other words, what is "Dutchiness," and how is it expressed? How does powwowing as an old "Dutch" tradition fit alongside food, craft, and language?

The book is organized into nine chapters. It begins with an account of my fieldwork experiences, then provides a comprehensive overview of powwowing. The structure and performance of powwow rituals are examined next, with ritual understood as a complex of behaviors aimed at mobilizing supernatural power. The fourth chapter examines powwowing's healing function, comparing it with biomedical practices and seeking explanations for its apparent efficacy. Chapter 5 gives cases of powwowing in Pennsylvania during the twentieth century and is followed by portraits of several contemporary powwowers in Chapter 6. Next, I suggest a cultural model of healing among the Pennsylvania Dutch that is based on survey and interview data, and then explain opposition to the practice. The concluding chapter poses some reasons that powwowing persists in an era of medicine that is based ostensibly on science and religion largely divorced from supernatural experience.

I am grateful to a number of people for assistance in writing this book. First, I must thank the series editor, Simon Bronner, for his initiative, invaluable editing suggestions, and tireless devotion to this project. I also want to thank all my consultants, who took time to share their personal and family histories with me. They have truly been my teachers. I also want to thank my dissertation committee at the University of Pennsylvania—Melvyn Hammarberg, David Hufford, and Frank Johnston. Their assistance in negotiating the hurdles of receiving my doctorate was invaluable, and they truly helped me grow as an anthropologist. I must also thank my friend Patti Kinlock, who helped me complete the final draft and made the computing and library resources of The Johns Hopkins University available to me. I am grateful to a number of other scholars for providing information and, in some cases, contacts to interview. These include C. Richard Beam, who with his wife Dorothy also graciously selected me to be the 2002 J. William Frey Lecturer at Franklin and Marshall College; William Donner; LeRoy Hopkins; Charles Wolf; and Don Yoder. And I cannot forget my friends at the Landis Valley Museum—April, Barb, Dusty, Jerri, Tim, Tom, and all the rest—where I served as Scholar-in-Residence in a hoary old library above the tavern. Last, but not least, I thank my parents, Mary and Jim Kriebel, who not only assisted me in my research but also have always supported me in whatever path I chose to follow in life.

ONE

ON THE TRAIL OF A LOST ART

"There's a shortage of holiness in Lebanon County," the elderly Eastern Mennonite man said. "You should put your faith in the Lord—not in witchcraft." He was warning me against inquiring too deeply into the affairs of Mrs. May, a woman who had practiced powwowing—traditional Pennsylvania Dutch spiritual healing—for more than twenty years in Lebanon, Pennsylvania, but had been arrested for charging money for fortune-telling. He explained that when other Mennonites had gone in to clean her house, they felt something wrong about it.

"She played around with everything—all the dark powers," he told me. We [Mennonites] believe there are many powers. And the second highest is very powerful."

"You mean the devil?"

He nodded. "You would do well to pay attention to the One Power."

I left Good's Store, where I had met him, shaken and concerned about how I should continue my research into powwowing, a traditional Pennsylvania Dutch healing practice often referred to as "white magic." However, the line between "white" and "black" magic can be difficult to discern. That same day another Eastern Mennonite, a young farmer named Chris Wine, had also warned me about powwowing, claiming not only that the devil was involved but also that patronizing a powwower or performing powwowing could lead to a dependence on magic to such an extent that it became impossible to live without fear. His words made a lot of sense to me and made me concerned about how I was to present my findings. I began to wonder if my other sources, the ones who spoke of powwowing as a gift from God—the One Power—were not themselves deluded and possibly under diabolical influence. This was clearly not an appropriate stance for a scientist to take.

That evening I placed a call to one of my professors, folklorist David Hufford, who, working at Hershey Medical Center (a degree-granting teaching hospital), has done a great deal of empirical research on supernatural phenomena and folk medicine, including powwow. David also knew of Mrs. May. He listened to my concerns without ridiculing them and told me I needed to trust my intuition in these matters—not to be afraid, but simply not to force myself to go anywhere where I felt uncomfortable for any reason. I left the conversation feeling more at ease. Perhaps I simply needed to hear a familiar voice that belonged to someone I could trust. In any event, I persevered.[1]

My encounter with the man at Good's Store was not my first brush with the supernatural during the course of my fieldwork, nor was it to be my last. I had felt it a few months before, when I interviewed a woman in her isolated farmhouse in Adams County. She demanded assurances that I was not working for the Commonwealth of Pennsylvania or for the Baltimore School of Massage, which she claimed had threatened to steal her secrets, and was satisfied only after I showed her my Penn I.D. card and signed a statement that read "I will not be responsible for anything said or wrote." Then she took me to her basement, where we sat in the darkness among her various homemade healing equipment and talked about how she had had several brushes with demons while she was being trained as a powwower. In fact, she told me the reason she did not follow through with the training was her fear of inadvertently becoming involved with black magic. At the end of this long, unsettling interview I stood on her porch and she bade me farewell with the words "We'll meet again." She pronounced them like a doom.

More recently, a woman contacted me begging me to help her find a practicing powwower. She had been suffering from what she believed was possession by the spirit of her deceased mother, a Pennsylvania Dutch witch. Her mother, she claimed, had hated her "because [I] was a girl" and because her mother, while alive, had put hexes on her. She had also sacrificed animals to the devil and kept jars of material from her victims under her bed. Now that she was dead, she had possessed her daughter, making her sick with illnesses that none of the physicians she had consulted could explain. At age fifty-five she was bedridden, almost completely paralyzed, and had suffered three episodes of "heart failure." When I asked why she believed all this was due to possession, she told me that she was a born-again Christian but that she could not stand the sight of a cross, spat up blood when ministers prayed over her, and snarled like an animal. She claimed that an exorcism performed by a Roman Catholic priest had been ineffective and that she was now was seeking help from every quarter, including powwowing. I was able to put her in touch with

1. I eventually completed the research that became the basis for my published dissertation, "Belief, Power, and Identity in Pennsylvania Dutch *Brauche*, or Powwowing" (Ann Arbor: University of Michigan, 2000).

a couple of powwowers, who paid her a house call but informed her that the process would take a long time, time she did not feel she had.

I do not mean to imply that I performed my research in constant fear of demonic forces. In fact, my fieldwork in the Pennsylvania Dutch heartland of southeastern and central Pennsylvania was overwhelmingly a joyous experience. I learned a lot about myself and made good friends with people who opened their lives and homes to me. But the presence of the supernatural was a palpable thing when I spoke to those who believed in the power of powwowing. The very air seemed heavy with it. This sense is magnified by the secrecy that shrouds powwowing today.

That secrecy dictated the methods I had to use. During my two years in and out of the field, I usually had to assume the role of a detective, developing leads, following them up, interviewing reliable and less-than-reliable sources. A typical trip into the Dutch country would mean booking an inexpensive motel room, one that preferably had a free local newspaper and free local telephone service. I would get a paper, scan it for ads that appeared promising, and then make calls. Rarely do powwowers advertise in the paper, but some practitioners—and clients—practice or make use of other alternative medical treatments, such as reflexology, therapeutic touch, and aromatherapy. I would also look for libraries, historical societies, and the like. Sooner or later, something would turn up—perhaps a lead from one of the listings, perhaps a knowledgeable person who overheard my conversation with a librarian, perhaps an old roadside store whose proprietor happened to know about powwowing. Everywhere I went, I asked about it. That was probably my most fruitful means of acquiring consultants.

About half of all the people I spoke with over the age of forty had heard of powwowing, and many of them had stories to tell—more about that later. But many others exhibited fear and suspicion when I mentioned the practice. For instance, when I called one reflexologist, she first denied ever hearing of powwowing, and then, when I explained the nature of my research, she remarked, "Well, that's very controversial, isn't it?" She still refused to see me, though. Another time when I approached an Amish furniture maker in Leola (Lancaster County) he turned his head to the side and looked down as he curtly denied knowing anything about powwowing. A Conservative Mennonite woman in Centerville (west of Lancaster) practically fled from me when I mentioned the practice.

This book is a passport to the secrets of the centuries-old art of Pennsylvania Dutch powwowing. It reveals the face of powwowing today, explores its historical roots, and introduces the real people who still practice this form of religious healing that some call "white magic." But before setting out on the journey, it is wise to get the lay of the land.

THE LAND AND ITS PEOPLE

While Pennsylvania Dutch populations are found all over Pennsylvania, as well as in many other U.S. states, most notably Maryland, Ohio, Indiana, Illinois, and Kansas, and in Ontario, Canada, the Pennsylvania Dutch "heartland" is southeastern and south-central Pennsylvania. This area's core includes Lancaster, Lebanon, and Berks counties but extends north into Schuylkill County, east into Lehigh, Bucks, Chester, and Montgomery counties, and west into York and Adams counties. Its total area is approximately four thousand square miles and falls within Pennsylvania's Piedmont Plateau. This was the setting for my investigation of powwowing.

The principal geographical features are the Red Hills in the east (northwestern Montgomery and eastern Berks counties), the Blue Mountain (actually a long mountain ridge) in the north (extending from Northampton County to northern Lebanon County, and the relatively flat agricultural area of Lancaster and eastern York counties. The land then rises again until it reaches another mountain ridge, South Mountain, in western Adams County. At that point the Appalachian Highlands begin, and the elevation of the land increases until it reaches the Allegheny Mountains, the backbone of the Appalachian chain, stretching northeastward across the state.

The farmland in this area, particularly in Lancaster and Chester counties, is among the richest in the world. The principal crop is corn, which has replaced wheat, the dominant crop during the eighteenth century, when most Pennsylvania Dutch settlement took place. However, wheat is still grown in the area, along with barley, soybeans, and alfalfa. It is a long-standing Pennsylvania Dutch belief that limestone soils are superior to other types of soil because it they have greater depth and hold moisture better.[2]

2. However, other kinds of soil can be as productive as limestone soils and alluvial bottomland.

Livestock raised by the farmers in this area include dairy cattle, beef cattle, poultry (chicken and turkey), pigs, sheep, and goats. The Amish in Lancaster County make abundant use of cow manure as fertilizer (as a summer open-air drive will readily confirm!). Since the period of earliest settlement, Pennsylvania Dutch farmers have been concerned with conserving and, if possible, increasing the fertility of the soil. They regarded the depletion of the soil that occurred with the use of southern farming methods as either sinful[3] or stupid.

There are no data on the proportion of inhabitants of the area who are Pennsylvania Dutch, although I estimate that approximately 50 percent of the inhabitants would claim Pennsylvania Dutch ethnicity if asked. Of the total Pennsylvania Dutch population, only 10 percent[4] are "Plain people," that is, Old Order and other Amish, Old Order or Conservative Mennonites, and various Brethren denominations,[5] the rest being what is variously known as "church people," "gay Dutch," or "fancy Dutch."[6] This latter group is mainly focused around membership in the traditionally Dutch churches: Lutheran, Reformed (now United Church of Christ [UCC]), Evangelical (now United Methodists), River Brethren, progressive Mennonite, and United Brethren (now United Methodist). Two of the six Schwenkfelder churches now worship with UCC congregations. While these churches are traditionally Pennsylvania Dutch, all have significant numbers of members who are not Pennsylvania Dutch.[7]

The emphasis on religion is typical of the Pennsylvania Dutch, most of whose ancestors left Europe to avoid religious persecution. For older people, especially, the church is still a main center of social activity, and the church affiliation of any one individual is known to others in the commu-

3. The Amish took this view because they regard a responsible use of the land as a divine command, issued in the book of Genesis with respect to the Garden of Eden and reinforced by Psalm 24, which states that "the earth is the Lord's" (Hostetler 1993, 114).

4. This percentage is a commonly mentioned figure, echoed by an official at the Landis Valley Museum (a historical museum and research library specializing in Pennsylvania Dutch culture) and confirmed by my own impressions acquired during fieldwork.

5. Other Plain groups, such as the progressive Mennonites, the Schwenkfelders, and the Church of the Brethren, lost their Plainness during the twentieth century.

6. These designations are not generally used by the non-Plain consultants with whom I worked, who simply referred to themselves as "Dutch" or, in a few cases, "Pennsylvania Germans." The Amish in Lancaster County typically refer to anyone who is non-Plain, including members of other Pennsylvania Dutch groups, as "English."

7. Including the First Schwenkfelder Church in Philadelphia, whose membership is now almost entirely African American.

nity. The church may play a lesser role in the lives of young individuals, although surveys still show a high degree of participation.[8]

Relations among the two kinds of Pennsylvania Dutch and other ethnic groups living in the area are generally friendly. The non-Dutch population (traditionally Scotch-Irish, but increasingly diverse) often consider the "Dutch" backward, giving rise to the term "dumb Dutch." Several consultants expressed embarrassment over their "Dutchified" accents. Possession of a Dutch accent did not necessarily mean knowledge of the dialect. In such cases, the accent was acquired despite efforts by parents to keep their children from learning the dialect, out of fear that it would mark them as backward. I have noticed that the Amish and the Mennonites I have spoken with have a markedly weaker accent than my non-Plain consultants, perhaps because they deal with native English speakers more often as part of the tourist trade.

The Plain people, however, are also caricatured quite often. One consultant indicated that the non-Amish population in Lancaster called the Amish "Jakeys," because Jacob was such a common male name among the Amish. At the Kutztown Folk Festival in Summit Station (Schuylkill County), a comic affecting a Dutch accent used the names "Jakey" and "Rachel" to refer to standard Amish characters.[9] It is interesting that one of my "gay Dutch" consultants indicated that she did not really consider Amish to be "Dutch" at all. The question of Dutch identity usually comes up when a Pennsylvania Dutch person describes another as "real" Dutch, or "he was an upcountry Dutchman."

The Pennsylvania Dutch are extremely conscious of their culture and its uniqueness. They form heritage clubs (such as the Grundsau Lodsch

8. Traditional secularization theory would hypothesize a lower level of religiosity among younger individuals. While a July 1999 Gallup Poll found that young people (ages eighteen to twenty-nine) view religion as less important than those age thirty and over, 84 percent of this group still rate religion as "very" (45 percent) or "fairly" (39 percent) important. Another Gallup Poll, in April 1999, found that teenagers consistently attend Easter services more than adults (50 percent of teenagers attend, and 40 percent of adults).

9. As of 2001, there was quite a feud going on between the organizers of this festival and a newer one in Kutztown. The "Kutztown Folk Festival" in Summit Station (which moved from Kutztown after a dispute with the Kutztown Fair Grounds) lays claim to being the original festival established by scholars Alfred Shoemaker, Don Yoder, and J. William Frey. It is run by Richard Thomas (known as "Little Richard"), a local entrepreneur. The newer one, the "Kutztown Pennsylvania German Festival," sponsored by Kutztown University, emphasizes Pennsylvania Dutch culture from an academic standpoint, whereas the Summit Station festival is geared more toward entertainment. The two festivals are held during an overlapping period in July.

[Groundhog Lodge] and the Schwenkfelder Exile Society), hold dialect events, such as *Versommlinge* (gatherings), and organize more academically oriented organizations, such as the Mennonite Historians of Eastern Pennsylvania, the Goschenhoppen Historians, and the Pennsylvania German Society, in order to preserve that culture. I have met several people, usually in their sixties and seventies, whom I call "local historians." Though not always self-taught, these individuals often serve as keepers of cultural lore. They are typically willing to help outsiders who are interested in learning about Pennsylvania Dutch culture, but they are wary of academic (particularly psychological and sociological) approaches to the subject.

THE ROAD TO REDISCOVERY

I first became interested in powwowing in my high school German class, when I had to do a project on German cultural traditions. Because I had a great love of genealogy and knew my family was of Pennsylvania Dutch origin, I decided to approach the assignment from that angle. I checked out Fredric Klees's *Pennsylvania Dutch* (1950) from the library and found a chapter on powwowing and hexing. Soon afterward, my grandfather told me that his parents used to use powwow to heal burns sustained by neighborhood children at their home in suburban Philadelphia. I was instantly intrigued. My father confirmed the story and told me that Granny, as we called my great-grandmother, could also use powwow to cause it to rain. He quickly added, however, that Granny had been a devoutly religious person and believed that the power she had came from God. Years later, when it came time for me to choose a study in the area of contemporary American magical practice, powwowing seemed a natural choice.

I began my research in August 1998 at the Schwenkfelder Library in Pennsburg, Montgomery County, where I found my first articles on powwowing, published in the newspaper *The Pennsylvania Dutchman* and its more academic successor publication, *Pennsylvania Folklife*. It was also at the Schwenkfelder Library that I had my first encounter with *The Long Lost* [or *Hidden*] *Friend*, one of the major "charm books," or collections of spells and recipes used in powwowing. *The Long Lost Friend* was written by John George (Johann Georg) Hohman and first published in Reading, Pennsylvania, in 1819, has gone through a number of reprints. I later learned that the eminent folklorist Don Yoder had traced its roots to two other collections of spells: *Albertus Magnus: Egyptian Secrets* and *The Sixth and Seventh Books of Moses*. Both of these have also been used by powwowers, although few will admit to owning a copy of the latter, which many Pennsylvania Dutch people consider a "hex book," probably because it contains formulae for conjuring demons.

It was at the Schwenkfelder library that I learned both of the enduring interest in powwowing and of the lingering suspicions about the practice. A young woman who worked at the library and was helping me with my research was interested in what I was doing. She asked about the practice, and I told her what little I knew. Then she looked at me and asked shyly if I had found anything in the Hohman book that could cure cancer. I searched the book and found nothing, leaving her disappointed and myself feeling sorry that I could not help her. The same day, I asked the elderly librarian, who was also a minister, whether he knew anything about powwow as a healing practice. His face assumed a serious expression as he said, "I think matters like that should be left to the church." That was the first indication I had of the long-standing negative attitude held by official Pennsylvania Dutch religion toward powwowing.

That day marked the start of a year-long search for a living powwower. I visited many libraries, colleges, and historical societies and accumulated many other documentary sources—other charm books, newspaper articles, letters describing powwow procedures, and so forth—that have helped paint a picture of the history of powwowing. I also began to network in the area, develop contacts, and conduct interviews. My last name helped me—there are a number of Kriebels in northwestern Montgomery County, eastern Berks County, and southern Lehigh County—so I seemed less of an outlander in that region.

But everyone I spoke with—scholars, local historians, former powwow patients, and relatives of deceased powwowers—told me the same thing: powwowing is a lost art. One local historian even gave me a timeline for when powwowing disappeared—in the 1950s and 1960s in Lancaster County, in the 1970s in Berks County, and so forth. But I remained convinced that a practice does not die out altogether in the space of thirty years, that there had to be someone, somewhere, still practicing powwow. Folklorist David Hufford agreed, noting that many others had cited the demise of powwowing throughout the twentieth century, only to be proven wrong. I myself found an 1895 newspaper article profiling a powwower who lamented the imminent disappearance of the practice.

Still, I was having difficulty finding a living powwower to interview. Mrs. May, the storefront powwower whom the Mennonite gentleman had warned me against, had been put out of business by the Commonwealth. According to an article in the local paper, an undercover policewoman had visited Mrs. May to have her fortune read and was informed that she was under a curse, which Mrs. May would be happy to remove for a fee. The policewoman immediately arrested her. The closest I could come to Mrs. May was an interview with the reporter who broke the story of her arrest. The reporter was unable to add much to the case report, although she did provide useful information about the powwowing activities of her grandmother, which I added to my case files. I should note that there is some dispute among the Dutch whether Mrs. May qualifies as a powwower—but more on that later.

I drove out to Mrs. May's house on Route 422, where she operated her fortune-telling and powwow business, and saw a big sign depicting the open palm symbol used by seers everywhere to advertise their trade and the words "Pow Wow" written above it. The house, though, was empty and the door was standing wide open. I did not enter. Later, I interviewed one of Mrs. May's powwow clients, who testified to the efficacy of her power in curing their son of a skin disease. The interview also substantiated an earlier report that Mrs. May was not Pennsylvania Dutch, but a Gypsy. According to David Hufford, Gypsies in the Dutch country had, in the past, sometimes set themselves up as powwowers without really knowing how to do it. However, one of my consultants reports that Mrs. May healed her son using what seemed to be powwowing.

I first encountered a powwower, an Old Order Amish woman whom I will refer to as "Leah Stoltzfus," in the unlikeliest of places—the Internet. An article about her in a midwestern paper referred to her practice as "Amish Voodoo" but clearly identified her as a powwower. I seized on this information and managed to track her down near a small village in Lancaster County. Outside her home, I conducted a brief initial interview with her, and then a more extensive interview in the waiting room of her home-based practice in January 1999. She agreed to the latter interview on the condition that I bring my mother along. I did not ask why, but I presume it had to do with concerns about her safety and the propriety of such a meeting. Fortunately, my mother is a good sport and she accompanied me, even asking a few questions herself. I was not, however, allowed to audio- or videotape the interview.

While I acquired a great deal of information that would prove useful later, and even participated in one of her diagnostic techniques—she claims to be able to detect pain—I left unsure whether her practice, which consisted mainly of silently laying on hands, qualified as powwow or not. It did not fit the conventional model of powwow ritual, nor did she herself describe it as "powwow" (when I asked why not, she said she was afraid folks would think she was "too New Age"). However, her Mennonite cousin who had pointed me to Leah definitely considered Leah's practice to be powwowing and definitely disapproved of it. Like the other Mennonites I interviewed, Leah's cousin believed it to be the work of the devil. I have since learned that Leah's simple healing practice does fit the model of powwowing as practiced by the Amish.

During that first year, I developed a good idea of what powwowing was and of what a conventional powwower might do, based on the reports of former clients and relatives of powwowers. However, I was still unable to track down a powwower who fit that conventional model, and I began to wonder whether the skeptics might be right after all. Maybe no one—except possibly Leah—powwowed anymore. Particularly frustrating was the fact that such well-known powwowers as Ruth Frey, Ida Wagner, and Preston Zerbe all died in the mid-1990s, just a few years before I had begun my research. On a visit to the Landis Valley Museum, where I was later to become Scholar-in-Residence, I learned that a powwower in the Lancaster area had died only two weeks previously.

It was not until fourteen months into my investigation, in October 1999, that I finally met a living powwower who followed traditional powwowing procedures. In fact, I met two of them, a husband-and-wife team living and practicing in southern Schuylkill County. I found them through a series of accidents. I was in Lehigh County, based in the small town of Fogelsville, outside the city of Allentown, and decided to drive to Center Valley and scout out some leads; one of my consultants had told me about her experiences being powwowed there in the 1930s. At an old Lutheran church—a *Friedenskirche*, or "peace church"—I interviewed a woman who had been powwowed as a child. She recommended that I try a small farming community northwest of Allentown called New Tripoli (pronounced "Trih-PO-ly"). I went there and drove through town all the way to Kempton and back again. On the way out I had spotted an old farm with the neatness characteristic of farms run by the Pennsylvania Dutch, and by the time I returned I had summoned enough courage to bother the residents. Through their screen door I interviewed the owners, an elderly couple, both of whom had been powwowed as youngsters. What was particularly interesting, though, was their mention of a man they knew who had bragged in a restaurant about being powwowed, claiming that two powwowers had cured his cellulitis. They turned out to be a husband and wife practicing powwowing in Schuylkill County, and I was able to interview them. I even received powwow treatment from the wife for my arthritis.

After that, it suddenly became easier to meet powwowers. Professor William Donner at Kutztown University introduced me to a powwower who had been interviewed by one of his undergraduates, and I was able to interview him in his home with his grandchildren present. He informed me that he had trained six to ten other powwowers in the area. Shortly after that, I found the locally published book *Powwow Power* (1988), which detailed the activities of the recently deceased powwower in the Lancaster area of whom I had learned at the Landis Valley Museum. According to the book, he had taught his widow how to powwow before he passed on. I was able to interview her by telephone and then went to see her as a patient. She informed me that she planned to pass the power on to her son, a man in his mid-thirties. Finally, I encountered the book *HexCraft: Dutch Country Magick* (1997), by popular neo-pagan writer Silver RavenWolf, which described her training as a powwow by Preston Zerbe of Adams County.[10]

In the space of three months, powwowing had changed in my mind from a relic that may or may not still exist to a living practice likely to continue into the foreseeable future. But what exactly is powwowing?

10. I was suspicious of the existence of Preston Zerbe when I first read RavenWolf's account, but I was able to confirm that Zerbe was a real powwower by talking with another of his powwowers-in-training.

TWO

A POWWOW PRIMER

The primary purpose of powwowing is to heal physical and spiritual illness. It can therefore not only cure diseases and heal wounds but also remove curses, or hexes placed on a victim by a witch. Secondary purposes include protection from evil forces, finding lost persons or objects, and bringing good luck. Powwow ritual can be simple (making a wart disappear by rubbing a potato on it) or highly complex (using a combination of complicated incantations, gestures, and sometimes material objects or substances to cure a range of illnesses). Powwow rituals derive from a number of sources, most notably the Holy Bible and the three charm books mentioned in the previous chapter: John George Hohman's *Long Lost Friend; Albertus Magnus: Egyptian Secrets;* and *The Sixth and Seventh Books of Moses*. Theoretically, anyone can learn to powwow, but some individuals seem to have a special aptitude for it. These may be individuals known to have power from birth (such as the seventh son of a seventh son) or simply those who show the ability to memorize complex powwow spells perfectly. Diverse methods are used to train powwowers, ranging from simple memorization of spells to a vision quest (an induced spiritual vision that helps the experiencer acquire supernatural power or attain a new social position). The general rule is that males must learn from females, and vice versa, but there have been exceptions to this.

Powwowing is not to be confused with the Native American "powwow," although individuals of Native American descent have practiced powwowing in the Pennsylvania Dutch tradition, and some powwowers claim that Native American spirit guides have assisted them in conducting healing rituals. While the origin of the term is obscure,[1] powwowing is known as *Brauche*, or *Braucherei*, in the Pennsylvania Dutch dialect. These dialect terms are often translated as "trying," although other meanings have been proposed, including "blessing" (as a mistranscription of the Hebrew *baruch*) and "needing or wanting" (from the High German verb *brauchen*), or "using" (from the High German verb *gebrauchen*). Prac-

1. It has been speculated that "powwow" may be a colloquialism or mishearing of the English word "power." Some powwowers have been called "power doctors," presumably because they have "the power." This term is also used in the Ozarks to refer to folk healers. Another possibility is that the term derives from a perceived similarity between Native American and Pennsylvania Dutch practices, or that the Native American term was used to cover any unusual, supernatural practices. This latter view is held by Studer (1980, 18).

titioners are referred to as "powwowers," the term used in this article, but also as "powwows," "powwow doctors," "*brau* doctors," "*Brauchers*," "*Brauch doctors*," "hex doctors" or, rarely, in Pennsylvania Dutch, *Hexenmeisters*. Those who oppose the practice use the terms "witch" or "sorcerer" or the Pennsylvania Dutch term "*Hex*."[2] The infinitive form of the verb "to powwow" in the dialect, is *Brauchen* ("to powwow" in English).

A WORKING DEFINITION

Powwowing has been defined in a number of ways. Probably the most widely disseminated definition comes from Don Yoder: "[Powwowing is] Pennsylvania's native brand of religious healing, on the folk-cultural level, using words, charms, amulets, and physical manifestations in an attempt to heal the ills of man and beast" (Yoder 1967, 39).[3]

Several elements of this definition require clarification and expansion. First, by focusing on healing, it does not acknowledge other uses. While healing appears to be the primary purpose of powwowing, possibly its only purpose at the present time, the practice has traditionally been used for other purposes too. These include protection from evil or misfortune, ensuring good luck in various endeavors, conveying information about the future, and finding lost persons or objects.

Second, "healing" should be understood in its broadest possible sense. Powwowing can be used to heal not simply physical ailments but also spiritual ailments. The powwower can make a wart vanish, but he or she can also remove a hex (a curse) on an individual and drive away evil spirits. Some consider hexing another function of powwowing, or even a synonym for powwowing, but that belief is far from universally held. Hexing is usually attributed to a witch, a figure who has traditionally occupied a very different social role from that of powwower. Powwowers typically oppose and neutralize the action of witches.

Finally, the term "religious healing," while accurate, does not include what can be legitimately viewed as a magical aspect to powwowing. Expanding and clarifying this definition would also permit an analysis of

2. These latter terms are more typically distinguished from and opposed to *Brauche*. For more details, see Chapters 7 and 8.

3. Yoder specifically defined "powwowing," rather than *Brauche*.

powwowing's relationship to "black magic" (*Hexerei*) and a comparison of powwowing with other magical practices in contemporary America (such as contemporary paganism). It could also contribute to a discussion of the relationships among magic, science, and religion.

The most expedient solution would be to change the adjective "religious" in Yoder's definition to "magico-religious." This, of course, requires definitions for "magical" and "religious." Many researchers have attempted to distinguish between the two. They may be distinguished in terms of their "function," so that magic may be considered to serve what anthropologist Bronislaw Malinowksi referred to as "empirical" ends (for example, finding a lost key, obtaining healing), whereas religion would serve "nonempirical" ends (for example, redemption, eternal life). Under this distinction, most acts of powwowing would be considered "magical" because they are intended to achieve a "this-worldly" effect. Another (and, in the case of powwowing, more useful) distinction would be to consider magic to constitute "coercion," or "expectation" : the magician mobilizes supernatural power in the expectation that it will be effective, generally using proven spells to obtain the result. Religion, on the other hand, would involve "beseeching" or "hope." A religious healer, for instance, might beseech God to heal, in the hope that God would be merciful and grant such a request. Powwowing has always accommodated both magical and religious attitudes, but during the twentieth century a shift from the magical to the religious appears to have taken place. A contemporary powwower does not generally use collections of written recipes or charm books. He or she approaches the task of healing not with expectation but with hope.

Before reintroducing Yoder's definition, however, it is necessary to make two further emendations. Yoder defines "powwowing" as a traditional Pennsylvania practice but not a specifically Pennsylvania Dutch practice. Indeed, a powwower could certainly be an individual who was not Pennsylvania Dutch but who had either learned powwowing from a Pennsylvania Dutch person or employed a folk-healing practice that superficially resembled powwowing. To situate powwowing within Pennsylvania Dutch culture, some acknowledgment of the practice's origin, which Yoder himself has traced, must be made. It is also necessary to define his term "folk-cultural" in a way that does not presuppose knowledge of the term "folk." For purposes of this study, I believe that the term "folk" refers to unofficial practices, chiefly oral, or customary practices.

By "unofficial," I mean all practices not given sanction by social institutions that serve as repositories of socially constituted authority. Unofficial practices are not sanctioned by cultural authority (for example, the American Medical Association) or political authority (for example, the Commonwealth of Pennsylvania). Widely held beliefs and popular practices are not necessarily "official." For instance, a belief in God is "unofficial" in American culture (although it is widely held), whereas it is "official" within the culture of the Roman Catholic Church.

With these emendations, the following working definition results from Yoder's original one: Powwowing is an unofficial traditional magico-religious practice—originating with and chiefly practiced by the Pennsylvania Dutch and emphasizing healing of humans and animals, but with other goals as well—that uses words, charms, amulets, and physical manifestations to achieve its objectives. Powwowing is also known as *Brauche* or *Braucherei* in the Pennsylvania Dutch dialect of German.

One final clarification is in order. While powwowers have often practiced herbalism as part of their healing activities (brewing teas, formulating "vitamins," and so forth), herbalism itself is not powwowing and therefore lies beyond the scope of this book. Our focus will be on the supernatural element, the "occult" level of folk medicine described by Cowen (1987, 87), because it is these "magical" or "spiritual" practices and beliefs that distinguish powwowing from other unofficial medical practices. However, it is important to note that powwowers did indeed employ herbal preparations and other home remedies, some of which worked but many of which were clearly valueless and even harmful. Some of these later home remedies, as Cowen points out (1987, 88–90), derived from outmoded medical theories and may be considered more a form of early biomedicine than any form of supernatural healing.

THE USES OF POWWOWING

Healing

Healing is far and away the most common use of powwowing, particularly if healing is understood to include the removal of curses (hexes). Powwowers who believe in hexes view hex removal as part of their healing practice. In fact, the principal purpose of a hex is to cause the victim to fall ill.

Powwowing has been used to treat a broad range of physical and psychological complaints. These include the following ailments, with those in italics being reported to me by consultants. The rest derive from documentary sources, most notably Barbara Reimensnyder's *Powwowing in Union County* (1982): arthritis, back problems, bee stings, *bloating in cattle*, *breast inflammation*, broken bones, *burns*, *cancer*, *consumption*, *cellulitis*, *corns*, *diphtheria*, *eczema*, epilepsy, *erysipelas*, *eye problems*, fever, *gall bladder problems*, goiter, *headache*, heart problems, *hex cures*, hip problems, *infections*, jaundice, *livergrown*, lockjaw, lumps, *mumps*, *measles*, *nervous conditions*, *pain*, *paralysis*, pleurisy, *pneumonia*, poison ivy, pregnancy (safe delivery), *preoperative preparation*, *preventive measures*, proud flesh, *psoriasis*, rat expulsion, *rupture*, shingles, snakebite, *sores*, *stitches*, sunsickness, surgery, *take-off*, *tapeworm*, *toothache*, trench mouth, *vaccination recovery*, *varicose veins*, *warts*, *whooping cough*, and *windgalls*. In my fieldwork, the most common of these ailments seemed to be warts, followed by hexes, burns, erysipelas, and livergrown, and the least common were cancer and heart trouble.

Skin problems seem to be by far the predominant class of ailment considered curable by powwowing during the twentieth century, constituting thirty-four out of the ninety ailments, amounting to 38 percent, recorded in my fieldwork or documentary accounts. If only purely physical ailments are considered (dropping out "hex removal"), this percentage rises to 41 percent. More than 40 percent of the skin ailments were warts. The second class of ailment, those specific to Pennsylvania Dutch culture, accounts for another 19 percent of the total. Together, these two classes constitute 57 percent of the ailments known to be treatable by powwowing.

Some of these ailments (such as livergrown and take-off) are limited to Pennsylvania Dutch culture. Others (such as rupture and sweeney) require elaboration because they refer to illnesses described in other terms by modern biomedicine. Readers desiring an explanation of these can refer to the Glossary of Illnesses in Appendix 2.

In some cases, the healer believes the disease is transferred to himself or herself (Hostetler 1993, 339). That may be part of the reason my consultant Mrs. Lenhart (York County) says, "You should be in good health if you want to do this." When I was powwowed by Daisy and Anita, I noticed them each making motions with their hands in between active healing, as if shaking off something. Daisy explained that doing that would reduce the risk of her being afflicted by my ailment. Whenever she powwows, she can feel the patient's pain and takes on the patient's affliction for a short time (up to two weeks). After that, it leaves her body and does not return.

In other cases, the illness is transferred elsewhere. Aaron Boehm claims that any illness he cures is sent to the moon. In Northampton County west of Raubsville and east of Gaffney Hill lies the Hexenkopf (Witch's Head), a hill that had a reputation for harboring evil spirits, witches, and demons and that was a site to be avoided by all (Wright 1988, 97). The legend is that local "powwowers" made it evil by transferring evil spirits that had caused illness from their patients to this hill. According to Wright, the local inhabitants blamed the evil spirits of the Hexenkopf for mysterious deaths, suicides, family problems, crop failures, and otherwise unexplained fires. Powwowing was indeed practiced in that area part of Northampton County from about 1750 onward. The most notable powwowers in the area were Johann Peter Saylor (1721–1803) and his son Peter (1770–1862), whose cures were legendary. I actually interviewed one of Johann's descendants.

Much hex removal is indistinguishable from normal healing, if a "personalistic theory" of illness causation is invoked (Foster and Anderson 1978). The powwower cures the illness by removing the evil spirit or hex causing it, as in the example above from Northampton County, in which spirits were cast out in order to heal people. However, powwowers also practice a different type of hex removal, in which the illness is not so much of the body but of the soul. Such hexes are typically long-lasting and often result in physical illness, which is understood to be a secondary development symptomatic of the hex but not the main purpose of the hex. The victim (who is said to be "*ferhext*") becomes fearful, loses confidence, often will not eat or drink, and has markedly diminished social contacts. In the dominant American culture, such an individual would be considered clinically depressed. One major difference between this kind of hex and the kind that brings on a specific illness is that in the latter the powwower diagnoses the hex and removes it in relatively short order, whereas in the former the victim is always aware of the hex by the time he seeks help from a powwower. The affliction of John Blymire, who participated in the 1928 murder of a York County man he believed hexed him, provides a classic example of this latter kind of hexing.

In order to remove the hex, the powwower generally (although not always) must know the name of the person who put the hex on or be able to identity an object that has been the proximate cause of the hex. Such an object might be a toy given a child, a doll, even a head of cabbage. This object must be removed from the premises or even destroyed in order to remove a hex. Another common way to remove a hex was to strike back at the hexer.

Protection

Protection most commonly involves the manufacture of items to protect the wearer or bearer from harm, although there are also incantations whose goal is also to create such protection. Such spells claim to provide protection from attack from humans or animals, fire, firearms, any harm while on a journey, harsh words, sickness or misfortune, tripping, and all weapons. Powwow spells may also be used in the fabrication of amulets or *Himmelsbriefe* (letters that invoke the protection of God).

To create an amulet, a powwower typically writes an incantation (usually incorporating a prayer or Bible verse) on a piece of paper, folds or rolls it up, and places it in a small bag that the client is to wear. My consultant Mrs. Schultz referred to an amulet made for her by a powwower ("*brau* doctor") in Center Valley, Lehigh County, as "a gigger."[4] This white bag contained a prayer or Bible verse that she was to wear as a protective device. The powwower Daisy Dietrich makes such amulets as well.[5] Her procedure is to write a Bible verse on a piece of paper and fold it into a triangle. Cowen also cites the use of a triangular form in the creation of amulets, which he refers to as "charms" (Cowen 1987, 94). Magical formulae dating from late antiquity, such as the well-known "Sator" square and "Abracadabra," were used in the fabrication of amulets. An example of these is reproduced below.

S A T O R
A R E T O
T E R E T
O T E R A
R O T A S

4. Mrs. Schultz (pseudonym) pronounced this word "djigger."
5. Pseudonym.

ABRACADABRA
ABRACADABR
ABRACADAB
ABRACADA
ABRACAD
ABRACA
ABRAC
ABRA
ABR
AB
A

Himmelsbriefe, literally "heaven letters" and usually referred to by English-speakers as "himmelsbriefs," are longer, not folded, and usually said to be copies of existing letters of protection, some claiming great antiquity. They are typically either posted in a house or carried on a person. The latter type generally protects against all harm. *Himmelsbriefe* may be plain or quite ornate, resembling illuminated manuscripts. They typically offer protection but also enjoin against impious behavior, such as failing to observe the Sabbath or disobeying the Ten Commandments. Tom Clemens, who is also one of Daisy's patients, carried a himmelsbrief in his wallet during World War II and credits it for his survival during landing at Omaha Beach and while in combat in Europe.[6]

Recovery of Property / Finding People

Powwowing can also be used to find property that has been lost or people who have left home. Mrs. Schultz recalls that her family went to the *brau* doctor in Center Valley in order to locate an uncle who had left the area and to assure the family that he was safe. At the time (she was six or seven years old), Mrs. Schultz thought it was all a waste of time, but now she is willing to believe it works and would go to a powwower "out of curiosity."[7] In another case, a powwower used *The Sixth and Seventh Books of Moses* to bring home a young man who was in a Virginia jail. *The Long Lost Friend* contains several spells for recovering lost property.

6. Pseudonym.
7. Mrs. Schultz has had a number of paranormal experiences since that time.

Bestowing Good Luck

Bestowing good luck involves rituals meant to ensure success in a given venture or to generally influence events so that their outcomes favor the subject. I have not found any cases of such spells being used, but they appear in charm books used by powwowers. For instance, *The Long Lost Friend* contains rituals for finding iron, ore, or water; obtaining things desired; catching fish; charming guns so that they will fire accurately; overcoming a man of superior strength; and other rituals for obtaining good luck.

Binding Animals and Humans

There are a number of spells for calming and binding animals. The famous incantation to stop a dog from attacking—"Dog, hold thy nose to the ground / God has made me and thee, hound" (Hohman 1971, 24)—was probably used. In one instance, the young John Blymire (later the chief defendant in the York Hex Murder Trial) was apparently able to stop a rabid dog by powwowing; at least one witness believed that he used the above incantation to do so. *The Long Lost Friend* contains spells used to control cattle, fish, and chickens, in addition to spells to be used against dogs. The book also contains spells to bind thieves. I have not encountered a powwow spell to control people other than thieves; that would be considered black magic.

Miscellaneous Spells

Other rituals contained in the charm books include spells for conjuring demons and angels, binding spirits, divination, mending objects, making good beer, and performing many other feats, but I have no documentation for their actual use.

PRINCIPAL WRITTEN SOURCES OF POWWOW CURES AND OTHER SPELLS

Because most powwowers have memorized the rituals they use, it is difficult to trace specific rituals to specific written sources. The living powwowers I know use a strictly oral means of transmission. Furthermore, many powwowers who practiced earlier in the century used recipes copied into notebooks, ledgers, diaries, and other repositories of personal writing. This is probably still the case, although I have been unable to document it, except in the case of sharing recipes for herbal mixtures and the like.

With this caveat in mind, the following works are considered the principal published sources of powwowing rituals, and most orally transmitted rituals probably have their origin in them. They are listed in decreasing order of importance.[8]

The Bible

The Bible is by far the most common source of powwowing incantations. Many of my consultants cited use of the Bible by powwowers as evidence that the cures must come from God rather than the devil, as some have accused. The fact that the cure was "taken out of the Bible" has also been used to explain why a powwower should not request payment (Reimensnyder 1982, 49).

Certain verses are considered effective for specific ailments. The most famous is Ezekiel 16:6, which is said to be effective when used by anyone, not just by practicing powwowers. It is also supposedly effective over great distances. The verse as it appears in the King James Version is most often mentioned (Reimensnyder 1982, 62): "And when I passed by thee and saw thee polluted in thine own blood, I said unto thee when thou wast in thy blood, Live; yea, I said unto thee when thou wast in thy blood, Live."

The Long Lost Friend

The Long Lost Friend (more accurately translated from the German, *Der lang verborgene Schatz und Haus Freund*, as *The Long Hidden Friend*) was written by John George Hohman in 1819 and first published in 1820 in Reading, Pennsylvania.[9] It has been reprinted in numerous German editions and twice translated into English, once in Harrisburg (1850) and once

8. Pennsylvania Dutch folk medicine in general drew on a number of different written sources beyond those mentioned here. For a good discussion of a number of these works, see David Cowen's "Folk Medicine of the Pennsylvania Dutch" (1987).

9. Much of the information in this section derives from Yoder 1976. Only the merest outline of Yoder's research is presented here.

in Carlisle, Pennsylvania (1863), the latter under the title *The Long Hidden Friend* (see Yoder 1976, 236).[10] All subsequent English editions derive from these two independent translations, but the Harrisburg edition is the only one still in print. A bookstore in Lebanon, Pennsylvania, checked with its distributor and informed me that the latest edition of the book was published in 1993.[11]

The Long Lost Friend is a collection of recipes, spells, and procedures, most of them invoking divine power. Hohman, an 1802 German immigrant who was himself an occult healer, borrowed heavily from other sources, especially the German charm book *Romanusbuchlein*, the "Romanus" book (Yoder 1976; Cowen 1987), which Cowen identifies as first published in Glatz, Silesia, in 1788, far from the Palatinate, where most Pennsylvania Dutch people originated.[12] He also borrowed from *Albertus Magnus: Egyptian Secrets* and other sources. Other than the Bible, *The Long Lost Friend* was the most common source of powwowing incantations. It also claimed to be in itself an amulet of protection for its possessor, and in one case (the York Hex Murder [or Witch] Trial) its destruction was supposed to lift a hex placed on another by its owner. While this book was used regularly by powwowers in the nineteenth and early twentieth century, it is not, to my knowledge, used by traditional powwowers today.

Albertus Magnus: Egyptian Secrets

The putative compiler of the charm book *Albertus Magnus: Egyptian Secrets* is the Swabian Dominican monk Albertus Magnus (A.D. 1200–1280), a saint in the Roman Catholic Church and known as a scientist, philosopher, and theologian. Albertus Magnus was known for bringing ancient Greek philosophical works, particularly those of Aristotle, from the Islamic world into Europe. While the book's true author (individual or corporate) remains unknown, the book does derive from European magical traditions.[13] Some of the spells even bear a strong resemblance to Christian magical literature from Egypt.

10. Yoder's article indicates the date of the Harrisburg publication as 1856, but the copy that resides at the William H. Welch Medical Library at Johns Hopkins bears the date 1850.

11. However, when I ordered that edition I received the 1971 edition instead, twice.

12. Although one group, the Schwenkfelders, did originate in Silesia, whence they emigrated in the early 1730s.

13. For the European background of the book, Yoder (1976) refers the reader to "Albertus Magnus" and "Kunst" in *Handworterbuch des Deutschen Aberglaubens* 1, cols. 241–43; and 5, cols. 817–36, respectively.

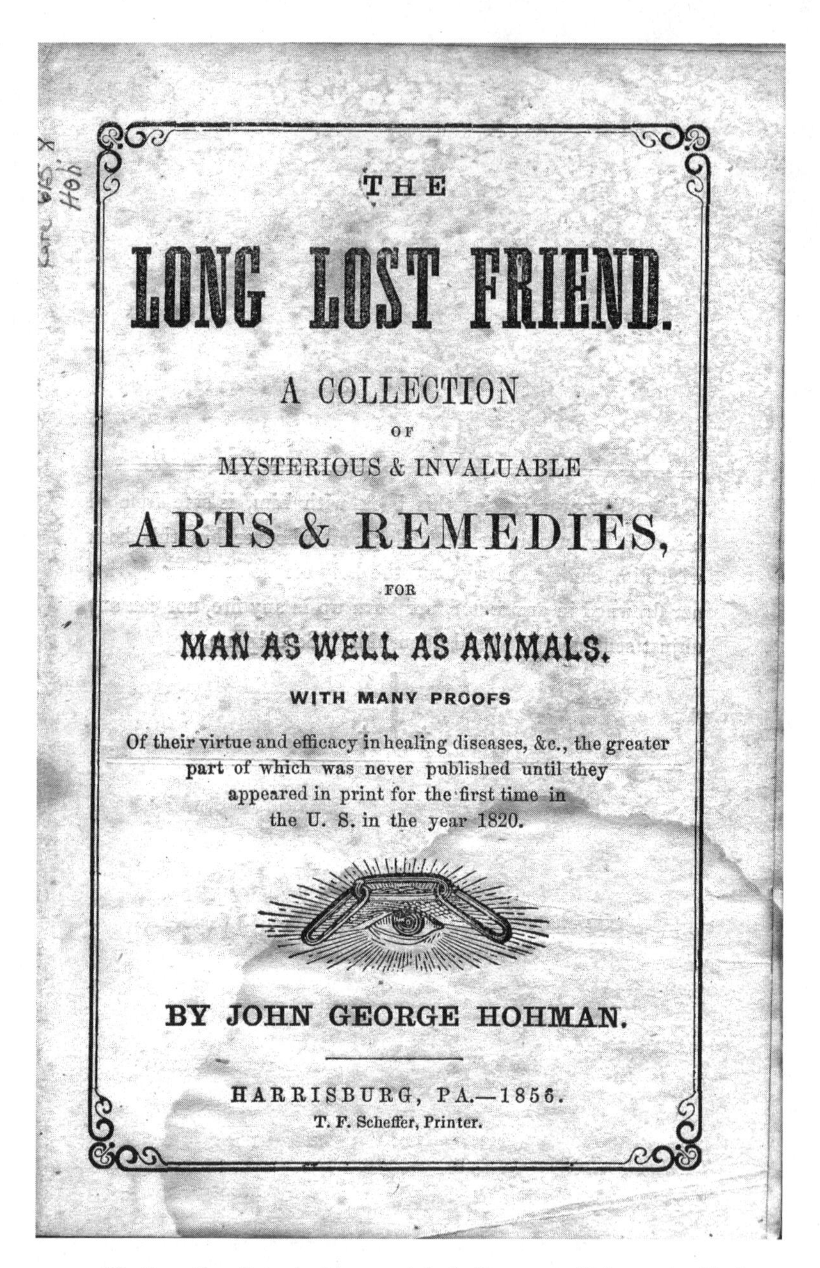
THE

LONG LOST FRIEND.

A COLLECTION

OF

MYSTERIOUS & INVALUABLE

ARTS & REMEDIES,

FOR

MAN AS WELL AS ANIMALS.

WITH MANY PROOFS

Of their virtue and efficacy in healing diseases, &c., the greater part of which was never published until they appeared in print for the first time in the U. S. in the year 1820.

BY JOHN GEORGE HOHMAN.

HARRISBURG, PA.—1856.

T. F. Scheffer, Printer.

FIG. 1. *The Long Lost Friend*, title page (1856). Courtesy of Mennonite Heritage Center, Harleysville, Pa.

Der
lange verborgene
Schatz und
Haus-Freund,
oder
Getreuer und Christlicher
Unterricht für Jedermann.

Enthaltend
Wunderbare und erprobte Mittel und Künste, für Gebrechen der Menschen und am Vieh.

Aus dem arabischen Schriften, des weisen Algemisten Omai Arey, Emir Chemir Tschasmir, ins Deutsche übersetzt und noch mit vielen andern Künsten vermehrt, welches zum Erstenmale in Amerika im Druck erscheint.

Herausgegeben von J. H........S.

Skippacksville, Pa. gedruckt bei A. Puwelle.
1837.

FIG. 2. German-language version of *The Long Lost Friend*, published in Skippackville, Pa., in 1837. Courtesy of Mennonite Heritage Center, Harleysville, Pa.

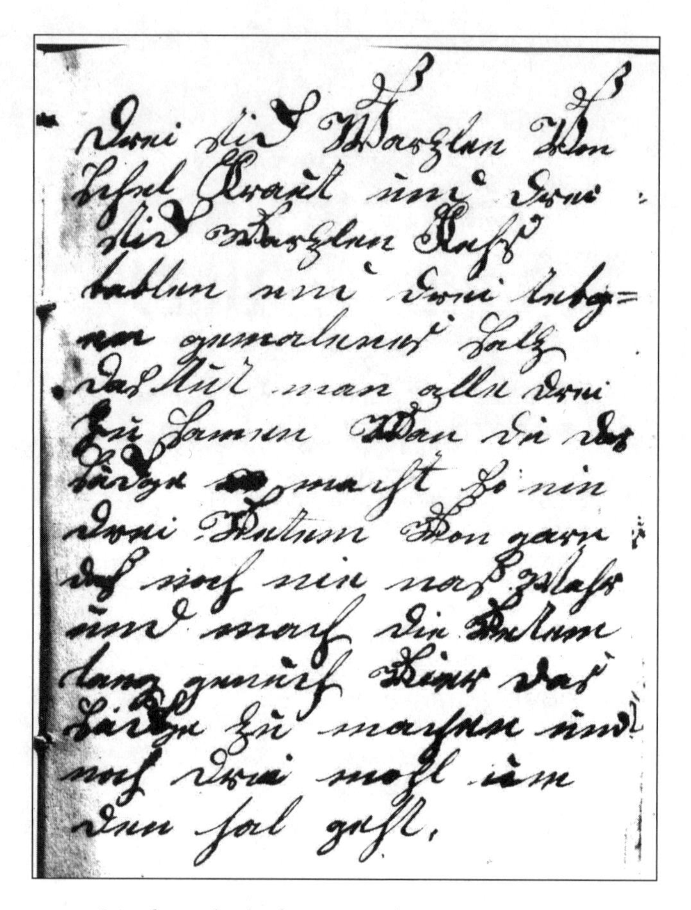

FIG. 3. Page from a book of powwow charms and recipes used by Joseph Overholt, c. 1855. Courtesy of Mennonite Heritage Center, Harleysville, Pa.

The 1900 edition is laid out much like *The Long Lost Friend* and contains "sympathetic as well as natural" remedies based in "white and black art." According to Yoder (1976, 242) the first American edition appeared in German in Pennsylvania in 1842 under the title *Albertus Magnus bewahrte und approbirte sympathetische und naturliche egyptische Geheimnisse fur Menschen und Vieh*, and the first English edition was published in Harrisburg in 1875.[14] A sample of recipes from the 1900 edition appears in Appendix 3.

14. In English the book is known as, *Albertus Magnus Verified and Approved Sympathetic and Natural Egyptian Secrets for Man and Beast.*

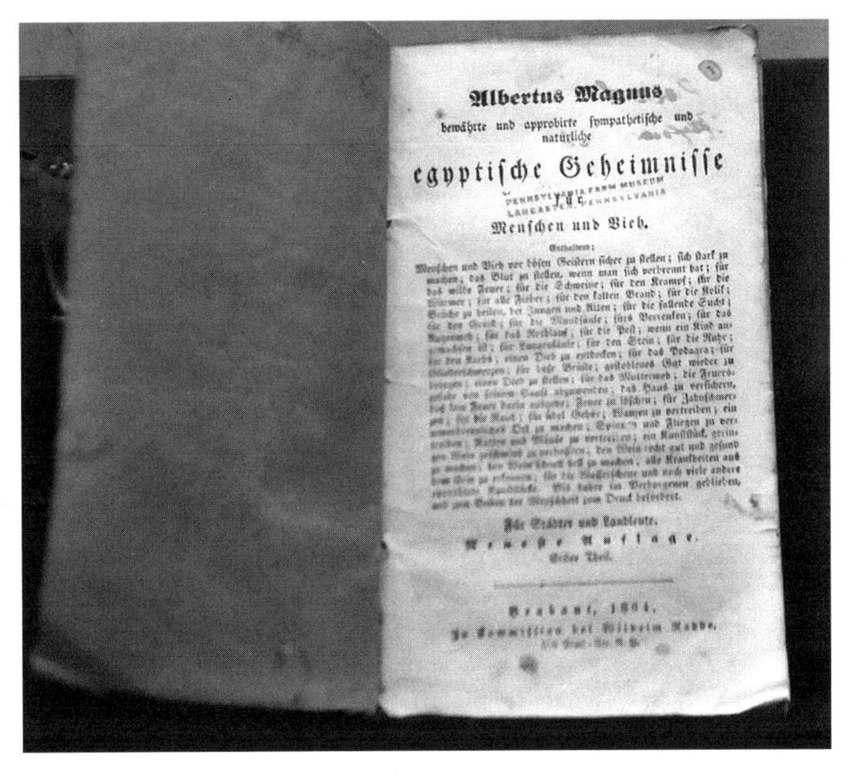

Albertus Magnus

bewährte und approbirte sympathetische und natürliche

egyptische Geheimnisse

für

Menschen und Vieh.

Für Städter und Landleute.

Neueste Auflage.

Erster Theil.

Brabant, 1864.

FIG. 4. A copy of *Albertus Magnus: Egyptian Secrets*, published in German in 1864. Landis Valley Museum library, Lancaster, Pa. Photo by David Kriebel.

The Sixth and Seventh Books of Moses

The Sixth and Seventh Books of Moses, a noncanonical text supposedly authored by the prophet Moses after the Torah, is considered more problematic than the others and is associated with black magic because it contains procedures for conjuring spirits. As its title implies, it contains two separate works, but it is always published in one volume. Few powwowers will admit to owning a copy or using it in their practice (but see case A27), and it is often considered a hex book. Mrs. Schultz recalls that when she was a little girl in the 1930s her neighbor (who was regarded as a witch) had a copy of the book and loaned it to her. When Mrs. Schultz's grandmother found out about it, she angrily returned it to the neighbor. Geraldine, a Pennsylvania Dutch woman who is also an amateur historian, has read some of the Albertus Magnus work but is afraid of this book: "I've never read the Moses book—frankly, I'm superstitious enough that I will not touch it, and I don't consider myself superstitious, but I do consider that—that there are powers on this earth that I don't understand and I'm not going to mess with something that I figure I'm too ignorant to mess with."

The Sixth and Seventh Books of Moses, like the Albertus Magnus work, derives from European magical traditions.[15] In nearly all other respects, however, this volume is quite unlike the other books in this section. While the others are fairly straightforward (if sometimes hard to implement) instructions and recipes, this book has the obscurity characteristic of many magical texts, both ancient and modern. It is geared toward what today would be called a "ceremonial magician," with many depictions of magic circles, seals, incantations, and other diagrams supposedly drawn from the Kabbalah, the Key of Solomon, and other ancient magical texts. The inscriptions and incantations include many of the mystical names of God, archangels, demons, and celestial bodies. My version also contains a treatise titled "The Magic of the Israelites." The language of the ritual instructions is mostly English, with some Latin, Greek, and Hebrew. The plates contain mainly Hebrew inscriptions, with some Latin characters. However, many of the characters are neither Hebrew, Latin, nor Greek; some resemble Egyptian hieroglyphs, and I have recognized characters that are identical in form with some from demotic Egyptian, a late form of the indigenous hieroglyphic Egyptian language.

Secrets of Sympathy

Secrets of Sympathy is one of a number of smaller charm books written by William Wilson Beissel of Leck Kill (Northumberland County) in 1938. Originally published as a sixteen-page chapbook, it was republished in 1998 as a section of the book *Powwow Power* by his great-nephew James D. Beissel of Willow Street (Lancaster County). I own a copy of the latter work. The spells ("sympathies") in this book resemble those in *The Long Lost Friend* and all contain explicitly Christian references drawn mainly

15. For the European background of the book, Yoder (1976) refers the reader to "Das sechste und siebente Buch Mosis," *Handworterbuch des Deutschen Aberglaubens* 6, cols. 584–93.

from events in the life of Jesus. It also includes a *Himmelsbrief*, a "Holy Fire-and-Pestilence Letter" to protect from illness and fire, which "the author" considered "the most important part of this entire booklet" (Beissel 1998, 33).

Yoder has identified the "sympathies" contained in this book as translations from another Pennsylvania Dutch work, *Dr. G. F. Helfenstein's vielfaltig erprobter Hausschatz der Sympathie; oder, Enthullte Zauberkrafte und Geheimnisse der Natur* (see Yoder 1976, 248 no. 24). This book was published in 1853 at Harrisburg by Scheffer and Beck in a joint edition with *Der lang verborgene Freund*. Like Hohman's work, this book claims to be itself an amulet of protection from harm for its possessor.

THE ROLE OF THE POWWOWER

While powwowers still practice today among Pennsylvania Dutch populations in southeastern and central Pennsylvania, the role of the powwower underwent radical change during the twentieth century. At the close of the nineteenth century, the existence of a practicing powwower in Berks County, Pennsylvania, was interesting enough to rate a long feature article in the *Reading Eagle*, but it was hardly news to the Pennsylvania Dutch people living there at the time. Today, however, even most of my Pennsylvania Dutch consultants do not believe powwowers still exist. That might be because there has been a decline in the actual number of powwowers, but the secrecy that surrounds the practice has certainly been a factor in the misperception that powwowing has vanished entirely.

The social position of the powwower varies. In the nineteenth century, most powwowers generally lived on farms or in isolated mountain areas. By 1929, however, based on reports from the time of the York Hex Murder Trial, many had moved into towns and even to cities, such as York and Lancaster. The notoriety of that trial and the mockery made of the "dumb Dutch" and their superstitions harmed the business of many powwowers. By the 1940s, powwowers were leaving urban areas. At the present time, all the traditional powwowers I am aware of live in rural areas or on the extreme outskirts of small towns. Difference in residence patterns is probably tied to the degree to which the powwower functions as a "professional" healer.

Before the twentieth century, the powwower's role in Pennsylvania Dutch society was not significantly different from that of the physician. That changed after the professionalization of biomedical practitioners, urged by the American Medical Association since its founding in 1847, took firm root in Pennsylvania and the country as a whole. From that point on, powwowing began to be seen as a mystical practice, and biomedicine as a scientific practice—another factor in pushing the "professional" powwower further from the center of Pennsylvania Dutch society.

In the twentieth century, powwowing has been practiced both by professionals and by laypersons, such as housewives. Unlike physicians, however, even professional powwowers cannot make a living on their healing practice alone, because the traditional mode of payment is a freewill offering—hardly the basis for a reliable income. Some powwowers even donate this money to the church. Therefore, the powwower must generally either have some other means of employment or be married to someone who does. Thus, all (or nearly all) powwowers play at least two roles, of which "powwower" is rarely the primary one, both because of the inadequate financial support powwowing provides and because of the secrecy attendant in powwowing. My consultant Leah Stoltzfus carries on a thriving powwowing practice just outside a small tourist town that appears to be largely unaware of it.[16]

Such variables as education, locale, and religious affiliation greatly influence reaction to powwowers. I found that relatives of powwowers and clients who visited a powwower as an adult generally had a much more favorable reaction to powwowers and a stronger belief in the efficacy of powwowing than did those with no experience with powwowing or who had visited a powwower as a child. They also had the general opinion that a "real" powwower must be a good person and behave decently; anyone claiming to be a powwower who lived a dissolute lifestyle (cursed, drank excessively, was not religious) was not considered a real powwower.

Several consultants who were powwowed as children reported being afraid of the powwower, who usually seemed to be odd in some way, whether by virtue of dress (one wore no shoes or socks), living conditions

16. "Leah Stoltzfus" is a pseudonym. The size of her powwowing practice is based on her own testimony. While she refused to give me specific numbers, her claim of having a large practice is validated by others in the community.

(in the mountains, away from civilization), or the mode of treatment (one was powwowed by having her face covered with a cloth).

GENDER AND ETHNICITY

There seems to be no correlation between gender and the profession of powwower. There are both male and female powwowers (and male and female witches as well). One of my consultants (Mrs. Lenhart) expressed the view that most powwowers she had heard about were men (as her family powwower was) and one (Leslie O'Keefe) said, "Every time I've heard of a powwow it was a woman," but I have no data to support either generalization throughout the culture area.[17] In fact, of the forty-five powwowers involved in consultant-reported cases during the twentieth century, twenty-four (53 percent) were female and twenty-one (47 percent) were male, an almost even split. Sometimes the nonprofessional powwower is referred to as the "grandmother type," but I have also seen nothing to suggest that most professional powwowers were male and that most nonprofessionals were female.

Most of my consultants have expressed the opinion that one need not belong to the Pennsylvania Dutch culture in order to practice powwowing, although one must generally know enough of the language to be able to use the appropriate incantations. For instance, I am aware of at least three African-American powwowers who practiced during the late nineteenth and early twentieth centuries, but in at least one case the powwower was half African-American and half Pennsylvania Dutch, a Lancaster woman who made her living from powwowing and became so prosperous she was able to own three houses. This was a remarkable achievement for any professional powwower, much less an African-American woman living in nineteenth-century America.

While knowledge of powwowing has always been available to anyone, regardless of ethnicity, it has also always been considered a specifically Pennsylvania Dutch tradition. Like many more-familiar American traditions (such as those surrounding holidays and meals), powwowing has its roots in German-speaking regions of Europe. However, unlike the use of

17. Both "Mrs. Lenhart" and "Leslie O'Keefe" are pseudonyms.

Christmas trees and eating scrapple, powwowing tended not to diffuse to the wider culture. Indeed, people who are interested in powwowing tend to be either those who want to preserve elements of Pennsylvania Dutch culture or those who see it as an exotic and hence interesting phenomenon.

PROFESSIONAL AND NONPROFESSIONAL POWWOWERS

Professional powwowers are distinguished by having large practices, having a special area of the house in which powwowing is performed, possibly with a waiting room, able to cure at least several illnesses, and having clients from outside the immediate neighborhood. Nonprofessionals, on the other hand, typically treat only their own family members, friends, and neighbors, usually specializing in a certain ailment. Nonprofessionals are rarely given a title, but when they are it is typically "Mr." or "Mrs.," or (in the case of an elderly woman) "Mother" or "Granny." Professional powwowers are often called "Doctor" or "Professor," the latter being applied only to males. The professionals may be further subdivided into those who perform it for money ("entrepreneurial" type) and those who do not ("traditional" type). The traditional type never specifies a fee, accepting money only when offered, but the entrepreneurial type often (and usually) does. Many individuals of the entrepreneurial type have been charlatans and indistinguishable from fortune-tellers and other scam artists, although some (such as "Professor" Howard Resh) seem to have believed in their powers.

Powwowers, like physicians, specialize. For instance, one consultant's father seemed to specialize in curing warts, my great-grandmother healed burns, and a mother-and-daughter team of Lancaster powwowers specialized in skin diseases. The contemporary powwower Aaron Boehm says he can cure only something that he can touch or that is evident from looking at the skin (skin diseases, varicose veins, and so forth).

Payment for powwowing services is handled indirectly. It is often expected but rarely requested. The normative view is that the power comes from God and that therefore no charge should be requested by the human who serves as a channel for divine power. Another reason has also been advanced for the nonacceptance of payment, namely, the Medical Practices Act of Pennsylvania, which specifically forbids anyone not meeting the definition of a medical doctor from practicing medicine (Aurand

1929, 10–14). That is why traditional powwowers will not make change when given money. Of course, powwowers of the entrepreneurial type have always had no problem charging for their services, handling the practice as a business.

SECRECY

A high degree of secrecy surrounds the practice of powwowing, and more so today than in previous times. During the course of my fieldwork, my inquiries were often met with suspicion, and I encountered a number of potential consultants who I believe lied to me about their knowledge of the practice. This widespread reticence to discuss powwowing is likely the result of two primary factors: the influence of Pennsylvania Dutch churches, especially the Conservative (Eastern) Mennonites (a Plain sect), and the consequences of the York Hex Murder Trial. All Conservative Mennonites I spoke with disapproved of powwowing and believed that its cures, to the extent that they work, come from the devil. The trial in York resulted in efforts to combat "superstition" with "scientific" education, beginning in the 1930s. This had the effect of attaching a stigma to those who practice powwowing or patronize powwowers. Later, I shall elaborate on secrecy as a response to secular and religious opposition to the practice.

THE RECRUITMENT AND TRAINING OF POWWOWERS

Because of the secrecy surrounding powwowing, the actual recruitment and training process is difficult to fully describe. There are a variety of beliefs regarding the qualifications necessary to be a powwower, ranging from the belief that anyone can learn it to the belief that one must have very particular qualifications from birth (for example, be the seventh son of a seventh son). Most who believe in the efficacy of powwowing have beliefs falling somewhere between these two extremes, so that some qualifications are necessary but may be minimal. A common belief is that to be a powwower one must believe in God, although it is theoretically not necessary to be a Christian (a Jewish person could do it, for instance), although reported cases consistently refer to the Christian beliefs of practitioners.[18] Calvin E. Rahn, himself the seventh son of a seventh son, believed one had to be born with the power and then "win your own private war with the devil just like I did" (Lewis 1969, 180).[19] Rachel Rahn claimed that the ability to stop blood was congenital and a requirement for further training as a powwower (Lewis 1969, 197).[20] Perhaps this was what she had in mind when she informed Hazel Sauer that she had the ability to become a powwower if she wanted to.[21] Some also believe the power is passed down through families (Lewis 1969, 11).

Other than powwowers who believe that the power runs in families or who otherwise train their own family members, some (like Rachel Rahn and Preston Zerbe) recruit from among their patients if they see someone whom they believe could learn the art. However, most training is at the initiation of the prospective powwower, who asks whether he or she can learn. Aaron Boehm did not hesitate to train another of my consultants, knowing that she would probably teach me.[22] He has also taught "six to ten" other people in Berks County to powwow.

A prospective powwower must be in good health, likely because the experience of healing drains the healer of energy, a sensation reported by a number of powwowers. As one Ohio powwower said, "A skinny person can't do it" (Studer 1980, 18).

Training procedures vary greatly, although one rule is nearly universal, namely, that only a woman can teach a man and only a man can teach a woman. The rule of cross-gender ("crossways") transmission is sometimes broken, as when Calvin E. Rahn (Lancaster County) taught his son Calvin M. Rahn, and when the ability to powwow was passed down in the male line through the Blymire family (York County).[23] Cross-gender transmission is used in other contemporary magico-religious practices, most notably in initiation into Wicca or similar neo-pagan sects.

Calvin M. Rahn claimed that when one powwower trains another the teacher gives up half his power to his student. He also indicated that the

18. The idea that it was necessary only to believe in God is held by Julius and Daisy Dietrich, who were taught that by Ruth Strickland Frey, as well as Anita Rahn. "Julius Dietrich," "Daisy Dietrich," and "Anita Rahn" are all pseudonyms. Ruth Frey is the real name of a renowned powwower.

19. "Calvin E. Rahn" is a pseudonym.

20. "Rachel Rahn" is a pseudonym. The actual woman shares a surname with "Calvin E. Rahn" but as far as I know is unrelated to him.

21. "Hazel Sauer" is a pseudonym.

22. "Aaron Boehm" is a pseudonym.

23. "Calvin M. Rahn" is a pseudonym.

two may end up becoming enemies (Beissel 1998, 54). However, this belief does not form part of the central tradition of powwowing.

Training time can take anywhere from a few minutes to a year. The training procedure used by Ruth Strickland Frey and passed on to Julius and Daisy Dietrich consisted of a ten-week program with all information imparted orally. When the initiate returned for the second session, he (or she) had to repeat all the incantations and gestures perfectly, as a sign the initiate was meant to become a powwower. Otherwise, training ceased and the individual was gently informed that he was not meant to learn and that there were other ways in which he could follow God's will. Every week of training, the initiate had to repeat back verbatim everything learned in all the previous lessons. Incantations that had to be memorized were mostly in English, but some were in Pennsylvania Dutch or German.[24] The cumulative memorization ensured that the powwower would be able to perform all the complicated hand movements and incantations deftly and swiftly (as Daisy was able to) without having to pause and remember or, worse, consult a book. This may have been intended to demonstrate the powwower's competence to the patient and therefore increase the patient's belief in the efficacy of the treatment and the powwower's power to heal.

Rachel Rahn also adopted a structured approach, believing that a prospective powwower must learn the cures for various ailments in a prescribed order. According to her, after learning how to stop blood (a congenital ability), the initiate's next step was to learn how to remove warts, then various other ailments, then the take-off, erysipelas, and tumors (Lewis 1969, 197). Because neither Mrs. Rahn, Daisy, nor Julius revealed anything more specific, it is impossible to accept or reject the possibility that all three used the same training program.

Aaron Boehm had an entirely different method. It was much briefer and easier, perhaps because he specialized in only one class of ailments, whereas Daisy and Julius can powwow for anything. Barbara Reimensnyder reports that she learned to powwow also using a simple method:

> It was so simple, so offhanded, so normal, that it took me by surprise and I said, "Does that mean I could powwow?"

24. The term used was "German," but many natives refer to the Pennsylvania Dutch dialect as "German."

> [Her consultant, Martin Steinbacher] chuckled, and said, "You could try." ["To try for," which is the English translation of *brauchen*, is another phrase used to describe powwowing.]

My female consultant and I had an almost identical experience with Aaron. I said, "Can she powwow now?" and he answered, "Sie kann brauch" (She can try).

Calvin E. Rahn's training method was the most dramatic. Being the seventh son of a seventh son, he was born with a great deal of power and struggled with the devil at a young age. He used this power as a "nonprofessional" powwower to minister to his family. When he decided to become a "professional," he realized he needed to increase his power and visited an elderly woman named "Amy" on Garrett Mountain in Cumberland County. He never tried to contact Amy before leaving home, because "I know'd in my heart she would" help him. When he reached her, she did indeed accept him and allowed him to stay in her shack. His account follows (Lewis 1969, 178–79).

> I stayed in that shack repentin' my sins day after day, hardly eatin' or drinkin' anythin' at all. This wasn't like attendin' a revival. This time I really searched my soul. Then, on the twenty-first day a miracle happened and I know'd I hadn't wasted those three weeks spent in prayer with that old lady.
>
> Suddenly I had a vision. I was in heaven at a table where the settin's were all in gold and everythin' was very beautiful. Saint Peter was sittin' at the head of the table. He spoke to me and invited me to set down with him and all the others.
>
> [At this point, Lewis reports that Calvin's voice fell to a whisper and he was crying, seeming oblivious to Lewis' presence.]
>
> I did what Saint Peter asked me and I set down with 'em all for a little while. Then he motioned me to get up and I did. I turned around and there, in front of me, was a long, long flight of golden steps. I know'd I was supposed to walk up 'em and so I did.
>
> At the top of the stairs was five Indians waitin' for me. They have been constant companions and guides through my life ever since.
>
> Once in a while, though, I'll send them off by themselves to

> help out some poor soul who's got a hex on him or is sick or somethin'. And once in a while, they'll go off on a mission of their own without tellin' me where they're goin.' But they always come back soon, every one of 'em.
>
> There they are now! There's Blue Cloud on his horse, there's Big Chief, there's the one I call Guardian Angel.

Of the other two, one was "just a little child—boy or girl, I've never been sure which. And the last one's not really an Indian, he's Hindu" (Lewis 1969, 179).

HEXING

Powwowing is related to but distinguishable from hexing or black magic. Black magic—*Hexerei* (hexing or witchcraft)—is practiced by witches, who put hexes (evil spells) on people. It is the opposite of powwowing, or "white magic." The view of most who believe in the efficacy of powwowing is that the powwower is the enemy of the witch, whose purpose is often to undo the witch's black magic. As one Pennsylvania Dutch woman, an amateur historian named Geraldine, notes, "The Pennsylvania Dutch feeling is that there are two life forces, *Braucherei*, the good life force based on Christianity, and *Hexerei*, or black magic, based in witchcraft. And I guess I kind of ascribe to that belief. And when it comes to anything that I consider black magic or devil worship or anything like that, I try to stay away from it. . . . I simply feel that I'm not smart enough or powerful enough to deal with it."

However, the relationship between powwower and witch is not always this straightforward, because the powwower (like the witch) uses supernatural power, and (as one consultant put it) "what he can take off, he can also put on." Another, who at one point started powwower training, was frightened off: "Back in the old days, I think powwow was great. I think it could be good today, but black magic is the negative part of powwowing."

In fact, when the powwower is called on to remove a hex from someone, he may use the power at his disposal to attack the hexer, in effect, putting a hex on the hexer. Therefore, the powwower does have the ability to throw hexes and is a potential danger himself. The murder victim

(Nelson Rehmeyer) in the York Hex Murder Trial was, according to the defendants' testimony, a powwower who placed a hex on another powwower (John Blymire), who himself evidently possessed the ability to hex people (Lewis 1969, 22–23). Therefore, the existence of black magic renders the powwower's position in the community problematic.

Witches—sometimes called "*hex* doctors," although the latter could also be applied to a powwower who removed hexes—were not well liked. They derived most of their income from hexing people whom others wanted to take revenge on. People always avoided a witch's house, because they believed that a witch would torment you for coming too close. Therefore, if a hex doctor wanted business, he had to travel (Shaner 1961).

According to local historian Richard Shaner (1961), one of the most famous was "Doc" Sterner, who lived high in the mountains above Kutztown. Working his way from Kutztown into the Poconos, Sterner usually managed to return home with enough meat and other foodstuff for a month. Local lore held that he had as many women as he wanted, and the men in the area believed he had a supernatural hold over women and could compel them to come to him.

In 1882 there was a rumor of a witch in Telford (Montgomery County). One resident went to a Philadelphia fortune-teller in an attempt to learn the witch's identity, whose influence was said to have affected various events. Witches also were said to be troubling the town in the 1920s.

COMBATING A HEX

The following account by William P. Shoemaker (1951) demonstrates that the witch and the powwower could be the same individual. It also presents a way an ordinary person could deal with a hex. I have condensed and paraphrased it here, but the basic narrative, including some of the expressions used, is preserved.

There once was an old woman in Berks County who everyone said was a witch. She has herself admitted being able to powwow for many ailments, but there were many people who would not even have her powwow their dog. She was always offering people large heads of cabbage that she raised herself, but no one who knew her reputation and believed in hexing would take one. One woman, who did not believe in hexing, did take a head of cabbage and placed it on a shelf in her cellar.That same night, one of the woman's three small children, a boy, began to cry uncontrollably. It appeared to his mother that he saw something that frightened him. She thought about the hex again and started to believe there might be something to the rumors. She immediately went to the cellar, took the head of cabbage, and found an old sword. She went into the backyard with the cabbage and used the sword to hack it into a thousand pieces. As she did this, she called the old woman's name, damning and cursing her and demanding that she stop tormenting her son and let him rest.

When the woman returned to the house, she found that her son had fallen asleep as if nothing was the matter at all. The other family members said he had become quiet as soon as she went out of the door (that is, when the cabbage was no longer in the house). However, they knew nothing about the cabbage or what she had done in the backyard until she told them afterward.

The next day, the old woman came to the house of the woman's neighbor and began to complain bitterly about her aching bones. The boy's mother overheard the conversation and heard the witch say that it felt as if her back were all chopped up and that she couldn't sleep that night.

One means of protecting a building from a witch is to place protective scrolls held by plugs of wood inserted in or near the windows and doors of the structure. I have collected two instances of this practice from Schuylkill County and one from Lehigh County. Daisy Dietrich reports using this method to protect a client in Schuylkill County several years ago. Mr. F provided the following account, relayed through his uncle.

F: My uncle told me that a friend of his across Schuylkill County had a large barn and had hex signs on it. But there were little square holes cut above each of the doors and windows of the barn. And in each one there was a little plug of wood the guy would pull out, and there was written in German special hex words to ward off the witches and evil spirits. At each of the animal stalls there was the same thing. And I asked him why the guy pulled it out. And he said that he had a very bad day that day [[after pulling out the plugs]].

David: So that's how he protected his barn?

F: By reading what was on the paper.

David: The little paper was inside like a cubbyhole in the barn that was plugged up with a piece of wood? Do you know what shape the paper was in?

F: It was rolled up in a scroll.

David: So it was a rectangular piece that had been rolled up?

F: My uncle went up there on business, but the man said, "Not a good day." So apparently the man was superstitious.

Darla Biehl of Allentown reports a similar procedure for keeping hexes out of a building, namely, folding pieces of paper into a triangles, placing three Xs on them, and placing the triangles in the windows. Daisy reports that she folds pieces of paper into triangles to make amulets of protection.

Geraldine reports a method to keep away witches: "I have heard of people who still believe that if you think a neighbor is a witch, you should put a broomstick across the door, because they will never step over it. I would say it's less than 5 percent of the population, tops, but there's always a few ultraconservative." She describes another method of protection: "I had a woman come in here and I truly thought that she belonged in a mental institution. And she would tell me things like, if the wind blew hard her mother would stand in a round rug because devils can't get through a circle, and all this type of thing, and this woman was really far out. I considered her over the line."

Darla Biehl, who had a younger sister who was hexed in the early 1930s and freed of the hex by a powwower, relates that her grandmother believed that if a hex victim traveled west and crossed two rivers, the evil spirits would fall out of the victim's body.

However, witches could be redeemed. According to Don Yoder's consultant, the well-known powwower Aunt Sophia Bailer, her brother John had a boarder who was a witch before he married Sophia's mother's maid and joined the church. Before that, as he was turning to God, he had difficulty finding peace with God for his previous actions. When Sophia was ten or eleven years old (around 1882) she heard him tell her mother that the devil used to come to him as he worked in the mines and made the coal so hard he could hardly pick it loose. The devil bothered this man every day to prevent him from turning to God. The last time, though, the man would not answer the devil; he found peace with God, joined the church, and lived a Christian life.

POWWOWING TODAY

While the practice of powwowing remains controversial, powwowers today resemble Christian faith healers more closely than folk magicians. Healing, whether physical or spiritual, is the main object of their practice. However, at least one prominent neo-pagan writer, Silver RavenWolf, has become a powwower, and she has reinterpreted the practice in magical terms, within the neo-pagan worldview. This appropriation of powwowing, however, has passed virtually unknown by those who operate in the traditional manner. And while there have been predictions of powwowing's imminent or actual disappearance for more than a century, those reports of its demise, to paraphrase Mark Twain, have been greatly exaggerated. Rather, powwowing may be expected to continue into the foreseeable future, if reinterpreted or driven underground, in a number of Pennsylvania Dutch communities.

THREE

POWWOW RITUAL: STRUCTURE AND PERFORMANCE

Powwowing is intimately tied to Christian belief.[1] Before a healing session begins, the powwower usually asks the client if he or she believes in the Christian doctrine of the Trinity. Most believe that faith in God—Father, Son, and Holy Spirit—must be shared by both healer and client if ritual power is to be successfully invoked and healing effected.[2] When faith is shared, both powwower and client are operating within the same symbolic universe. Cosmological beliefs also influence ritual elements. For instance, the "three highest names" (the Christian Trinity) are often used in incantations, many of which incorporate Bible verses. The number three, said to symbolize the Trinity, is ubiquitous in such sacred formulae. Finally, the question "Do you believe in God?" when asked, marks both powwower and patient as part of a sacred community and establishes a sacred ritual space.

Unlike most Christian healing traditions, powwowing makes use of elements that seem to belong more to Western magic, such as certain material components (eggs, lengths of string, and so on) and the inscription of protective circles around the afflicted (Foster and Anderson 1978, 72). By "Western magic," I refer to the long tradition of magical practice dating to the Mediterranean basin during the Hellenistic period, with roots in Greece and Egypt. This tradition was carried forward into the Christian world. For instance, there are many examples of magical texts from Roman Egypt in which God, Jesus, and various saints are invoked to bring about some magical effect.

These texts are quite similar in form to many powwowing spells. The distinction between Western and non-Western forms of magic is that the latter rely on the invocation or manipulation of animistic spirits while Western magic relies on spells that are transmitted orally or through written sources and that often make use of impersonal deistic powers, such as the elements or astral forces. The distinction between powwowing and other Western magic traditions is that the theory of powwowing requires the cooperation of God, while most Western spells are effective in and of themselves, even those including Western symbolism.

1. Of the seventy-five cases with data on the religious content of *Brauche* ritual, fifty-three (71 percent) showed evidence of Christian symbolism. See Table A19 in Appendix 7 for more details.

2. According to Clarence Kulp Jr., some believe that only the powwower needs to have faith (Kulp 1978).

Powwowing thus can be considered a ritual healing practice that resembles Western magic in its use of some incantations and material components but is firmly grounded in a Christian cosmology as expressed through words and symbols. The powwower regards God, not himself or herself, as the source of power. However, while some scholars, popular writers, and those who condemn the practice may consider powwowing a form of magic, that label appears to be completely rejected by powwowers and their clients, some of whom refer to it as "divine healing" (Studer 1980, 18). For them, powwowing is a natural religious practice that serves God and does not conflict with science.

The powwower is on the side of God when confronting the powwower's opponent, the witch or witch doctor.[3] The witch is the opposite of the powwower in every respect. The powwower serves God and acts as a channel of healing, where the witch's abilities ultimately come from the devil. The powwower gives God all the credit for successes, but the witch claims all the credit. The powwower was traditionally a respected member of the community and was considered almost a holy person, whereas the witch was traditionally excluded from the community, considered strange, and feared.

The presence of a religious practice with magical trappings within predominantly Protestant populations suggests to Don Yoder that it represents a Roman Catholic practice that went underground after the Reformation. Yoder interprets the Catholic use of ritual blessings and sacramentals as implying a belief in the "holiness of material objects." This belief encouraged the principle that supernatural power could be mobilized for healing through the mediation of material objects and human healers. That notion is basic to what Yoder terms "magico-religious" folk medicine (Yoder 1990, 95).

The Reformation, in renouncing the Pope and the Catholic hierarchy, took the more radical move of severing symbols from their referents. That is why anthropologist Mary Douglas finds it understandable that antiritualist Protestants should find little difficulty in turning to Eastern religions, claiming that the path of Protestantism leads to a rejection of "first the Eucharist, then inevitably sooner or later the Incarnation; for the same social process which made the first repugnant was bound to lead to a rejection of the other" (Douglas 1996, 168).

3. Although "hex doctor" is sometimes used to refer to one who can remove hexes, such a person is typically also able to function as a witch.

Yoder notes that as part of their program of deritualization, Protestant church authorities rejected religious healing, leaving it for lay practitioners. He notes that folk healing was driven underground in Protestant Europe, to emerge in such practices as powwowing that exist apart from official religious authorities (Yoder 1990, 95). It is therefore not surprising that most opposition to powwowing arises from the most radical Protestant sects—Anabaptist groups such as the Mennonites and the Amish—and that powwowing should secretly exist within such communities.

THE MECHANICS OF POWWOW HEALING

Powwow healing is typically performed in close proximity to the patient. The powwower must at least be able to see the patient, and in cases of rituals involving somatic components (gestures or body positions) must be very close to the patient, in some cases actually touching the patient's bare skin. However, there are cases when powwowers can heal remotely. Daisy Dietrich requires only the patient's full name and ailment to be able to heal someone she has never met. She also must know what time the ritual is to take place and specifies that the patient must sit in a chair, face east, and hold a Bible, just as if he or she were physically present. Aunt Sophia Bailer, Don Yoder's powwow consultant, told him how she stopped the bleeding of a man seriously hurt in a mine accident ten miles from her home (Yoder 1967, 40). There was no time to take her to the scene of the accident, so the miner's friends phoned Sophia, and she powwowed for him. All she needed was the baptismal name of the patient. In this case, the patient knew someone was praying for him. The serious bleeding stopped, and he recovered.

Many procedures in healing rituals are repeated three times—again, most likely symbolizing the Holy Trinity in Christian theology. The "three highest names"—Father, Son, and Holy Ghost—are often included in published powwowing incantations and are said to be repeated at the end of a ritual. However, in twentieth-century powwowing, particularly toward the end of the twentieth century, any incantation "spoken" was inaudible to the patient and considered a secret that must be kept.

Many powwow cures are contained in charm books such as Hohman's *Long Lost Friend* and other documentary sources, such as recipe books, diaries, and accounting ledgers. These written rituals, which I shall call "spells" or "recipes," depending on whether they involve actual healing or the compounding of healing mixtures, respectively, contain a number of actions, which I shall refer to as "ritual components."

Ritual Components

I have grouped ritual components into three major categories: "verbal components" (meaningful utterances, including incantations), "somatic components" (meaningful movements of the powwower's hands over the patient's body or the patient's body position), and "material components" (the manipulation or application of material objects or substances). These components are frequently combined in a ritual, but they do not have to be.

It is important to bear in mind three points regarding ritual components. First, they are components of behavior, not particular patterns or objects. The latter I term "elements." Thus, the sign of the cross is an element of a ritual's somatic component (for example, drawing the sign of a cross), and an egg is an element of a material component (for example, having the patient place an egg in his mouth). Second, both powwower and patient make use of such components, although they differ in purpose: the powwower's components are active, shaping how the ritual is conducted, whereas the patient's components are passive, forming part of the initial conditions for the ritual (for example, verbal declaration of a belief in God or placing the patient's body in a certain position). Third, to be considered present in the ritual, components must be meaningful in themselves rather than merely a necessary adjunct for another component. Thus, the utterance "Please sit in that chair and face east" does not qualify as a verbal component but rather is an adjunct to a somatic component (sitting facing east). In the same manner, merely rubbing spittle on the skin is not a somatic component, but rather is necessary in order to apply spittle, an element of a material component. If, however, the rubbing described a meaningful pattern, such as the sign of the cross, the action would include a material component (the application of the element "spittle") and a somatic component (the hand movement describing the element "cross").

An example from a familiar ritual is helpful here. A Roman Catholic

Mass (or most Protestant communion services) contains the following verbal, somatic, and material ritual components:

Verbal components: Reading the liturgy (by the celebrant) and appropriate responses (by the communicant). An element of the former would be the phrase "The Lord be with you," and an element of the latter would be the words "And also with you."

Somatic components: Kneeling, holding hands in the prescribed manner to receive the host in bread or wafer form, making the sign of the cross (by the communicant). Elements would be the kneeling and hand positions, or the sign of the cross.

Material: Placing the host on the hand or in the mouth of the communicant, giving wine to communicant (by the celebrant). Consuming the host by letting it dissolve in mouth without chewing (by the communicant). Elements would be bread (or wafer) and wine.

Verbal Components

Verbal components used in powwowing employ utterances or written spells. Elements of verbal components include words, whether audible or subvocal, that the powwower uses as part of the powwowing ritual. They may be simple or complex. In the latter case, they are usually uttered (or subvocalized) in concert with a somatic or material component. Subvocal or whispered incantations are the norm, pronounced so that the patient cannot hear them. They may also include utterances by patients declaring or assenting to belief in God.

Somatic Components

Somatic components used by powwowers are movements of the powwower's hands over the patient's body or placing hands on the patient's body. The former is the most common type of powwowing procedure, reported in 80 percent of the cases, including my own experience as a powwow patient. The latter is much rarer and closely resembles the form of religious healing known as "laying on of hands." Somatic components may be used by patients as well. These always involve the patient's assuming a certain body position.

Hand Movements

Hand movements are a type of somatic component in which the hands are moved over the body of the patient in a fashion that appears to be symbolic or that otherwise carries some significance not related to the application of a substance (see material components, below). Often these movements are performed while murmuring an incantation that the patient cannot hear well enough to understand or that makes no sense to the patient. The hands of the powwower usually cover most of the patient's body, most often working from head to foot. Special attention is paid to any part of the patient's body that the patient indicates is the site of the illness or pain. During this procedure, the patient is sitting or lying down. Three contemporary powwowers I interviewed—Daisy and Julius Dietrich (Schuylkill County) and Anita Rahn (Lancaster County)—use this method exclusively.

Laying on Hands

Laying on hands is a somatic component that involves the powwower's placing his or her hands on the patient's skin at the site of the problem and either holding them there or rubbing them. An incantation may or may not be used.

Body Position

Body position refers to the positioning of the powwower's or patient's body during the ritual. Most often it is the patient who assumes a certain position as directed by the powwower. Daisy Dietrich, for instance, told me to sit in a chair and face east, then to stand up. Elaine Madeira was instructed by Mrs. A to lie down on her back.[4] In such cases, the body position is not part of the ritual per se, but allows the powwower to conduct the ritual. If the patient does not assume such a position, the ritual cannot proceed. However, when a powwower assumes a certain body position, it is a part of the ritual, just as much as hand movements and laying on hands are.

Material Components

Material components are procedures that involve the manipulation of material objects or substances, including rubbing those objects or sub-

4. "Mrs. A" is a pseudonym.

stances on the body. This is frequently combined with an incantation. It is distinguished from the somatic component of hand movements in that the latter involve movements that appear to be symbolic or otherwise have significance in themselves. Published collections of charms (see below) contained recipes that often instructed powwowers on how to use such elements. Some of these are listed below:

Eggs

Eggs are the most common material objects used in powwowing. I have collected cases in which they were used alone or with a cord or string or with needles or pins. The egg is often thrown into a stove, presumably to destroy the problem that the egg had come to represent. Mrs. Lenhart cited a cure for stomach problems in which her powwower Mr. Rodenbaugh[5] used a raw egg to cure her and her husband.[6] In it, Rodenbaugh tied a red silk string around an egg and placed it in a wood stove. Cures for stomach problems most often use this procedure, but it was also used to treat psoriasis. A similar procedure was used in Maryland to diagnose "marasmus," a wasting away of the body,[7] in young children (Hand 1980, 114).

In one hex removal case, the powwower instructed the victim of the hex to urinate on an egg, stick a needle in it, then bury it. Shortly after the victim performed this procedure, the hexer appeared, demanding to know where the egg was buried and complaining that she was unable to "go to the bathroom," presumably to urinate.[8]

The egg, in such cases, seems to function as a *Zwischentrager*, or intermediate agent of disposal (Hand 1980, 3). Such objects take on an illness, which then is cured when the object is cast away or destroyed. This

5. Pseudonym.

6. Her stomach problem had been especially bad, according to the powwower, after the egg broke and blew ashes out the front.

7. This term "marasmus" (take-off, or decline) has been used as an equivalent for the Pennsylvania Dutch *abnemme* (*abnehme*, *opnema*) (Fogel 1915, 276).

8. The consultant could provide no explanation for this procedure, but in European and Euro-American magical healing traditions, pins may be used in "nailing" or "plugging," a procedure in which the hair, nails, blood, expectoration, or even the breath of the sick person is implanted into a tree (Hand 1980, 87). Pins are also known to be used to harm an individual if inserted into a poppet or other object representing the victim (Hand 1980, 222). The pin may have represented a kind of "plugging" of the hexer's body (represented by the egg), with the urine indicating the kind of affliction the hexer was to suffer. An alternative possibility is that the pin may have been meant to fix the urine onto the egg as a characteristic of the egg, and the burial may have been intended to prevent the hexer from "finding" urination.

would be an example of "contagious magic," one of Frazer's two main branches of "sympathetic magic," in which a quality is transferred from one object or being to another by virtue of having once been in contact (Frazer 1922, 37–38).[9]

The egg is also a common symbol in religious and magical practice, both Christian and non-Christian. In her book *An Egg at Easter*, folklorist Venetia Newall notes that the egg has been a symbol of life[10] in many cultures throughout the world, including those of the German-speaking homelands of early Pennsylvania Dutch populations. As a symbol of life, the egg could become a vicarious human sacrifice (Newall 1971, 69) used to propitiate evil or protect a building by incorporation in the structure's foundation (46–50). Thus, the egg would seem to be a particularly appropriate intermediary agent for use in a healing ritual. The Christian context of the powwowing ritual fits nicely with this conception, because Christ himself served as a substitute sacrifice for the whole human world. Indeed, the egg has long been viewed by Christians as a symbol of the Resurrection of Christ (West 1989, 58).

String, Thread, or Measuring Tape

Mrs. Lenhart said Mr. Rodenbaugh also cured her of stomach fever and the "take-off" by measuring her with a measuring tape from the top of her head to her feet. This method is also documented by Reimensnyder in Union County for the "take-off." A powwower describes the method: "I'd start at the crown of the head. You laid them on the belly. You measured the back . . . clear down to the heel. Then you measure the length of the foot. Then you have to take the string seven times into the length of their foot. . . . What's over shows how bad they had this falling away of the flesh. . . . The take-off, that's what we used to call it" (Reimensnyder 1982, 112–13).

This use of measuring with thread is a well-documented method of diagnosing the wasting illnesses variously known the "take-off" (*opnema, abnemmes*), "flesh decay," "go-backs," or "short (or long) growth" throughout Pennsylvania, as well as southern and midwestern states

9. I shall employ Frazer's terminology because it is a useful shorthand for describing common magical practices across cultures and is undoubtedly familiar to many readers, but I do not accept Frazer's general theory of magic, religion, and science, which has been amply shown to be, at best, an oversimplification that ignores key features of practice and belief.

10. Eggs may also be symbols of creation, the sun, and immortality in many cultures throughout the world.

(Hand 1980, 110). The popular belief is that the height (measured from head to toe) should be seven times the length of the foot (measured from heel to toe). Deviations indicate "short" or "long" growth. Other methods of body measurement, used in Germany, Scandinavia, and the Slavic[11] regions, have been reported in Pennsylvania, Maryland, and Virginia but are otherwise unattested in the United States (Hand 1980, 109–10).

Thread could also be used to heal, as well as diagnose, illness. Used in this way, it fits within the genre of "passing through," in which the sick individual passes through an object (such as a horse collar, a hoop, or the crotch of the tree) or between the legs of a table, an animal, or a human. Hand (1980, 112), cites a classic case of powwowing using thread in this way. In his example, the measurement is performed as described above, then a loop is made and the child is passed through nine times. The thread is then placed somewhere so it will wear out fast. In such a ritual, the thread, like the egg, functions as a *Zwischentrager*, for when the thread wears out, the child is cured.

The use of thread as a symbol is ancient and generally means a mystical connection of some sort. The Upanishads use thread (*sutra*) as a metaphor for the connection between the temporal world and the "other world" (Chevalier and Gheerbrant 1996, 991–992), while the Zohar suggests that it symbolizes ties between the spiritual, biological, and social planes (Circlot 1983, 341). In magical rituals, as Mircea Eliade has noted, thread can be tied into bonds or knots that may either protect against illness, sorcery, or wild animals or restrain human enemies, living or dead, from causing injury (Circlot 1983, 192). In cases in which color is prescribed, that color is almost always red, with obvious connections to blood and life.

Beyond these general possibilities, specific explanations can be offered for the use of thread in curing erysipelas and the "take-off." The typical thread used in powwowing for erysipelas, or *rote laufa*, a red inflammation of the skin, is a length of red silk. This is an apparent use of sympathetic magic (Hand 1980, 113), using the homeopathic principle of "like cures like." I want to emphasize the word "apparent" because this is an external ("etic") view; powwowers would not use the term "magic" to describe

11. Citing Phyllis Kemp's 1935 work on healing ritual of the Southern Slavs, Hand (1980, 110) notes that Pennsylvania Dutch practices of measuring the wrist, elbow, and foot are "reminiscent of a South Slavic cross-measurement, namely, from the right great toe to the middle finger of the left hand, and vice versa."

what they do, and at least today they do not think in terms of such "principles."

In the case of the take-off, Pennsylvania Dutch folklorists Thomas Brendle and Claude Unger suggest a more general motivation behind measuring, that of temporarily creating a likeness of the sick person:

> At the present time when we [Pennsylvania Dutch] speak of taking a photograph we use the word *abnemme*. Similarly, when a person was measured from the crown of his head to the sole of his foot and crosswise from tip to tip of his outstretched arms—the height is to be as great as the width—he is *abgenumme*, measured off or taken off. His correct likeness is taken. In that likeness his diseases are tied with knots. Symbolically a rebirth is represented. (Brendle and Unger 1935, 147)

This explanation suggests that what is created in the measuring process—the "likeness" of the person being cured—is the important part of the ritual and that the disease may adhere to that likeness rather than to the actual victim. When an ill person was measured in medieval and Renaissance Germany and Scandinavia and found to have unequal height-width proportions as described by Brendle and Unger, above, he was said to have "lost his measure" and to be in need of healing. While Hand notes that this concept is not known in the United States (1980, 108), it may survive implicitly in powwowing rituals of measurement that create and then discard a likeness reflecting "lost measure" and illness.

Saliva

Saliva can be used as a kind of healing salve to cure a problem visible on the skin, such as warts or peeling skin. In most cases, the saliva is that of the powwower. This fits nicely into the Christian background of powwowing, because in the Gospels Jesus (sometimes called "the first powwower") used his saliva to heal the blind (John 9:6). It is also in accord with a broader tradition that saliva and other healing bodily emissions, to be effective, should be from a person known for innocence, moral excellence, or virtue (Hand 1980, 48–49). A powwower, as a channel of divine power, would seem to qualify.

Along with blood, mucus, urine, and other body secretions, saliva is viewed in many cultures as a magical agent of transmission because it is a substance that has been in the body but can leave it and potentially enter another body. While some other magico-religious traditions also give saliva the power to heal, this is not a universal attribute. Some traditions view saliva as a destructive substance that can pass on disease or symbolize insult (Chevalier and Gheerbrant 1996, 822).

Potatoes and Pennies

Both potatoes and pennies were used to remove warts by rubbing. The healer would rub the affected area with either a potato half or a penny and then instruct the patient to bury it in his backyard. When a potato was used, tradition held that when the buried potato rotted, the wart would go away. Hand reports a similar procedure from North Carolina, in which an Irish potato was rubbed on warts and then placed in a sack, which was then placed in a fork in the road. In that instance, whoever picked up the sack got the warts (Hand 1980, 2).

This principle of contagion is also present in the use of pennies in powwowing. Pennies were considered to "carry" the wart, and if they were not buried they were to be set aside and not used, because whoever received the penny would develop a wart soon after. In both such instances, potatoes and pennies may be viewed as *Zwischentragers*.

In the case of pennies, rubbing was not always performed. In such cases, the healer said he would "buy" the wart from the patient. There is disagreement about whether these wart procedures are actually powwowing or simply a "home remedy."

Table or Chair Legs, or Horse Collar

The practice of passing a child around a table leg, a chair leg or rungs, or through a horse collar, usually three or nine times, is most commonly used to cure livergrown or the take-off. Like passing a child through a loop of thread, these are forms of the curative practice of "passing through" documented throughout Europe and North America (Hand 1980). When a horse collar was used, often the collar had to be warm, suggesting contact with the animal itself. In such cases, the collar may serve as a substitute for being passed under the legs of the horse (Hand 1980, 163).

The similarity of such practices around the world, where they can use a bewildering array of objects (windows, doors, hoops, pant legs, stones with holes or clefts, bushes, crotches of trees, animal or human legs, a hank of yarn, even women's underwear), suggests some cross-cultural reason for their use. Possible candidates include the idea that the disease is "scraped off" the person who is passed through and magically transferred to the object, or that the object represents a barrier to pursuit by illness-causing evil spirits (Hand 1980, 171–72). The most obvious explanation is that it symbolizes rebirth, an explanation advanced by a number of authorities, including Brendle and Unger (1935, 147). None of these explanations can be adequately tested, although the last one fits in most easily with Pennsylvania Dutch ideas of disease causation and healing. In any case, even if passing through a horse collar or around a table leg began as a symbol of rebirth, it is certainly not seen that way now. It is simply viewed as a prescribed healing method passed down from long ago.

Stones

Powwowers were known to use stones in performing their rituals, either to increase their power or for special purposes, such as relieving pain. Sometimes such stones were considered one-of-a-kind items, as with the stone passed down to John Rhoads from his mother and with Preston Zerbe's "divinity stone." The name may have been inspired by the stone's use in divination, a practice used routinely by one of Zerbe's students. In various cultures, stones have been used for this purpose, as well as for healing, through rubbing the diseased area with the stone and then discarding it (Chevalier and Gheerbrant 1994, 937–38; Hand 1980, 20). In such cases the stone serves as a *Zwischentrager.*

Religious Objects

The Bible is sometimes used as a ritual element. It may be held by the patient or by the powwower, or placed under a pillow to ward off hexes. One powwower I interviewed insisted that her patients hold a Bible in their laps as powwowing was being performed; if the Bible shook, it indicated that the patient lacked faith. One Catholic powwower routinely used holy water in her rituals (Lewis 1969). While the sign of the cross is made in many powwowing rituals, to my knowledge an actual cross has not been used in powwowing.

Animal Parts and Excreta

Substances such as urine, cow dung, cat's blood and hair, and the bladder of a hog have all been used in powwowing rituals. The use of animal parts or fluids is common in healing traditions worldwide, though less so in the United States because the animal was often killed to collect such materials and because a strong Christian tradition in this country has deemphasized animal sacrifice. When sacrifice is made, the animal should be perfect in some way. For instance, a powwowing ritual to cure erysipelas and consumption requires the blood of a black cat whose coat contains no white hairs (Hand 1980, 196). On the other hand, I collected an early twentieth-century powwow cure for an injured foot that required the patient to walk in cow dung in a field—no particular cow was specified, and certainly none was killed.

Hot Coal

Hot coal was typically used either to produce sparks by blowing on it or to produce smoke. The antipowwowing preacher Daniel Weiser theorized a "like cures like" rationale for this action in curing erysipelas, so that one would "fight fire with fire." However, the practitioners themselves did not subscribe to this invoking of the Frazerian "law of similarity." The purpose of creating smoke is unclear, although in one case a powwower was trying to get the cooperation of "the spirits." Smoke is often associated with spirit(s) and, as such, is used in Native American ceremonies (Chevalier and Gheerbrant 1996, 890) and "high church" religious services. Both may have influenced the development of powwow ritual.

Geological Features or Astronomical Bodies

Certain locations, such as a hill or the moon, may be used as a "sink" for illnesses removed. The powwower would cure by sending the illness to the designated location. The Hexenkopf ("Witch's Head"), a hill in Northampton County, is probably the most famous example of such a place in the Pennsylvania Dutch heartland. The Hexenkopf was said to have become a place of evil because of all the evil spells that had been removed and deposited there by powwowers (Heindel 2005).

Magical Items

I have collected one case in which possession of a certain item is sufficient to allow a person not trained in powwowing to powwow. This derives from the late nineteenth-century newspaper account of the activities of "Doctor" John Rhoads.[12]

12. More information on Rhoads appears in Chapter 5.

Rhoads made what he called "Rhoads bundles," with which anyone could "pow-wow." He sold these "by the dozen to people all over Eastern Pennsylvania." These consisted of packets "an inch long and 1/4 inch in diameter," and the illustration in the article shows a miniature scroll consisting of "3 hollow pieces of the stalk of an old herb wound with a piece of red flannel and tied with an ordinary brown string" ("Magic Healing" 1895–99).

Rhoads gave a Rhoads bundle to a reporter from the *Reading Eagle* with these instructions: "Whenever you have anything sore about any part of your person run the end of the packet in the blood of suppurated matter of the wound or sore until the little hollows at both ends are filled with blood or pus. Then put the packet to some place where neither sun or moon can shine upon it. Keep the 'bundle' thus hidden away until the wound or (unreadable) is healed and then burn it. It is a sure cure. The sore so treated always commences to heal from within outward. When it looks healed on the outside you can rest assured it is healed" ("Magic Healing" 1895–99).

Use of Ritual Components

Both the powwower and patient use certain ritual components, much as actors in a theatrical production will use a certain gesture or prop in a certain way. The nature of the use varies with the situation and the actor.

Components Used by the Powwower

Verbal components, when used by the powwower, articulate a statement relating the ailment and the cure, ranging from Aaron Boehm's simple incantation to the complex series of utterances in English, Pennsylvania Dutch, and High German used by Daisy Dietrich. Incantations may be in oral or written form, the latter often being used in the fabrication of amulets. The incantations specified in Hohman's *The Long Lost Friend* fall into two categories. Incantations using religious imagery usually either relate the patient's ailment to a similar one dealt with by Jesus or to a biblical event or location (such as the rivers flowing from Eden), or simply invoke the blessing or power of Jesus or the triune Christian God. Incantations that do not include any obvious religious imagery are usually simple statements such as "It is all over!" and are usually combined with material components.

Somatic components used by the powwower (hand movements and laying on hands) establish a connection between powwower and patient. The most direct connection is the laying on of hands, a religious healing practice with a long history in official and unofficial Christianity. I have had the priest at an Episcopal church in Baltimore lay hands on me as part of a healing service. The gesture had overtones of concern and care. Leah, who uses this method, explicitly likens it to a gesture of affection by a mother caring for a child: "When we were sick, my mother rubbed us. It's my instinct to do that." Hand movements may not involve actual contact with the body, but they may outline it. In complicated rituals, hand movements describe signs (such as the cross) over the body of the patient, appearing to consecrate it. In such cases, the hands of the powwower are the medium through which the body of the patient is brought into the sacred realm and connected to divine power.

In the contact established by the powwower's somatic components there is a danger to the powwower, who may catch the patient's ailment. To safeguard against this, the powwower may at intervals remove his or her hands from the patient and make "shaking off" or "wiping off" motions. This motion implies a belief that the faith of the powwower plays a role in determining whether he or she will catch the illness or other ailment afflicting the patient. For instance, John Hickernell, of Schaefferstown, reports that his uncle Harry was good at curing erysipelas but nine out of ten times would catch the disease himself. Another powwower, Eliza Hartman, believed that this was because Harry's faith was not strong enough. Because of this danger, one of my consultants said, "You should be in good health to do this [[powwowing]]."

Material components employ elements that appear to play an iconic role, standing for various things. For instance, a wooden figure could be made to stand for a witch, so that whatever was done to the figure was done to the witch (and thereby caused the witch to remove her own hex from a victim). Other stand-ins for witches include a cabbage grown from the witch's garden, a raw egg, and a lock of hair. As Barbara Reimensnyder noted (1982, 104–5), this procedure falls under Frazer's concept of "sympathetic magic," that is, it uses objects having a "sympathy" for, or similarity to, other objects or bodies. Some powwowers use the term "sympathies" to refer to any powwowing ritual (Beissel 1998, 31) and Hostetler defines powwowing as "sympathy healing" (1976, 252–53). Other substances (the *Zwischentragers* discussed above) seemed to have the ability to take on the illness, and fall under the Frazerian category of "contagious magic." For instance, a wart could be "transferred" to a potato, a string, or a penny. "Infected" potatoes and strings would then be buried and the wart would disappear when they rotted. Pennies "carrying" warts were said to be contagious, so whoever picked the penny up would get the wart.

At least some of the material components may relate to specific Christian ideas about the self. For instance, if the "passing through" rituals indeed suggest rebirth, as Brendle, Unger, and others have proposed, they may be enacting a pervasive Christian symbol—the "second birth" in Christ. As is well known in American culture, many follow the New Testament injunction "You must be born again" (John 3:3). Saint Paul, in his letter to the Roman church (Rom. 6:4) equated this rebirth with a death to sin, paralleling Christ's death on the cross: "We were buried therefore with him by baptism into death, so that as Christ was raised from the dead by the glory of the Father, we too might walk in newness of life." It is also noteworthy that early Christian tombs usually bear inscriptions describing the day of the person's death as his "birthday."

Components Used by the Patient

Patients' use of ritual components is always at the direction of the powwower and nearly always forms part of the conditions necessary for the ritual to take place, rather than part of the healing mechanism itself. In a few cases (such as the patient's verbal components noted below), the patient uses verbal or somatic components in an active way, as part of the ritual. In many cases, however, the patient is required to use no ritual components at all, the conditions for the ritual being limited to the agreement between powwower and patient that the ritual should be performed.

When used by the patient, verbal components are usually limited to types of statements: declaration of belief in God and the patient's full name. If the patient is a Christian, the name given should be the name under which the patient was baptized. These statements carry religious affirmations designed to situate the patient within the community of believers. They are usually omitted in consultant descriptions of rituals, being mentioned only in response to a question. If patients are directed to use a verbal component in an active way, it generally involves a religious utterance, such as the Lord's Prayer or using other words from the Bible.

Patients may also be directed to use a somatic component, nearly always body position. Within this category, I include actual positions of the body and injunctions about motion or use of senses (go or don't go somewhere; look or don't look at something). Sometimes the patient must sit in a certain way (most commonly facing east), occasionally in a special chair, such as the "powwow chair" on display at the Schaefferstown Museum. The patient may remain seated during the entire ritual or be directed to stand at intervals. When a patient is directed to stand facing the moon (as Aaron Boehm directs his patients to do) or to lie prone, sometimes with eyes closed, the position is held by the patient throughout the ritual.

Patients may also be asked to provide the elements of the material components, which are then used by the powwower. (Although when the powwower cannot be present, he or she directs the patient to manipulate the elements in a certain way.) I have counted such actions as part of the powwower's material component because the patients are acting as the powwower's helpers in such cases, not as patients.

Consultants, even powwowers, could throw no light on the significance of these postures. However, Ruth Frey and Daisy Dietrich's insistence that the patient hold a Bible containing both Old and New Testaments throughout the ritual was clearly religious—Daisy used this also as a means of determining sincerity of belief because it was believed that unbelievers could not hold the Bible steady. The direction east signifies rebirth in many religious traditions and is also the direction of the Holy Land from the United States. Traditionally, Christians were to be buried facing east, as well. A secure explanation, however, remains elusive.

The Special Status of Material Components

Of the three categories of components used in powwowing, material components are the least easy to explain in the context of contemporary religious, as opposed to magical, practice, particularly within the predominantly Protestant populations living in the culture area. The use of verbal formulae is easily likened to prayer, and the practice of laying on of hands is well attested in Christian religious healing practice since the days of Jesus and is used today by many clergy, and the hand movements often include crosses. While some material components (such as Bibles, when used as objects rather than texts) are clearly religious, it is difficult to see the Christian connotation of eggs, string, excrement, pins, and so forth. Some material components, such as the act of sticking pins in wooden dolls, recall voodoo practice (itself a partly Christian religion, but not recognized as such by most of the Pennsylvania Dutch) and therefore smacks of magic.

Moreover, the use of magic, unlike religion, cannot easily be reconciled with the present scientific-technological worldview dominant in American culture. While both religion and magic are situated within a supernatural worldview, belief in an omnipotent deity whose ontological status is generally considered a question unanswerable by science is quite different from the belief that stepping in cow manure with an open cut on your foot will cause that cut to heal.

STRUCTURE AND SEQUENCE OF RITUAL

Powwowing rituals do not accomplish their restoration through noticeable preliminal, liminal, and postliminal phases; as noted above, biomedical treatment offers better examples of such a structure. However, there is a typical sequence, beginning with a therapeutic interview in which certain minimal information about the patient is revealed, then the healing itself, which involves the use of one or more ritual components, and finally the payment itself. The effect of the ritual is typically delayed, and repetitions may be necessary for healing to be accomplished.

A powwow ritual performance typically begins with a brief therapeutic interview in which the powwower is told the patient's name and ailment. Generally, the full name is required, but some hold that only the Christian (first) name is needed, because "the name one was given at birth followed the individual through eternity" (Kulp 1978). Some powwowers, such as Daisy Dietrich, claim to be able to sense illness or injury during the course of the ritual, giving the interview a diagnostic as well as curative function. As Tom Clemens, one of Daisy's clients, notes, referring to Daisy and Julius, "They can tell you what you got. They get the same pain you've got."

Knowing the ailment in advance allows the powwower to concentrate on the area afflicted. At this point, some powwowers will ask the patient whether they believe in God, but, as mentioned above, this is not always done. Daisy questioned me about my beliefs, Anita did not. In emergency situations and in the simplest ritual performances, the question is not asked.

The use of this question, however, does point to the common belief that one must believe in God in order to be healed. A belief in the Christian doctrine of the Trinity is not always necessary—for instance, Daisy and other powwowers believe that a Jew may be healed by powwowing. There is also a belief that one must believe in the efficacy of powwowing, or in the powwower's power, in order to be healed. This belief-about-a-belief is not as commonly held as the first one, and I do not have any accounts of powwowers' asking patients "Do you believe in me?" or "Do you believe powwowing works?" although I have accounts that include the simple question "Do you believe?" or the statement "You've got to believe" without saying to what the belief refers. The belief that one must believe in the powwower's power to heal probably originally began as a conflating of two other beliefs, that one must believe in God in order to be healed and that the powwower is a channel for God's power. This belief-about-a-belief could potentially represent a skeptical statement invoking a form of the "placebo effect" to explain the success of powwow healing. But such "scientifically based" explanations for powwowing's success must be relative latecomers to the native system of beliefs, because the common belief that powwowers can heal animals (who presumably cannot "believe," as humans can) is attested at least as early as the early nineteenth century). Incidentally, because the healing of animals represents a kind of baseline case for nonplacebo healing (healing absent belief), experiments with animals could reveal whether such nonplacebo healing actually takes place.

The ritual that follows the therapeutic interview uses at least one of the three components described earlier: verbal (incantations), somatic (hands coming in contact with or moving above the body), and material (manipulation of material objects or substances, such as eggs, string, potatoes, or saliva, including rubbing them on the body). More complex rituals use at least two of these components.

During the ritual, the number three figures prominently, a fact traditionally explained with reference to the Christian Trinity. Daisy, for instance, does three rituals in one session, taking breaks between sessions to get rid of the patient's ailment by making "wiping off" and "shaking off" motions. She also insists that patients undergo three treatments. Aaron Boehm performs his ritual facing the moon three times. Many simple powwowing cures (such as passing a child around a table) are performed three times. Many of the spells in the Hohman book use the number three. For instance, the cure for a sore mouth (Hohman 1971, 21), which is only one of many involving the number three, reads:

> If you have the scurvy, or quinsy, too
> I breathe my breath three times into you.

Nearly all the spells in Hohman book end with three Latin crosses. I have found the row of three crosses following handwritten spells in an account ledger that once belonged to the Light family and now resides at the Lebanon County Historical Society.

Following completion of the ritual, payment may be rendered. Only powwowers who practice the most complex rituals generally expect payment, perhaps because the ritual takes effort and requires training to use. A powwower will generally not request payment, under the theory that God did the actual healing, but a "freewill" offering may be given, and many clients believe that the treatment will not work without payment.

During the entire ritual, the patient is completely passive, becoming the site of the powwower's performance. The patient must follow all instructions given by the powwower, but these are typically minimal ("stand up," "sit down," "hold the Bible"). The objectification of the patient ends with payment. At that point, the roles are reversed and the patient is in control, deciding whether or not to make an "offering." That signals that the ritual is complete.

PERFORMANCE GENRES

I have divided powwowing rituals into three genres and refer to them as Types I, II, and III. Type I rituals are simple, easy to learn, and almost always used by nonprofessionals. Type III rituals are complex, difficult to learn, and always used by professional powwowers. Type II rituals form an intermediate class, comprising relatively simple rituals that are quick and easy to learn yet used by professionals and nonprofessionals. In the cases I studied, there appeared to be a marked correlation between professional status and a higher genre number.

The three genres are described below, along with a case list and a description of a typical performance. Cases lacking sufficient detail to classify them as a specific genre have been omitted, along with the one case in which I attempted to powwow myself. Descriptions of typical performances are based on interview and documentary accounts but should not be construed as ideal models of the genres.

Type I Rituals (Simple)

Type I rituals have the following features:

- They use no more than two ritual components, usually only one.
- They do not use verbal components.
- They are typically limited to one ailment (most often warts).
- They address ailments that are never potentially life-threatening.
- There is never any payment.

Examples of Type I rituals are passing a child around a table leg to cure livergrown, and wart removal by rubbing with a potato or penny.

In the typical Type I performance, the powwower will ask the patient what the problem is and, without many preliminaries, begin a simple ritual to cure it. The rituals often include a material component but rarely a somatic one. Material objects used are most commonly potatoes, pennies, string, or, in the case of livergrown, a table leg. Ailments are typically minor, the most serious being livergrown. There is no payment, not even a donation. Most often the patient and the powwower are either relatives or neighbors.

Type I rituals appear to be the most common, despite the relatively low number of such rituals collected in the case list. I attribute this bias to the fact that many consultants consider Type I rituals to be merely "home remedies," not powwowing. Therefore, potential consultants would reply in the negative when asked whether they knew anything about powwowing. Consultants who did consider Type I rituals to be a form of powwowing often reported having an older relative or neighbor powwow for some ailment, mainly to remove warts or cure livergrown. There are so many varieties, and the typical case is so generic, that no specific variations can be pointed out. If a Type I performance did not work, the nonprofessional powwower might refer the patient to a professional powwower he knows.

Type II Rituals (Simple, with Some Complex Features)

Type II rituals have the following features:

- They use no more than two ritual components (except in rare circumstances).
- They typically include a verbal component.
- They are typically limited to a single class of ailment (for example, skin diseases, bleeding problems, problems caused by poor circulation).
- There is rarely any payment.

Examples of Type II rituals are the all-purpose rituals used by Aaron Boehm and Leah Stoltzfus: blood-stopping using the "Live in spite of your blood" verse from Ezekiel (16:6), and burn-healing.

In the typical Type II performance, the patient is seen by the powwower in a special area or treatment room. The powwower asks the patient what the problem is, then lays hands on the affected area and murmurs a simple subvocal incantation. The entire ritual takes a few minutes. There is no payment.

Type III Rituals (Complex)

Type III rituals have the following features:

- There is no limitation on use of ritual components.[13]
- There is no limitation on ailments to be cured.
- Payment is often expected, but not requested, unless the powwower is of the "entrepreneurial" type.

Examples of Type III are the rituals performed by Daisy Dietrich and Anita Rahn, which will be more fully described in the next section. In most cases, the Type III ritual is used only by professional powwowers.

In the typical Type III performance, the client is seen by the powwower in a special room of the house separate from the main living

13. Examples of such complex assemblages include the rituals used by Ruth Frey, which included verbal components (powwower and patient) and the somatic components of hand movements and body position; and the rituals of Mrs. A, who used verbal, somatic (hand movements), and material (powder) components.

quarters. This may be an enclosed porch or a small room close to one of the entrances. The powwower asks the patient's name and what the problem is, if the patient has not volunteered the information already. The patient then sits in a chair or lies down, depending on what the problem is. The powwower runs his or her hands over the body of the client, usually lightly touching the client's body, with special focus on the area of complaint. All the while, the powwower is speaking subvocally so that the patient cannot hear what he or she is saying, even when the powwower's lips are inches away from the patient's ears. Each movement is performed three times. After running hands over the patient, the powwower will make wringing motions with them in order to shake off the affliction removed from the client. At various points of the ritual, the powwower may draw signs of the cross on the patient's body. At the end, the powwower will run his or her hands over the entire body of the patient.

The ritual typically takes between fifteen and twenty minutes but can be longer if many specific areas of the body are affected. Once the ritual is complete, the patient will typically leave money for the powwower, although the powwower is not supposed to ask for payment.

MY OWN EXPERIENCE

At this point it might be useful to describe my own experience as a powwow patient. As part of my field research, I was treated by several powwowers, and I shall describe two of these treatments below.[14] The first, by Schuylkill County powwower Daisy Dietrich, took place in three parts, although only one was at Daisy's home. The other two were remote sessions in which she powwowed for me remotely at my home in Baltimore. The second was by Anita Rahn, a powwower in Lancaster County. I emphasize that these accounts are not intended as "evidence" of the efficacy of powwowing, but merely first-hand accounts of a ritual performance by an observing patient.

The first session with Daisy Dietrich took place immediately after my interview with her and her husband, Julius. I did not tell her in advance

14. I selected these treatments because they are rituals that have been passed on through multiple generations and likely include few idiosyncratic innovations. They therefore would be representative of performances in the mainstream tradition of powwowing.

that I would be requesting treatment, but merely asked her to work on me. She agreed, on condition that I follow up with two more treatments, once a week for the next two weeks, making a total of three treatments. After the third session, I was to rest for three weeks and let her know if I needed more treatments. I asked if Daisy could perform the other two treatments remotely, as my teaching duties required that I be in Baltimore those weeks.

Daisy: Well, we can set up a time today before you leave. And as long as you're here then I can pray for you. And we can never go behind. We must always stay ahead at exactly the same time. So that's no problem.
David: So you would set up a time today?
Daisy: For the following week.
David: So we would start the following week and do it then?
Daisy: Well, I can go over you today and then the following week, Monday again, and then the following week again on a Monday.
David: And I would hold my Bible at that time?
Daisy: Yes. . . . The Bible has to have the Old and New Testament.

I informed Daisy of my ailment—arthritis—and told her that I had seen some physicians about it. Daisy has to know the specific ailment, and she cannot stop in the middle of a ritual if the patient informs her he has another ailment as well for Daisy to cure.

She began by having me sit in a chair holding a Bible, then asked me whether I believed in God. I told her yes. She explained:

Daisy: You ask them first before you even start. In the majority of the time, if a woman or a man do not believe, you can actually feel it. They have a very hard time holding the Bible, for one thing.
David: Hmm. You mean like they start to shake or something?
Daisy: Right. Or they're very uneasy.
David: Are there other telltale signs that a person doesn't believe?
Daisy: Just the feeling that I get.

I asked Daisy if I had to concentrate on anything while she went through the ritual. She said no. As I worked, I was torn: then I wanted to be a good observer and record everything in my memory, but at the same time I wanted to have the experience of being powwowed. It proved to be a difficult balancing act. I probably paid more attention to observation than participation as the ritual was being performed.

She placed a pillow at my feet and knelt on it, starting at the top of my head and working downward.[15] I could see her mouth moving, but I heard nothing but the faintest hint of a whisper, even though it was only a few inches from my ears. I could understand then what powwowing patients meant when they described not being able to hear what was being spoken. Meanwhile, her fingers flew over my face, lightly touching it and making what appeared to be some kind of symbol. She continued down my torso, and then I could tell she was making the sign of the cross, four times in a "Z" pattern—right shoulder, left shoulder, right waist, left waist. She continued down, focusing on my hands, where I had told her my arthritis mainly was. I could see her making circular motions. She continued down my thighs and legs, all the way to my feet, making long strokes down my shins. Then she stood up and walked behind me and began at the crown of my head. At this point during the second segment, I thought I heard her pronounce the word "bless." That was the only time during the ritual that I could actually make out what she was saying. When she worked down to the neck, she told me to stand up, and then worked down my back, then hips and legs again. I do not recall her touching the genitals or buttocks. She told me to sit down again and came around in front to do what I later learned from her was "the blessing," the invocation of God the Father, God the Son, and God the Holy Spirit.

During the breaks, Daisy stood up and told me I could set the Bible down. (I was glad it had not shaken in my hands.) She made brushing motions over her arms and hands, shaking them out. When I asked, she explained that was to prevent my arthritis from coming into her.[16] She could still feel it, she said, commenting on how she could sense it in her hands, but then explained that by brushing it off it would go away more quickly.[17] She said the pain is terrible when she works on cancer patients.

15. Afterward, I asked a few follow-up questions. For instance, when I spoke to Daisy's husband I asked whether her kneeling in front of me had any significance—a possible association with the Gospel account of Jesus' washing the feet of the disciples occurred to me—but he informed me that it was simply for her convenience.

16. Later, another powwower, Tom (pseudonym), who had learned the art from Daisy, told me that what entered the unprotected powwower was only the sensation of having the patient's illness, not the illness itself, and that such sensations were only temporary.

17. No evidence for supernatural power is implied in this comment. I had already told her that the pain was in my hands.

I got the impression from her tone of voice and facial expression that she was sincere and genuinely found it an unpleasant experience to work on such patients, partly from the pain and partly from sadness that the person had such an affliction.

During the ritual, I felt an intermittent cold sensation around my hands, but I attribute this to the rapid movement of Daisy's hands, which could have stirred up the air in the vicinity of my hands. The sensation also occurred after she had told me patients sometimes feel a sense of cold.

Daisy claims that she can diagnose as well as heal when she performs a treatment—she can feel is something is wrong. I asked her, with some trepidation, whether she had sensed anything else wrong with me. She told me no, which I found a relief. However, she said she did sense "a lot [of pain] behind the eyes," which she attributed to arthritis. At the time, this seemed to be a false diagnosis, but immediately after the treatment, I had one of the worse migraine headaches I have ever had, one that caused me to cut short an interview with one of Daisy's patients.

At the end of the session, I slipped ten dollars under Daisy's Bible when she wasn't looking.

The following two sessions with Daisy were performed remotely while I was at my house in Baltimore. They took place the following two Mondays at 8:30 A.M. I sat downstairs in my house in a straight chair, held my Bible, and closed my eyes. I cannot report any particular sensations, other than that I did feel a start on the first session at a certain time, forty-five minutes after the session had started. I also found these long-distance sessions much more difficult than the in-person session, because I had no breaks between segments. I did not want to move without knowing exactly when Daisy was taking a break, which was impossible.

This experience as a powwow patient did not result in healing. I still have my arthritis, and I still take medicine for it. At the time I saw Daisy Dietrich, I was feeling no arthritis pain at all, which I attribute to the fact that I was taking "Excedrin Migraine" (a mixture of aspirin, acetominophen, and caffeine) every day to help ameliorate the pain of a fractured tooth. When I graphed my pain on a scale of one to ten, I rated that day a "one." However, within a few days I had a root canal in the fractured tooth and the tooth pain went away, causing me to stop taking the Excedrin. Once I stopped taking the anti-inflammatories (NSAIDS) my joint pain began to steadily increase. To test Daisy's healing, I did not take any other medication during that two-week period. While my arthritis did not go away, I did notice that it diminished on the days on which I had my powwowing treatments.

About two months after seeing Daisy, I was able to visit Anita Rahn in Lancaster County for powwowing treatment. When I saw her, I did not mention that I had already received a treatment from Daisy, although I did mention that I had been to see physicians and received medication that harmed my stomach.

She saw me on her enclosed front porch, which was much smaller and less well kept than Daisy's had been. And whereas Daisy was quiet but responsive and friendly, Anita was somewhat taciturn. (Part of that might be because her husband had recently died, at age sixty-one.) Inside the house, I could hear a television tuned to an episode of *Fox Kids*, an afternoon series for children, and every now and then a younger woman's voice. I presume her daughter-in-law and grandchildren were inside the house and probably live there, because Anita said "we" when referring to residents of the house, and four cars were parked in the small parking lot in front of the house. Also in front of the house was a yard bounded by a chain-link fence and containing two dogs—a black lab and a lab/doberman mix. They greeted me with raucous barking.

Anita had a chair set up facing the window (facing east) and told me to sit in it. After a brief period of small-talk, initiated by me, we began:

David: Do you need to know my medical history?
Anita: Just tell me what's wrong.
David: Well, I have arthritis in my hands mainly, also in my right knee a little. I used to have it in my foot, then it went away, but it's started to hurt more recently. I'm seeing a physician and I'm taking medication that hurts my stomach. I also have migraines.
Anita: Is that all?
David: That's the major stuff.
Anita (*wryly*): That's enough, huh? Just relax.

She stood behind me and ran her hands over my head to my shoulders. Her hands were warm and gently pressed against my scalp. I felt a slight but distinct tingling sensation in my scalp. She was completely silent. She performed this movement three times, the third time pressing the palm of her hand against my forehead.

Then she walked around and placed her hands over mine, running her palms slowly across the top of my hands. She also did this three times, but the third time she did not touch my skin, keeping her hands three to four inches above mine. When she removed her hands, she made a subtle but noticeable "wringing off" gesture, as Daisy had done to shake off my ailment from herself.

Anita then knelt down and ran her hands along the tops of my shoes, then up to my knees. She likewise made this movement three times. At that point, I had a good view of her mouth and I could not see the lips moving. After that, she stood in front of me and outlined my entire body with her hands, moving symmetrically down from the crown of my head. When she did this, her hands were not touching me at all. When she had finished this, she made another wringing gesture.

Anita then went behind me and performed the same kind of outlining of my body. Then she drew what felt distinctly like three crosses on my back, followed by a larger cross covering most of my back, possibly elaborated with other symbols.

"That's it," she said, walking around to face me. I asked her whether she could tell if everything was all right with me otherwise. "Everything's all right," she said quietly.

I paid her ten dollars and asked, "Is this okay?" She said, "That's fine" and took it from my hand. I thanked her and asked whether I could refer my consultant Geraldine (Lancaster County) and a friend from Baltimore to her. She said yes.

I left, exchanging pleasantries with her and saying, "I hope I can reduce my medications." She answered, "I hope so too."

Unfortunately, Anita was likewise unable to relieve my arthritis pain, and clinical examination revealed that I still had the condition after treatment.

FOUR

POWWOWING, MEDICINE, AND THE ACT OF HEALING

The relationship between powwower and physician in the Pennsylvania Dutch heartland was far different in the eighteenth and nineteenth centuries from what it is today. That was a time when many physicians grew herbs and prepared their own remedies, much as powwowers did, and, like powwowers, most rural physicians did not charge for diagnostic or healing services, but only for the materials used. Most physicians practiced without formal medical training, and the title "Doctor" could be applied to various kinds of healing practitioners, including powwowers. The concept of licensure, introduced by the American Medical Association at its formation in 1847, was bitterly resisted by many physicians throughout the nineteenth century (Weiss and Lonnquist 2000, 29). Up to the mid-twentieth century, physicians would often refer patients to powwowers for treatment, and powwowers would visit hospitals to perform their procedures over patients.

There are three related reasons for this changed relationship: the progressive domination of scientific thinking in various areas of knowledge, including medicine; the push for professionalization of medicine; and the concomitant decline in diversity of biomedical practice. It is important to remember that today's physicians represent only one kind of biomedically oriented practitioner: the academically trained and licensed possessor of a medical degree. These were known as the "regulars" or "allopaths" (Cassedy 1991, 33).

While proclaiming a scientific basis for their work, these "regulars" tended to be divided into those who followed dubious theoretical systems (such as bleeding or purging) and those who proceeded by a process of trial and error, without regard for experimental controls. Success was measured by amounts of blood drawn and quantities of drugs given. Some of these drugs were quite strong and dangerous. For instance, Cassedy notes that prescribing substances such as calomel (mercury), medicinal alcohol, and opium was common (Cassedy 1991, 29). This was true until at least the mid-nineteenth century, when allopathic medical advances in Europe began to be adopted by regular American physicians.

Other biomedical practitioners included the so-called sectarian physicians—homeopaths, hydropaths, and Thomsonians. Homeopathy, which is still practiced today, sometimes under the term "naturopathy," was a system created in the early 1800s by German physician Samuel Hahnemann;

by the 1820s and 1830s it had gained popularity among many regular American physicians (Cassedy 1991, 37). In fact, one of the two regions in which homeopathy was first introduced to the United States was near Allentown, in the Pennsylvania Dutch heartland (Kett 1968, 134).[1] The basic doctrine of homeopathy is "like cures like,"[2] so that a disease was treated by administering small doses of drugs that produced symptoms similar to those of the disease. Unlike allopathic medicine (a term still used by homeopaths today for "regular" physicians), homeopathic remedies were at least rarely dangerous. And like the academically trained regular physicians, homeopaths claimed a scientific basis for their work and tended to be intellectuals.

Hydropathic medicine had a completely different basis for healing than homeopathy, although it too had its origins in German-speaking Europe. Its basic principle, developed by Silesian farmer Vincent Priessnitz, was that the combination of water, applied internally and externally, and good hygiene could cure all disease. According to Cassedy (1991), by the mid-nineteenth century the "water cure" was the preferred therapy for upper- and middle-class Americans, particularly women. Hydrotherapy remained popular until the latter part of the twentieth century and, as I observed, is still being used in the Pennsylvania Dutch heartland.

The "Thomsonian System" devised by Samuel Thomson, a man without any formal education and described in Reuben Chambers's 1842 volume *The Thomsonian Practice of Medicine*, invoked the humoral theory that "heat is life and cold is death" (Chambers 1842, 149). Therefore, Thomsonian medicine opposes the practice of bleeding on the grounds that "it lessens the heat and gives double power to the cold." Moreover, it held that all life consists of the four elements of the classical world: earth, water, fire, and air (Chambers 1842, 155), each having its corresponding humor (melancholer, phlegm, choler, and sangue).

THE SCIENTIFIC STATUS OF BIOMEDICINE

The hostility of modern medical schools and many of their graduates toward "folk" medical practitioners such as powwowers on the grounds

1. The other was New York City.

2. This is identical to the "law of similarity," which Frazer identified as characteristic of "sympathetic magic."

that the latter are "unscientific" was far from universal until well into the twentieth century.[3] However, pre-twentieth-century biomedical practice, whether "regular" or "sectarian," cannot be considered "scientific" either, self-serving claims to the contrary.

Nineteenth-century biomedical practitioners, such as Simon M. Landes, proprietor of the Ephrata Hydropathic Institution, used religiously based theories to justify their healing methods. Landes's 1853 book, *The American Improved Family Physician or Home Doctor*, opens with a religious justification for the advancement of hygiene, which he terms "preserving health" (Landes 1853, 3):

> I beg all men that have not yet learned how to preserve health, to take the subject into view and study it. For the Lord has made all things natural. He not only asks man to study the Bible, but learn all good things, and do them, and leave the evil. Also, the Lord has created the world and all therein, and has pronounced it good; and why, if he has pronounced it good, shall we pronounce it bad? Also, the Lord has made man and woman, and directed them what to do; but did they do it, do we do it at present? No! we eat daily of the forbidden fruit and we even do not know it. Therefore now is the time to learn, how to live to keep principally in good health. For as sure as we eat of this forbidden fruit, so surely we shall and will be sick. Some people are praying daily for good health? Reflect a moment and see whether it is not a sin to pray for good health if we don't live according to the laws of nature? We oftentimes destroy our own health by nothing but what enters our mouth.

Landes extends the argument from food to "pure air, cleanliness, exercise, &c." and immediately launches into a set of remedies involving baths, drinking water, douches, wraps and packing in sheets, and enemas ("injections"). Landes's remedies are no more based on the principles accepted in modern scientific medicine than are Hohman's. For instance, Landes recommends that croup be treated by wrapping "very cold cloths" around the patient's throat while bathing the patient's hands and feet in

3. It is interesting that the trend now is shifting toward greater acceptance of what are now termed "alternative" or "complementary" therapies by medical professionals.

warm water. He also claims that an emetic and an enema "will arrest the disease" if used with "other means" (Landes 1853, 27). However, once "the preternatural membrane" has been formed, the disease is fatal unless the membrane is "expectorated in fragments." Landes recommends similar treatments for "inflammation of the larynx" (26), bronchitis (27), "inflammation of the lungs" (28), pleurisy (29), "inflammation of the heart" (pericarditis) (29), "inflammation of the stomach" (gastritis) (30), "inflammation of the liver" (hepatitis), and a host of other ailments, sometimes adding doses of herbals to supplement the usual cold wraps, warm baths, and emetics. Even cancers were to be expelled by means of douches and enemas (140). However, for some cancers an application of sulfurated lead, zinc, caustic potash, or other caustic agent to the cancer is prescribed (141).

All Landes's treatments appear to be aimed at expelling or destroying something harmful that has entered the body. His earlier religious statements suggest that the aim of this purification of the body is to cleanse it from sin and return it to its natural state. The role of the physician, in Landes's system, is to restore the patient to a state of health that sickness had disrupted. In doing so, the physician also restores and affirms the natural order ordained by God.

Not all Pennsylvania Dutch physicians made such an explicit connection between physical and spiritual health. Thomsonian medical practice, for instance, included curative methods similar to those urged by Landes (wraps, emetics, enemas) but invoked no supernatural entities or powers. Both Landes's hydropathy and Thomsonianism emphasized cleansing the body of impurities, but whereas Landes stated that the goal of this cleansing was to expel sin, the Thomsonians claim that the goal was to expel "poison and death" from a stomach that was "already in a state, more or less morbid, and actually in need of an effectual cleansing by emetics, rather than to be made the depraved receptacle of such filth [mucus and phlegm]." While some partisans of Thomsonian medicine have attempted to link it with Landes-like ideas linking health and spiritual redemption (Chambers 1842, 261–63), the system does not depend on any religious models for its justification.

Nor do the veterinary guides published in the mid-nineteenth century show much connection between biomedicine and religion. While J. S. Skinner's edition of Clater and Youatt's *Every Man His Own Cattle Doctor*, published in Philadelphia in 1844, includes a preface (by Skinner) justifying the care of animals on account of God's concern for them, no theological connection between physical and spiritual health is attempted.[4] Moreover, earlier editions of the book have no religious language whatsoever. Nor does Pennsylvania Dutch veterinarian John Mohr use religious language in his *Medical Guide in Treating All Internal and External Diseases of Horses, Mules, and Neat Cattle*, published in Reading, Pennsylvania, in 1866.

The lack of religious language does not mean that the recommendations in these guides are any closer to those of modern scientific medicine than Landes's volume. In fact, these works have more in common with Hohman's *Long Lost Friend* than they do with the latest edition of the *Merck Manual* or *Physician's Desk Reference*. All these nineteenth-century works contain lists of recipes for folk medicines, most of which would not be prescribed by a physician today.

It is understandable that during this period many people in this area chose to patronize a powwower rather than a physician. American biomedicine during that period was only beginning to understand disease processes. In doing so, it went through many fads, ranging from the purgative treatments of Landes and Kellogg (of Kellogg's cereals) to Thomson's botanicals, to Fletcher's emphasis on completely chewing all food until it became liquid (resulting in infrequent and relatively fragrant bowel movements). The lack of reliable medical treatment was exacerbated by the split between scientist (physiologist) and clinician in biomedicine, which was much more pronounced than it is today, and by the many false starts and blind alleys into which medical research was led by the various philosophical theories of the day, such as the notion that humors must be balanced in the body.

Probably the most successful physicians were those whose practice most closely resembled powwowing. These individuals, termed "eclectics" by Cassedy, tried, like homeopaths, to steer clear of "strong medicine" and, like the Thomsonians (and powwowers) made use of herbal remedies (Cassedy 1991, 38). Such physicians focused on treatments that seemed to work, without bothering to find out why. In short, the hostility and skepticism that physicians in the culture area now have for powwow was absent a century ago, probably because biomedicine itself was more art than science and because biomedical cures were limited in their effectiveness and many times more dangerous to the patient than the disease itself.

4. This is the first American edition of a book that had already gone through nine English editions. Francis Clater was the original author, but the work Skinner published was based in part on the seventh English edition, a version "edited, revised, and almost rewritten" by William Youatt in 1832.

Advocates of eclecticism, or "reform" medicine, founded medical schools that, before the Civil War, scandalously admitted women. This controversy died down after the war, but it points to an interesting phenomenon, what I call the "defeminization of medicine." One factor that distinguished regular physicians from sectarian physicians and powwowers before the twentieth century was the role of women. In regular medicine, nearly all the physicians were white and male. And as more and more medical concerns, even traditionally female-controlled processes such as birthing, came under the authority of regular physicians, women found themselves relegated to a peripheral role in health care. The professionalization of medicine as allopathic medicine, and the delegitimation of competing biomedical practices, which had lower barriers against women practitioners, only exacerbated this gender divide. Women were not admitted to the American Medical Association until 1915, sixty-two years after its founding; and until 1940, women never made up more than 6 percent of medical school graduates (Cassedy 1991, 94–95).

However, as we have seen, women could be powwowers, and in as great a percentage as men. This is true for other magical or mystical healing practices in the United States. It is significant that the predominately male medical profession that had fought so hard against "quackery," as it termed competing biomedical practitioners up to the nineteenth century, should turn its attention to powwowing in the twentieth. It is also tempting to suggest that the purpose of professional academic biomedicine was to create a male monopoly on healing in order to suppress the influence of women healers. But this is an unwarranted conclusion. The reason for the monopolistic behavior of what we now called scientific medicine could also have been a desire to eradicate harmful practices, an honest attempt to place medicine on a more scientific footing, or an attempt to increase economic gain for all its practitioners. Most likely, all these factors, including gender and racial discrimination, played a role, and individuals motivated by diverse reasons found that they had a common goal: to create one professional standard of medical practice.

THE IMPACT OF THE PROFESSIONALIZATION OF MEDICINE ON POWWOWERS

The impact of the professionalization of medicine, beyond reducing the diversity of health-care choices, also suggested criteria of legitimacy for all varieties of healing: healing should be grounded in science, limited to people with a certain educational background, and authorized by appropriate licensing procedures. Powwowing, like competing biomedical practices, met none of these criteria. Moreover, it was practiced in a completely unregulated manner by men and women, as well as by people of all nationalities.

Because powwowers did not engage in direct competition with allopathic practitioners, however, powwowing posed less of a threat to organized scientific medicine. While during this period powwowers lived in relatively urbanized areas and operated storefront practices, most were nonprofessionals serving their own families, friends, and neighbors.

Moreover, the science behind allopathic medicine was not placed on a secure empirical footing until after the Civil War, when the expanded use of microscopy helped establish the bacteriological theory of disease causation, a theory that has become part of American culture in general. Two additional key developments were the founding the Johns Hopkins Medical School in Baltimore (1876), which emphasized the use of scientific principles in medicine, and the establishment of the American Association of Physicians (1885), whose goal was the "advancement of scientific and practical medicine" (Lester King 1991, 222). By the opening of the twentieth century, scientific medicine was clearly the dominant biomedical approach in urban America. Yet, powwowing and other magico-religious healing methods were still quite prevalent in the areas outside the cities.

As long as there was medical diversity in the United States, accommodating many types of biomedical and magico-religious healing practices, there was little pressure to eliminate powwowing. Moreover, while many practitioners used the word "science" to describe what they did, controlled laboratory experimentation and scientific testing were not a major part of any form of medicine. Even regular physicians were trained more in anatomy than in laboratory science, emphasizing description rather than explanation. Thus, there was no rigorous testing of treatments. Finally, before medicine became scientific in more than name, its chief concerns were effecting cures or following a certain medical theory. Once it became scientific, these concerns lost their centrality. The priority of science is truth, not practicality, and so scientific medicine had to be less concerned with healing than with knowledge. And theories in science are not philosophical systems to be followed with fidelity. They are explanatory frameworks to be discarded when shown to be inadequate.

Thus, to the scientists of medicine, powwowing became not a competing medical approach but a set of beliefs that were not scientifically testable and that conflicted with a worldview in which miracles simply did not happen. To the wider society, which had seen the fruits of scientific knowledge in the form of advanced technology and which embraced the myth of progress, powwowing was outmoded superstition. Like root doctors, fire doctors, rubbing doctors, granny women, power doctors,[5] and all the other traditional magico-religious healers in the eastern United States, powwowers began to be seen as less reputable than the white-coated, degreed "real" doctor. Physicians who followed the professionalized scientific model believed it was their duty to stamp out "quackery" and "to protect the community from practitioners who rejected the advances of scientific medicine" (Barney 2000, 61).

THE EFFECT OF THE YORK HEX MURDER TRIAL

In this climate, the 1929 York Hex Murder Trial took place, throwing an unfavorable light on powwowing and its practitioners. While this trial will be discussed in greater detail in the following chapter, I shall summarize it here. The case involved a York County powwower and his teenage accomplices who were convicted of murdering another powwower. The motive for the murder was that the victim had supposedly hexed all three of the defendants, who had visited his house with the intention of making him lift the hex and ended up killing him.

When reporters from New York, Philadelphia, and Baltimore descended on York, Pennsylvania, where the trial was held, the result was a series of sensational reports portraying the Pennsylvania Dutch as backward people mired in superstition. Local officials reacted defensively, ordering a program of scientific education to eradicate this "superstition." Today, perhaps folklorists or anthropologists would enter the discussion and explain powwowing in its cultural context, but in 1929 the social pressures to conform to the ideology of scientific progress were too great. It was at that time that powwowing began to go underground and that

5. The similarity of the term "power doctor" to "powwow doctor" is probably not coincidental, even though "power doctors" are found hundreds of miles from Pennsylvania, in the Ozarks. As anthropologist Jean Moser points out (Barney 2000, 26), by the early twentieth century Hohman's "powwow book" served as a critical reference for many Appalachian people.

powwowers retreated from population centers, shrouding themselves and their practices in secrecy. Magical trappings, such as spell books and material components, ceased to be used as frequently, and the practice underwent a shift toward religious healing.

POWWOWING AND BIOMEDICINE TODAY

Despite that shift, powwowing has persisted. As Susan Stewart has argued (1976), powwowing has long been a rational health-care choice for rural populations in Pennsylvania. Given the unreliability and danger of biomedical treatment until the early twentieth century. it made sense to consult a powwow before seeing a physician. Memories of such treatments survived the professionalization of medicine and influenced decisions well into the twentieth century. This is not to say that powwow cures were intrinsically safer or more reliable, but gestures, incantations, and the use of objects served a ritual function, and even if they were not successful in healing the patient, at least in and of themselves they could do no physical harm. The same could not be said for biomedical cures, such as purging, bleeding, or trephination. And there was also the issue of ease of treatment—powwowing was, at least usually, available for free, and one might have to look no farther than one's own home for treatment. The services of educated physicians were more difficult to secure, both because of their expense and because few physicians were available in isolated rural areas (Barney 2000, 27).

Today, the situation is quite different. Biomedicine has been put on a more scientific basis and is more reliable and available. In fact, it is much more readily available than powwowing. Knowing this, it is reasonable to wonder whether powwowing today is still a viable health-care choice. To get a rough sense of this, I distributed a questionnaire to my informants and to others who identified themselves as "Pennsylvania Dutch," to have them indicate the order in which they would visit a number of different health-care practitioners. I asked them to respond twice, indicating their choice of health-care provider from one to ten if (a) they knew what was wrong with them already and (b) if they did not know what might be wrong with them. I listed certain occupations and permitted write-ins. I also asked them to indicate if they would never visit a certain type of healer. I listed four different types of healer in the questionnaire:

1. Biomedical (physician, osteopath, nurse practitioner). One respondent added "special tests," which would fall into this category.
2. Physical—nonmystical[6] (chiropractor, massage therapist, reflexologist).
3. Physical—mystical (acupuncturist, therapeutic touch).
4. Spiritual (powwower, hex doctor, religious healer).

It was clear that there were no a significant differences in responses to the two questions. I therefore combined the results in one table. I also noted that there were few responses beyond the fourth-choice level. This makes sense because in practice few would be familiar with more than four types of healing practitioner, and in most cases no more than two. Because there is little difference in the minds of many among the individual types of practitioners (physicians versus nurse practitioners, powwowers versus hex doctors or religious healers) and because I was evaluating the popularity of alternatives to biomedicine, Table 1 groups practitioners by category. It depicts choice of practitioner and was drawn from the combined table.

Table 1 shows that biomedicine, now licensed, regulated, and backed by science, is the medical treatment of choice for contemporary Pennsylvania Dutch populations. Even among those who knew something about powwowing, biomedical practitioners received sixty-five combined first-choice responses (thirty-three if the ailment was known, thirty-two if it was not) compared with only one first-choice response for powwowing, or

Table 1. Medical choice survey of Pennsylvania Dutch respondents familiar with powwowing, 2000

	Order in Which Respondents Would Visit Each Type				
Type of Practitioner	1st Choice	2nd Choice	3rd Choice	4th Choice	Never
Biomedical	65	6	2	0	0
Physical (nonmystical)	4	39	24	9	12
Physical (mystical)	2	3	4	5	17
Spiritual	1 (1)	9 (5)	15 (10)	2 (0)	43 (15)*

* Eighteen out of these 43 points came from responses to "hex/hex doctor," which no respondent selected as a first to fourth choice.

6. The term "mystical" refers to any medical theory that explains illness and healing by recourse to the supernatural or any nonmaterial "energy." However, "nonmystical" does not mean "scientific" or "evidence-based."

spiritual healing in general. No respondents indicated that they would never see a biomedical practitioner, giving biomedicine the most positive score, while many said they would never see a spiritual healer, whether powwower, witch or hex doctor (which received the most negative votes), or religious healer. However, it does appear that Pennsylvania Dutch people will seek powwow treatment (or spiritual healing in general) if other treatments have failed. The bias in this sample—in favor of those who know something about powwowing—only further supports the contention that biomedicine has supplanted powwowing as the treatment relied on most in the face of illness.

Yet, it is also true that most of these respondents did not realize that powwowing was still being practiced, and it is possible that this knowledge would have changed their responses. Many times, those I interviewed or addressed in public lectures asked me whether I knew of any practicing powwowers. I have received a number of requests for powwow referrals, and I often joke that I seem to have become a sort of powwow broker. So while Pennsylvania Dutch people today share the dominant culture's preference for biomedical treatment, there remains an interest in, and at least some measure of demand for, powwowing.

POWWOWING AS AN ACT OF HEALING

The experience of being sick is always an infringement on our sense of control. Biomedicine and some brands of religion represent attempts to deny that infringement and claim that we can explain and to an extent exert control over the experience.[7] Biomedicine attempts to control the experience of being sick by explaining the disease, typically relying on theories of disease causation—such as infection by microorganisms, genetic predisposition, or poor diet—that have become part of medical culture and that may or may not be backed up by laboratory data. Physicians and other biomedical practitioners attempt to alter that experience by exerting control over the patient's body, whether by prescribing pharmaceuticals

7. "Biomedicine" refers to what is otherwise known as "Western medicine," "scientific medicine," "cosmopolitan medicine," or, in the vernacular of American culture, simply "medicine." "Biomedicine" is the term most often used in medical anthropology, and it condenses the most meaning into the shortest space. "Bio-" implies science, and "medicine" implies healing. I use the term "healer" to refer to all modes of remediation of culturally defined physical, psychological, or spiritual ailments, including biomedicine and powwowing.

or performing procedures. Modern biomedical, or allopathic, treatment has focused on curing the organism—the body—rather than on addressing spiritual or psychological dimensions of illness. Indeed, in hospitals, among physicians, nurses, and other biomedical personnel, the patient is referred to by disease or procedure, not by name: "the appendectomy in 540." The analogy of the body to the automobile—a machine that must be serviced and repaired by a mechanic—is often drawn, with the "driver" being the mind or soul, a matter for other specialists. Perhaps this dualistic view is necessary, given the invasiveness of biomedicine, which requires biomedical practitioners to become desensitized to what they are doing.

Some religions attempt to control the experience in similar ways, although explanations and methods of controlling the body are different from those in medicine. For instance, some religions explain disease by postulating behavioral causes for illness. The ancient Israelites and some fundamentalist Christians have attributed certain serious conditions to sin, provoking divine punishment, while Christian Science, Science of Mind, Scientology, and various New Age groups emphasizing doctrines of karma blame illness on the patient's negative thoughts (attracting the disease to the body or causing the mind to think itself sick).[8] Religions may control the body in the healing process by prescribing fasting or other penitent action or by requiring that the patient kneel or otherwise demonstrate humility as a condition for being healed.

Powwowing, considered a healing practice, bears some resemblance to medicine. Unlike many forms of healing, it only minimally attempts to control the experience of sickness. Its theories of disease causation never blame the patient for the illness and rarely offer any explanation at all for the experience. Powwowers can diagnose; I have been treated (for arthritis) by one who claims to be able to sense the presence or absence of pathology in her clients' bodies, and indeed claims to feel the symptoms of the condition she is curing. But they do not theorize a cause at variance with those suggested by medical professionals.[9] The only instance in which an explanation is offered is in the case of hexing, which will be dealt with separately below. In such cases, an individual is blamed for

8. Biomedicine certainly includes a behavioral component as well, for example, failing to wash one's hands, handling dirty surfaces, or coming in direct contact with an infected person. Behavior patterns are the central focus of the study of epidemiology.

9. In fact, none of the powwowers and their clients whom I interviewed have any reservations about the efficacy of medicine, and most have a family physician.

causing the illness.[10] The powwower exercises a degree of control over the client's body, instructing him or her to sit or stand in a certain way or to face a certain direction, and sometimes prescribing vitamins or various chemical mixtures in the same way that a physician might prescribe a pharmaceutical. However, there is no attempt to assert control by claiming credit for healing. In fact, the powwower who is practicing the craft in the traditional manner always gives the credit to God and never asks for remuneration for what he or she has done.

HOW DOES POWWOWING HEAL?

There are numerous testimonials about the success of powwowing. In examination of eighty-nine twentieth-century powwow cases involving healing, successful healing was reported to occur in more than eighty of them, a success rate of 90 percent.[11] A successful healing was defined as the alleviation of symptoms. In most cases, successes were not verified by laboratory tests or medical examinations by physicians. While it is impossible to test the veracity of every such report, I can say that those that derived from interviews are unlikely to be the result of intentional misrepresentation or some sort of hallucination. Errors of memory may certainly have occurred (reported events took place as long ago as 1910), and although I have tried to reduce ramifications (information added after the experience) as much as possible in recording the cases, it is difficult to eliminate entirely. Still, the high success rate requires explanation. Possible explanations include spontaneous remission, "placebo effect," healing by means of supernatural intervention, and concurrent but unreported biomedical treatment. The last option assumes that information has been withheld by the consultant, whether through lapses in memory or deliberate omission of facts, and is therefore a kind of hypothetical error in the data rather than an explanation. If no other reason exists to assume that information has been withheld, this option must be rejected as an argu-

10. Not all powwowers and their clients believe in the existence of hexes. Most of my consultants regard hexing as a part of the past, something that people no longer believe takes place.

11. In order to be considered a "case," an account of a powwowing event had to meet four criteria: the event had to be at least roughly datable, the illness had to be identified, the outcome had to be known, and there had to be some detail on the powwow procedure itself.

ment from negative evidence. However, the other three possibilities must be considered.

Spontaneous Remission

Spontaneous remission, or the coincidental resolution of symptoms that would have abated without any kind of treatment, is most likely in the case of minor ailments, such as warts. The criterion for inclusion is whether a given ailment is believed by those unfamiliar with powwowing to resolve without assistance, given sufficient time. Of the cases collected, 16 percent involved the treatment of such ailments.

If spontaneous remission is invoked, it can have no cause-and-effect connection with the act of powwowing itself, so that resolution of the condition is a mere coincidence. Time frame is important here: if someone powwows a patient for Illness A and Illness A is resolved immediately after powwowing, it is reasonable to conclude that the powwowing was the cause of the cure. If a week passes, it is a little less reasonable. If three months pass, it is much less reasonable to conclude that the act of powwowing caused the illness to resolve (although some do credit powwowing with curing illnesses when the time gap between ritual and cure is months in length). Because the criteria for ruling out spontaneous remission are not well defined, it is difficult for researchers to eliminate it as a possibility for any illness, although patients do it all the time.

The Placebo Effect

The term "placebo effect" refers here to the power of belief to affect the body. It derives from the response of the patient to inert substances (placebos) administered as if they were medicine. The purpose of administering placebos is to test the efficacy of pharmaceuticals—any significantly improved patient response above what is elicited by the placebo is considered evidence that the pharmaceutical works. However, the fact that any placebo works at all is surprising, because there is no pharmacological reason why it should work. There have even been cases in which placebos have been known to work better than the pharmaceutical being tested.

According to Ernest Rossi, the placebo effect has been known to affect the autonomic nervous system (hypertension, stress, cardiac pain, blood cell counts, headaches, pupillary dilation), the endocrine system (adrenal gland secretion, diabetes, ulcers, gastric secretion and motility, colitis, oral contraceptives, menstrual pain, thyrotoxicosis), and the immune system (common cold, fever, vaccines, asthma, multiple sclerosis, rheumatoid arthritis, warts, cancer) (Rossi 1993, 15). This list includes many ailments that have been successfully treated by powwowing. The placebo effect has also been known to influence surgical outcomes, to show up in biofeedback instrumentation, and to help with psychological treatments. Even the action of making an appointment to see a doctor has been known to provoke a placebo-like response.

The placebo effect has been studied by social and behavioral scientists, as well as by physicians and physiologists. In 1985, psychologist Frederick Evans studied data from twenty-two double-blind studies conducted with five analgesics and found that placebo response was remarkably consistent, constituting from between 54 percent and 56 percent of the pain reduction of the drugs (Rossi 1993, 16). For instance, 56 percent of the pain-reducing effect of morphine was due to placebo effect. Evans also studied data from ninety-three double-blind studies of antidepressant psychotropic drugs (such as tricyclics), finding that 59 percent of the antidepressant response was due to placebo effect, and thirteen studies of lithium, finding that 62 percent of the response was placebo effect. Evans also studied nonpharmacological therapies—in thirteen double-blind studies of insomnia treatment techniques, 58 percent was accounted for by placebo response.

Even differences in the color of pills can generated a placebo effect. In a 1972 study by Honzak, Horackova, and Culik it appeared that yellow capsules and white capsules were the most effective in relieving symptoms and that red pills and gray pills precipitated the most side effects (cited in Hahn 1995, 90). A University of Alabama study (Benson 1997, 55) found that white pills were associated with analgesic action, lavender with hallucinogenic effects, and orange pills and yellow pills with stimulant or antidepressive action. I conducted an interview with a retired physician who practiced in Reading, Pennsylvania, who reported giving pills of different colors to patients with correspondingly different results, even though all the pills contained the same pharmaceutical.

A 1978 study by Levine, Gordon, and Fields showed that dental patients whose pain after tooth extraction had been significantly diminished by placebo medication suffered increased pain after being given naloxone, a compound that blocks the analgesic effects of opiates (cited in Hahn 1995, 90). This suggests that at least some placebos function by stimulating the release of endogenous opiates. Benson (1997) has proposed that a "relaxation response" exists in humans that is a relaxed physical condition elicited by mental focusing and related to the placebo effect (which Benson calls "remembered wellness") (1997, 20).

Sammons's study of "fire drawing" traditions in North Carolina and wart removal suggests that hypnosis may play a role in spiritual healing practices. In firedrawing, the "fire doctor" talks the "fire" out of burns, thereby relieving the pain and speeding the healing of burns (1992). Fire drawing is an especially significant practice for comparative purposes, because the beliefs surrounding it and the rituals it uses closely resemble those associated with powwowing. Wart removal is also important because that is one of the most commonly cited examples of the use of powwowing. According to Sammons, hypnosis has been used to successfully treat both burns and warts, although the mechanism by which it accomplishes these effects has not been demonstrated (1992, 63). However, Sammons suggests that hypnosis helps heal burns by inducing vasoconstriction, or narrowing of the blood vessels, to reduce inflammation and then vasodilation, or widening of the vessels, to reestablish metabolic homeostasis (maintenance of a stable and optimal internal environment) in the area of the burn, paralleling the standard burn treatment in sports medicine (64). Sammons's proposed mechanism for the ability of hypnosis to heal warts is less specific and could apply to a wide range of placebos, namely, that hypnosis stimulates the immune system to fight the virus that causes warts (66). It is important to note that these proposed mechanisms do not explain why such healing processes should have been initiated by hypnosis (or any placebo) in the first place. They merely describe what occurs once the body begins healing itself.

Placebo effect cannot, by definition, occur in the absence of prior belief or in cases in which the patient was unaware that he or she was being treated. In cases in which animals are healed, clearly there can be no "mind-body" interaction actuated by belief, because animals do not "believe" the way humans do. To be more concrete, a horse that is successfully powwowed cannot be said to be healed because that horse knew about powwowing and expected to be healed, thereby stimulating his immune system. While the issue is not nearly so clear-cut, successful healing of those unfamiliar with powwowing (such as small children) or those who do not believe in the power of powwowing cannot be attributed to the power of belief, because the expectation of healing is absent. For these instances, we have to admit that healing cannot be due to belief or any other cultural factors or rely on other explanations. However, placebo effect may offer a reasonable explanation in many other cases, particularly when the ailment is culturally defined (for example, livergrown or the take-off). Culturally defined ailments were treated in 19 percent of cases collected.

The salience of the placebo effect in powwowing can be tested by looking for a relationship between prior belief in powwowing and successful healing outcomes. Within the limits of this study, belief in the efficacy of powwowing appears to be related to experience as a powwow patient, while those who were never powwowed for an illness have significantly less belief. Prior belief in the efficacy of powwow appeared to have no influence on judging the success of a given powwow ritual. This suggests that belief may arise from the experience of being healed, not that beliefs produce the experience. David Hufford found a similar phenomenon when analyzing other supernatural beliefs, such as those surrounding "Old Hag" supernatural assault events, which are reported in many parts of the world with no cultural term for the phenomenon (Hufford 1982).

Older consultants showed greater belief in the efficacy of powwowing than younger ones, probably as a result of greater exposure to the practice. Cultural factors that might be expected to produce greater belief in the efficacy of powwow, such as lower education level and use of Pennsylvania Dutch dialect as a first language, showed no significant correlation with belief in powwowing.

Healing by Spiritual Intervention

Many researchers would discount this explanation without further evaluation under the assumption that spiritual intervention either cannot occur or, if it does occur, cannot be substantiated or distinguished from other causes and is hence beyond consideration by science. However, to do so would require acceptance of either one of these claims, which themselves are really untested (and perhaps untestable) assumptions.

Because supernatural intervention is an extraordinary claim, for it to be considered at all the act of healing must include some additional evidence suggesting that the supernatural was operating. The best evidence would be what Hufford calls a "direct supernatural experience," in which the action or presence of spiritual entities was detectable to the senses in a way that would intuitively suggest the supernatural (1995). An example of such an experience would be a person seeing a ghost. Unfortunately, the experience of being powwowed is rarely (if ever) a direct supernatural experience, because there are few sensory elements beyond the mundane observation of gestures, lip movements, or the manipulation of material elements. It becomes what Hufford calls an "interpretive supernatural experience," that is, an event in which the supernatural element is inferred rather than directly observed. Such indirect experiences provide a much weaker foundation for concluding that supernatural forces or entities may be operating.

For now, the most prudent approach appears to be to search for other explanations first, and in cases where the explanations seem improbable or impossible, leave the question of causation open, to admit (but not claim or attempt to prove) the possibility of spiritual intervention.[12] It is worth noting that a recent review of randomized, controlled trials on distant healing (which occurs without direct contact between healer and patient) suggests that healing methods based on nonmaterial mechanisms at least warrant further study and that such mechanisms may not just be discounted (Astin et al. 2000).

ASSESSING THE EXPLANATIONS

The data at hand suggest that powwowing is used mainly against ailments that are not life-threatening and that can respond to the stress level of the sufferer (such as skin conditions), that tend to resolve spontaneously (such as warts), or that are not documented outside the culture and may be produced by cultural factors. Cultural factors appear to play a strong role in defining which ailments are considered treatable by powwowing. But is powwowing actually more successful against skin diseases and culturally defined illnesses than against other ailments? To test this, I looked at twentieth-century cases I had compiled that did not involve powwowers themselves as patients and divided them into two classes: skin conditions or cultural illnesses, and other conditions. I then compared the success rates of the two classes: 94 percent success against skin conditions or

12. For more on the assessment of supernatural experiences, see David Hufford's 1995 "Beings Without Bodies," in Walker 1995.

cultural illnesses and 82 percent against all other conditions. This suggests that powwowing *may* work better against these ailments than against others,[13] but there is no strong reason to conclude that it does.

Beyond errors introduced by the nature of the interview data, it is especially important in this instance to heed the old adage "Correlation is not causation" in interpreting this result. While it may be that the expectation that powwowing can cure such ailments actually produces the cures through reducing stress and stimulating the immune system, it may also be that the demonstrated effectiveness of powwowing has resulted in the expectation that it will cure. And we cannot rule out other explanations, even those that presently may seem exotic.

IDENTITY WORK IN POWWOW HEALING

The act of powwow healing is more than a restoration of bodily health. It also defines the relationship of a powwower to the patient and the relationship of each to God. It is, in fact, a negotiation of identities and constitutes what anthropologist Anthony F. C. Wallace (1965) refers to as "identity work." Much of the discussion of the various kinds of identities in this section derives from his work.

In powwow healing, the two main actors are the healer and the client, although the former very rarely (for example, Leah Stoltzfus, Calvin M. Rahn) may be assisted by family members, and the latter may have friends, family, and other supporters present. However, the presence or absence of additional persons associated with the patient is strictly at the discretion of the powwower, with some (such as Mrs. A) forbidding it. In the believer's view, a third actor is also present in powwowing rituals—namely, God, who is the source of the powwower's power.

There is a difference in the two kinds of identities being negotiated in the healing situation. The powwower's social identity—that is, how he perceives himself or herself functioning in the role of healer—is at stake. Because social identity affects personal identity, the powwower's personal identity is at stake too, but only indirectly. For instance, failure to successfully heal directly relates to his performance of the role of healer, a matter

13. If the samples had been random, there would have been a one in ten chance that the difference between the success rates was caused by chance. That is not particularly impressive, but it suggests that further research is in order.

of social identity. This, in turn, has consequences for the powwower's relationship with God, a matter of personal identity (and social identity in the putative supernatural society of the kingdom of God). It may also affect how people view the powwower as a person; for example, the powwower could not heal because he is not sufficiently religious or is not living an appropriate lifestyle. Such perceptions, while social, affect personal identity.

Despite these indirect effects, the powwower's personal identity is shielded. In fact, failure in a healing performance may not even significantly affect the powwower's social identity, depending on such factors as the magnitude of the success or failure and the number of other clients, or patients, past or present, on whom his social identity rests. The client has no such protection, at least in the interaction with that particular healer. Whether the healing succeeds or fails must affect the client as a person, regardless of which social identity he assumes. Every failed healing confirms the person's identity as a sick person. Should the powwower fail, the patient may (or may not) have recourse to other healers, but the more healers who see the patient and fail, the more closely the patient's real identity approaches his feared identity. For the powwowers who have unsuccessfully treated such a person, the process works in reverse. The more independent failures occur in treating a single patient, the more the stigma of failure is removed from the powwower and placed on the patient. Thus, in a repeated series of failures with different powwowers, the "antitherapeutic" process for a patient becomes a "therapeutic" process for those treating the patient.

The identity relationship with God is affected in similar ways. A successful powwower may be seen as a person of faith by others in the community, that is, as someone with a close relationship with God and endowed by God with power. In fact, this judgment may be correct within the framework of Christian belief, because the powwower may begin to see the working of God in his successes and indeed become a person of strong faith. Thus, the elements of the personal and social identities reinforce one another in a positive feedback loop: success leads to real faith (as part of the personal identity) and perceived faith (part of the social identity). Perceived faith leads to public confidence in the powwower's cures, increasing the placebo effect and thus the number of successes. Similarly, an unsuccessful powwower is often considered to be a person who is out of favor with God, as evidenced by the lack of power in his cures, leading to low confidence in cures (both by powwower and by the public), leading to fewer cures.

John Blymire, the chief defendant in the York Hex Murder Trial, suffered the worst of both worlds. As a patient seeking to have a hex removed, the more failures occurred, the worse life became for him. The only solace he had was shortly after he was married, but that happiness was short-lived, for he came to mistrust his wife following treatment by Andrew Lenhart. As a powwower himself, Blymire found himself losing patients and unable to cure the ones he had. As he puts it, "A stronger power than I had got hold of me; tormented me almost every day of my life from then on. I couldn't eat, I couldn't sleep, my skin was getting too loose on me and I had the *abnehmes*. I couldn't take away anybody's hex no more and I couldn't put none on" (Lewis 1969, 22–23).

It is little wonder that when Blymire was finally told who was responsible for the hex and how to remove it, he took action. Although it is extremely doubtful he intended to kill Nelson Rehmeyer, the man whom Mrs. Knopt claimed had placed a hex on him, he reported feeling much better afterward.

The identity states of the two main participants in the healing ritual (beside God, whose real, claimed, and ideal identities are the same) are as follows.

1. Patient (relevant aspect of personal identity)
    - Real identity: sick person
    - Claimed identity: patient
    - Feared identity: incurable sick (or hexed) person
    - Ideal identity: well person
2. Powwower (relevant aspect of social identity)
    - Real identity: performer of a powwow ritual
    - Claimed identity: powwower
    - Feared identity: unsuccessful powwower
    - Ideal identity: successful and respected powwower

Each state of the powwower's social identity has implications for the powwower's personal identity. The parallel states of personal identity for the powwower would be as follows.

Real identity: a previously successful channel for God's power / one who considers himself a religious person

Claimed identity: a channel for God's power / a religious person
Feared identity: an unfit channel for God's power / a falsely religious person
Ideal identity: a good channel for God's power / a religious person

The process of healing itself constitutes the identity work required to increase the value distance between "real" and "feared" identity and to decrease the value distance between "real" and "ideal" identity for both healer and client. This is the exact opposite of the "antitherapeutic" situation, in which the ritual performer (such as a witch) is attempting to harm the other individual (the victim). In that case, there is identity conflict, and where one loses, the other wins. But healing is a cooperative venture; the client must want to be healed, the healer must want to heal, and an avenue for healing must be available.[14]

However, just because the healing process is a cooperative one does not mean there are no power inequalities in the relationship. The powwower, like any healer, whether a physician, a *curandero*, a fire doctor, or a shaman, generally holds a position of superior power vis-à-vis the client. Even in the extremely rare cases when he depends on patients for his livelihood, one patient carries only so much weight in that equation.[15] The powwower, by virtue of his special competence and power, holds authority to which the client must submit, although the power inequalities are less than professional healers in some traditional societies, such as the Apache and the Inuit, who often require clients to humble themselves before them and pay high fees (Foster and Anderson 1978, 112). This kind of extreme power inequality does not apply to powwowers, because God does the healing and for that reason they are not supposed to take personal credit for the healing or charge a fee.

The "identity work" involved in powwow healing makes use of the "claimed identity" of both participants, which pulls the "real identity" closer to the "ideal identity" and farther from the "feared identity." The claimed identity serves as a symbol of the ideal identity, a promise and

14. For instance, there have been cases in *Brauche* when the healer and client are one. That both sets of identities are present in one individual presents no difficulties, because one self can have many self-images that make up the "total identity" (Wallace 1967, 65).

15. Although in the case of scientific medicine the threat of malpractice suits may exercise a balancing influence.

encapsulation of what is to come. Both the claimed and the ideal identities of powwower and patient are complementary. In the antitherapeutic process (hexing), the claimed identities may also be complementary, but the ideal ones are not. A witch may present himself or herself as a powwower, someone who heals, but the hexer's ideal identity is that of one who gains power over the patient. A witch-victim relationship is masquerading as a powwower-patient relationship. An example of this is found in John Blymire's life story. Blymire was supposedly involved in a powwower-patient relationship with Nelson Rehmeyer, but came to see the relationship as that of the witch-victim kind. In the antitherapeutic process, the claimed identity of neither actor points to the ideal identity. For the patient, the claimed identity of patient facilitates the movement to the feared identity, not to the ideal one. For the witch, the claimed identity of powwower may help him achieve the ideal identity of powerful witch, but it does not have any real connection to it.

The terms of the healing process and the stakes involved are related to the sacredness of the ritual itself. When the sacral qualities are emphasized, by the presence of such symbols as crosses or pictures of Jesus on the walls, or by requiring the patient to hold a Bible or asking the patient whether he or she believes in God, the ritual takes place in a sacred space containing only powwower, patient, and God. In such an atmosphere, the ritual acquires a heavily sacramental nature, with the powwower functioning as priest, and the patient functioning as supplicant. Only the powwower can dispense divine healing, and hence the powwower's authority is increased in the eyes of the patient. The belief of the patient empowers the ritual and allows the patient to accept the healing offered. The two participants reaffirm the sacred cosmos by playing roles previously set out in the Bible: the powwower as Jesus (sometimes called "the first powwower" and the patient as one of the people healed (and saved) by Jesus. Like Gospel accounts, the healing is done not merely to cure a fellow human being but also to celebrate the presence of God. The powwower seeks to imitate Jesus and the legendary powwowers of the past who appear to function as saints, each serving as an exemplar of the ideal powwower.

The above description is most clear when viewing the actions of professional powwowers, people most likely to be given the titles "*brauch doktor,*" or "powwow doctor," because the rituals they use are more elaborate. Yet the simplicity of the powwowing genres used by nonprofessionals mirrors the simplicity of the healings in actual Gospel accounts.

The symbolism of crosses and the number three fits this model well. The connection of material components is more problematic. The transfer of an ailment to a material object, such as a potato or penny, does not fit this model well but does appear to fit the "magical" models of contagion (Hand 1980, 20). To be sure, the medieval church considered certain objects holy, but such objects had some symbolic or historical connection to Christian belief systems. The color red is often used in powwowing ritual, possibly representing the blood of Christ but possibly simply representing blood in general, or something else entirely. As noted in Chapter 3, however, some material components used in powwowing do seem to carry Christian ideas of rebirth, with implications for the self.[16]

The possibility that faith may be embodied in a patient suggests that the "sacredness" of the "self" is something that is a given in Pennsylvania Dutch culture and may be used by the powwower to restore the patient. McGuire and Kantor (1988, 238) suggest that Christian healing (which would include powwowing) seeks to cultivate a self in a subordinate relationship to God. My data tend to support this position. But the actions of the powwower, while affirming the sacredness of the body and the relationship of self to God by means of Christian symbolism, do not impose a sacredness by means of prescription or discipline. For instance, a patient is not instructed to pray, or abstain from sin, in order to be healed. The body, possibly because the New Testament considers each believer to be a temple for God (1 Cor. 3:16), "naturally" responds to the healing power of God as channeled by the powwower. And just as the body's response is natural, so too is the impulse to heal. Leah Stoltzfus compared her laying on hands to the gestures of affection shown by a mother for a child: "I think it's the natural thing to do."

16. Thomas Csordas's work on charismatic healing (1994) provides a good comparison with powwowing, particularly with regard to the self and "healing of memories" in charismatic practice, although I do not subscribe to the "orientational" view of the self that Csordas uses.

FIVE

POWWOWING IN PENNSYLVANIA

The story of powwowing in Pennsylvania is the story of individuals and of cases. What follows is neither a detailed chronology nor a social history, but rather an attempt to characterize 250 years of powwowing by looking at various periods, personalities, and narratives. From Mountain Mary in the colonial period to the infamous John Blymire to "Aunt" Sophia Bailer, this chapter provides biographical sketches of well-known and colorful powwowers during the past 250 years. It also describes some of the most dramatic cases of successful powwowing from the late nineteenth century to through the twentieth centuries. These include a mysterious powwower's intervention to save a man on the verge of death, the events leading up to the York Hex Murder Trial, in which one powwower was convicted for killing another in order to remove a hex, and a duel between a powwower and a being she described as "the devil" (she won, but was left with a noticeable scar).

FROM MOUNTAIN MARY TO JOHN GEORGE HOHMAN, 1770–1819

Powwowing has been practiced in Pennsylvania since the first German-speaking Protestant settlers arrived in the eighteenth century. Before the twentieth century, powwowing was practiced routinely by the descendants of these European settlers. Folklorist Don Yoder considers powwowing to be based on ancient religious healing traditions sanctioned and even blessed by the Roman Catholic Church but was driven underground among Protestant populations, such as the Pennsylvania Dutch, and placed into the hands of lay practitioners (Yoder 1990, 95).

Yoder's tracing of powwowing to pre-Reformation church practices and beliefs is supported by the invocation of Christian saints in powwowing incantations and the way in which beliefs about saints help define the social identity of the powwower (Yoder 1990, 201–3). As Yoder notes, healing was often attributed to Christian saints before the Reformation. Some powwowers also came to be viewed as saints, such as Yoder's own consultant, "Aunt" Sophia Bailer, who was known as "the Saint of the Coal Regions" (Yoder 1951). And in fact, as already noted, many powwowers consider Jesus to have been the first powwower, because of the many people he healed by the power of God.

Powwowing certainly existed in southeastern Pennsylvania by 1750, and there were a number of well-known practitioners. Sometimes, as in the case of the Saylors, a family acquired a reputation for effective powwowing. Johann Peter Saylor (1721–1803) had a practice in Northampton County and passed the power on to his son Peter (1770–1862), whose cures were legendary. However, probably the best-known powwower of this period was a woman called "Mountain Mary."

Mountain Mary

Mountain Mary, known in Pennsylvania Dutch as *Barricke Mariche* and in German as "*die Berg Maria*," was reputedly a hermit and a "holy woman" who lived in the Oley Hills about five miles northeast of Pikeville and two miles north of Hill Church in eastern Berks County. Her given name was Anna Maria Jung (Jungin, with the feminine German suffix). Accounts of her life differ, but most agree she was born to a German family in Europe and fled with them to Philadelphia shortly before the American Revolution. Her legend emphasizes the suffering she faced during the war, including the death of her husband (or, possibly, fiancé), Theodore Benz, the latter having fought in the Continental Army.[1]

Mary Young, as she was called after anglicizing her name, never married after Benz's death. Rather, she lived alone in the mountains tending a "magic" herbal garden and was reputed to have "wide and astonishing knowledge of the medicinal value of her roots and herbs," through which, some claim, she performed miraculous cures (Burch 1938).[2] At an early age, she became known as a "holy woman" who read the Bible and performed Christian "good deeds." Prayer was an integral part of her practice. Her fame spread far beyond the Oley Hills, and she saw patients from distant areas. She did not require payment for her services. Mountain Mary died in 1819 at the age of seventy, the same year that John George Hohman's *The Long Lost Friend* was first published in Reading, Berks County.

Today, Mountain Mary is considered a semi-legendary figure, in no small part because of the body of literature that has grown up around her,

1. Some (such as the "The Belles of Berksiana") claim that her family landed with her but that her father died during the Revolution. Others, such as Ludwig Wollenweber's romanticized account (Yoder 1990, 213), claim that her family perished during the crossing to America and that she arrived alone.

2. Others, such as Miller (1912, cited in Yoder 1990, 217), omit any supernatural reference when discussing her cures.

including two poems, an account by Quaker writer Benjamin Hollinshead, a highly sentimentalized 1880 novel by Ludwig Wollenweber, and several newspaper articles.[3] In 1934 the Berks County chapter of the Daughters of the American Revolution erected a monument to her (Yoder 1990, 213–17). She is portrayed as a "powwow doctor" at the Goshenhoppen Pennsylvania Dutch Folk Festival by Veronica "Ronnie" Backenstoe.[4]

FROM HOHMAN TO THE END OF THE NINETEENTH CENTURY

The nineteenth century saw a continuation of traditional powwowing, helped along by the publication of John George Hohman's book, *The Long Lost Friend.* Powwowing was performed by "professionals," some of whom are described below, who were renowned for their power and drew a wide clientele, but also by members of many Pennsylvania Dutch families, who treated family, friends, and neighbors. With Hohman's book and the Bible, incantations and recipes were available to cope with many kinds of troubles against which biomedical practice and theories of the day were of little help.

However, opposition to powwowing began to be seen during this time. Probably the most effective and vociferous opponent of the practice in southeastern Pennsylvania was the Reverend Daniel Weiser, a Lutheran or Reformed clergyman. Weiser also recorded a number of cases of powwowing, some of which appear below, but always in a skeptical and hostile manner. His rhetoric described believers in powwowing as ignorant, and the practitioners as both ignorant and evil: "Witches hate schoolhouses, as well as water and daylight." He claimed that powwowing was in "direct opposition to the Divine Record" (Weiser 1868, 6).

In addition to Hohman, some of the more prominent powwowers during this period were Peter Bausher and "Doctor" John Rhoads, who were both profiled in newspaper articles in 1895, at which time they were elderly. Bausher lamented that he was one of the last powwowers, and the

3. Yoder 1990 describes these in more detail.

4. Ronnie, a Pennsylvania Dutch woman, dresses in early American garb to play her role, wearing spectacles and holding a corncob pipe in her mouth. In this costume, she strongly resembles the figure in a drawing entitled "The Powwow-Doctor" from Don Yoder's collection, used as the lead illustration in an article in *Pennsylvania Folklife* (Dieffenbach 1975–76, 29). Ronnie performs simulated powwow cures by using hand movements and prepares herbal remedies. She originally prepared for her role by reading articles on powwow.

art would be lost after his generation passed away. This belief that powwowing is dying out or has died out is a common one today as well.

Peter Bausher

According to an 1895 newspaper account, Peter Bausher lived in a rough-hewn log hut at the base of the Blue Mountains (described in 1895 as "a half-century at least behind the times") in northern Berks County three miles north of Strausstown.[5] He was "a famous powwow man" and never charged for his services, although he accepted freewill offerings. When he was younger, "it was nothing for him to go twenty miles away into the forest to powwow for some afflicted sufferer." However, he was elderly at the time of the interview and rarely ventured out.

Bausher said he learned powwowing from his father, who had learned it from his father. For 150 years, he claimed, "the Baushers of my family knew the prayers for various cures," meaning that the ability to powwow was passed through the male line. Bausher, who used no herbs or medicines, stated, "Powwow healing is by faith and prayers. We do it all in the German language." He reported curing hemorrhages and burns ("I have frequently stopped a serious flow of blood in a minute after powwowing. Pains from burns I cure the same way"). He also cured "erysipelas, wild fire, felons, lameness, sprains, poison plague, and many other afflictions, such as wasting away of the nerves, quickly disappear with powwowing."[6] He went on to note that all the incantations had to be memorized and "said silently." He believed that the words he used had originated with his great-great-grandfather. "What they were when he first used them, I don't know, but they have been changed, no doubt." He attributed this to mistakes in pronunciation and memorization and believed that some of the words had completely changed by his time.

Bausher wanted to pass the ability to powwow on to his eldest son, who wanted nothing to do with it. The paper quoted Bausher as saying, "Of course, I can tell a woman, but not a man, except my oldest son.[7] Man tells woman, and woman tells man. In this way these powwow

5. Unfortunately, I can give no citation—the body of the article was preserved at the Berks County Historical Society in Reading, but no identifying information as to the name of the paper or its date of publication had been preserved.

6. "Wild fire" is a synonym for erysipelas.

7. This latter mode of transmission also was used to pass the practice from Anita Rahn's father-in-law to her husband.

secrets are passed from one to another, but must not be written down. You must know them by heart." This cross-gender method of transmission is traditional in powwowing, as is the idea that training must be done orally. The notion that an eldest son can learn has been believed by some but cannot be considered typical.

Regarding the procedure, Bausher said, "You must be near the person and see him when you powwow for him or her. . . . Sometimes injuries are blown upon when we powwow, or the hand is passed over the injury lightly, during the operation of powwow."

Bausher did not believe that powwowing could cure "typhoid fever, diphtheria, or any dangerous disease like that"; his advice, then, is "to send for a reputable doctor at once, and don't bother with powwowing. But there are some things doctors can't touch. Powwowing can heal and cure every time."[8] Bausher claimed to have thousands of proofs of the efficacy of powwowing and offered to provide the names of "hundreds of the best farmers of Berks, Lehigh, and Lebanon counties who have unalterable faith in powwowing." He held that the patient must believe in powwowing for it to work: "The patient, of course, must have, first of all, the strongest faith in the powwow."

Bausher absolutely denied performing black magic: "I only try to cure people and help the afflicted. Heaven knows, there is enough suffering in the world." He did believe in evil spells and spirits as a cause of illness, and that powwowing can combat those, saying, "Many a person declining to the grave under a strange, unknown spell is helped, and the consuming evil spirit within him is driven out by prayer or powwow alone."

Bausher believed (wrongly) that he was one of the last powwowers remaining. As he told the reporter, "I must find someone to give my secrets to. I might not be able to rest in peace in the grave if I died with all the precious cures unrevealed to someone worthy to hear them, remember them, and practice them for the benefit of suffering mankind."

"Doctor" John Rhoads

John Rhoads, known as "Doctor Rhoads," had a large powwowing ("powwow") practice in Berks County during the latter half of the nineteenth

8. I suspect that Bausher may have meant or uttered these statements as two connected clauses, which were then misinterpreted during the editorial process at the paper. In my interpretation, Bausher would have said, "But there are some things doctors can't touch [[that]] powwowing can heal and cure every time."

century[9] and was the subject of a newspaper article in the *Reading Eagle* more than a century ago ("Magic Healing" 1895–99). He lived on the side of a mountain off present-day Route 73, between Pleasantville and Shanesville in Rockland Township, Berks County. His home, a small shanty with a rough kitchen addition, accommodated a large family, although it was unclear from the article how many of his thirteen children still lived with him and his second wife, the first wife having died childless and at a young age. Rhoads encouraged the reporter who interviewed him to take his photograph, but the newspaper printed an ink sketch rather than the photograph.

Rhoads's mother, a renowned "practicer of the magic art" in Rockland township, as the *Eagle* article describes her, taught her son how to powwow. Hundreds of people in eastern Berks County would visit her for relief from all sorts of diseases. According to Rhoads, the mode of transmission was from mother to son, and only one son could learn the art.[10]

Rhoads said he never charged for his services. "People are expected to give as much as they can afford or what they feel they owe me." He later declared, "I could make lots of money by putting some of my articles on the market, but I don't believe the gift was given to man to use as a means to make money, and consequently I will never do it." He also believed he would probably lose his "power" if he used it to make money. The payment he did receive for "medical services" was insufficient to support his family, and he worked as a laborer much of the time.

He was called away at all hours of the night to distant places, Rhoads explained, and he said that he always dropped what he was doing and went. He believed that if he refused to go he would probably lose his power. But Rhoads would refuse to powwow for anyone whom he knew had ridiculed the practice in the past, and he could not be persuaded by money to alter that policy.

The article continued: "[Rhoads's] word is the supreme law in that section. His alleged curative power causes his offspring to look upon him with an awe so poorly concealed that a man with half an eye can readily

9. Rhoads's surname is Welsh, not Pennsylvania Dutch. However, because he learned powwowing from the mother, and given the intermarriage known to have occurred between different Protestant Euro-American groups at this time, it is likely that his mother's family was Pennsylvania Dutch.

10. Cross-gender transmission is the norm, but it is rare to find it limited to a single family. The idea that only one son can learn from his mother is unique to Rhoads's account.

grasp the humor of the situation." Rhoads is described as intelligent, interesting, and "much better posted on the affairs of the world than his home surroundings would suggest." Rhoads had boasted that he had saved his children's lives on several occasions by powwowing, including an instance when he successfully powwowed four or five of them for typhoid fever. He also asserted that he had "cured eighteen prominent Reading people of stricture," and he offered to provide their names as proof.[11] Before being treated by Rhoads, these individuals had spent hundreds of dollars on physicians without result.

Sample Cases

Case 1: Healing Burns (mid-1800s)

This case, from the Welsh Mountains of Pennsylvania, involves a powwower who worked with a physician (Gourley 1936). Until the mid-twentieth century, this kind of cooperation was not uncommon.

A "German" woman burned her hand seriously on hot huckleberry juice.[12] A physician treated her hand and informed her it would take three weeks to heal. A day later he returned and noted marked improvement. On the fourth day the burn was almost entirely healed. The woman was nervous during this visit and seemed to want him to leave.

Shortly, the "powwow man," whom the woman referred to as "the other doctor," arrived. The physician asked whether he could watch the treatment and learn about it, and the powwow man obliged. The powwower used a salve but claimed it was not as effective as "sympathy." Then he recited a mixture of "Dutch and dog Latin" over the burned hand.

The powwower seemed happy that his cure was more efficacious than the doctor's.

The woman wanted both doctors to remain on the case, and they agreed to return four days later. At that time, when the physician arrived the powwower was already working on the woman's hand. (The physician later learned that the powwower had been coming every day since

11. See Appendix 2, "Glossary of Illnesses." In this case, the term "stricture" probably refers to a digestive problem that today might be called "constipation" or possibly "irritable bowel."

12. "German" probably means Pennsylvania Dutch here.

the first.) At that point, the wound was entirely healed and the woman was able to return to work.

The powwower gave the physician the recipe for the salve, but when the physician tried it on another patient, it worked no better than his own. The physician believed that the powwower had deliberately omitted some secret healing substance from the recipe.

Case 2: Cure for a Horse's Lameness (mid-1800s)

This is one of a number of skeptical accounts presented by the antipowwow minister Daniel Weiser that emphasize that powwowing is no substitute for the healing power of God, but powwowers, particularly today, would claim that their practice is a manifestation of God's healing power.

Weiser once met on the highway (presumably King's Highway) a "simple-hearted elder" of his church who noticed Weiser's horse was limping. This elder, the story notes, had the previous week refused to observe National Fast Day and never believed in observing that day. The elder asked Weiser why he hadn't done something for the horse, to which Weiser replied that he had done nothing because of his "ignorance in veterinary science." The elder offered a "sure and sartin cure," which consisted of words to be spoken three times. Weiser "of course, suspected some miserable powwowing" because the elder had mentioned "the sacred number three," but he listened, and the elder related the following cure.

> Tomorrow morning, before the sun rises—if it is cloudy, wait for the first clear day—take up a stone that is partly buried in the earth. But be very particular in noticing the exact habit of the stone, so that you may precisely replace it again. Stand as near to the lame limb as you well can, and stroke it three times downward, from the shoulder to the hoof, saying as often these words:
>
> Blut und Fleisch! Mark und Bein!
> Schwimm starker als ein Stein!
>
> [Blood and flesh! Hoof and leg!
> Be stronger than a stone!]

Weiser, however, immediately decided not to do this, telling his horse, "G'long, Bill. It's enough if you are lame. Your master need not turn into a fool to boot."

When he told his family over supper, Weiser's servant ("our man, Friday") overheard and went out to the stable to do as the elder suggested. The next time he saddled the horse, Weiser found it entirely cured. Friday was "grinning and swinging his hat over the wonderful cure wrought." Weiser, however, explained the cure as a natural healing after rest, citing the example of another horse with the same problem that "an educated veterinary surgeon" diagnosed with "dislocation of a very small bone in the lower joint." The veterinarian prescribed rest for that other animal and predicted the problem would "just as suddenly leave the horse as it came unexpectedly by it." Weiser notes that this veterinarian "was intelligent and candid," and his prognosis turned out to be correct. He proclaims, "One single veterinary surgeon in a neighborhood is worth more than an untold multitude of miserable powwowers." This naturally begs the question of why Weiser did not take the second horse to the same veterinarian, but it is possible the latter's services were not available at that time.

Case 3: Remote Healing of Injuries, Including Hernia (1895)

This case shows how powwowing can be done remotely, without the physical presence of the powwower, and illustrates the Christian spiritual component of powwowing and its connection with prayer. It is clear that both powwower and patient shared in the Christian conception of Jesus as the source of all healing.

The case is described in two letters from the powwower Samuel M. Musselman in Center Valley (Lehigh County) to two of his clients, Jacob and Maria Mensch of Skippack (Montgomery County). Jacob Mensch was a Mennonite minister. The letters derive from the Jacob Mensch Collection of the Mennonite Heritage Center and were written in German. I am grateful to Dr. John Ruth for furnishing me with these letters and an English translation.

I have reproduced the letters in their entirety because they provide a description not only of the rituals but also of the way in which a powwower at the turn of the century sought to present himself to his clients.

When he refers to powwowing, Musselman uses the Pennsylvania Dutch terms *Brauch* and *Brauchen*.

> February 18, 1895
>
> Peace be with you.
>
> Beloved friends Jacob and Maria Mensch, with these few lines I let you know that I, God be praised, am still in usual health, and I hope these few lines will find you the same. Your letter dated February 14 came to hand, in which I read of the condition of your injuries. I have carefully *Brauched*, and I think it must have helped. May the Lord grant his blessing thereto. It is he who can help, and no human. We can only do our duty. Now I will *brauch* over, or yet another time. Sometimes that has to be. But I can not now *brauch* again until the first Friday in the new moon—that is the first of March, and I won't be finished with *Brauchen* until the 24th of May [seventy-five days], and after May 24 write me again how it is, and if it isn't good, then I will *brauch* the 3rd time, which I nevertheless hope will not be necessary.
>
> Now I must hasten to close my writing, since time does not allow me to write more today. I would have, indeed, much more to write, and would much rather speak with you by mouth, of the pilgrimage to the land of eternity, which is my element, and my heart's joy, and I fully believe that if we could converse orally with each other we would have a pleasant time. But we will seek to meet each other there where peace endures forever. In closing, yet another greeting of love:
>
> [The following is an English translation of three rhyming German couplets.]
>
> > Herewith I want to close my page,
> > And greet you again from my heart,
> > And counsel you to fight on,
> > And strive under Jesus' banner,
> > Strive nobly, then follows the reward,
> > And after the battle the crown of victory.

So much from your friend and well-wisher
Samuel M. Musselman

June 11, 1895

Much loved friends J. and M. Mensch,

Peace be with you.

May the Spirit of the Lord rest upon us here in time and there eternally through Jesus Ch. Amen.

With these few lines I let you know that I, God be praised, am still in normal health and hope these few lines find you also in health.

Further, I let you know that yesterday I received your letter dated the 7th of June, and with regret saw that you have not been healed from your injuries. What the reason is I do not know. Now I will *brauch* yet again. But send me your names again. As you write, let no letter be missing in the name. Perhaps there is somehow a mistake in the name as I have it; and write it for me exactly as you can where your hernia is. Write your wife's birth [maiden] name; then I will *brauch* once again. That is all I can do, but it is God who can help. May the Lord grant his blessing thereto. I will *brauch* again on the 28th of June, and will finish with *brauchen* on the 26th of August [sixty days]. Then write me again, and if it should still not be good, which I certainly hope, but has nevertheless become significantly better, then I will *brauch* once again, if the Lord grants me life and health. In closing, another greeting of love. So much from your well-wisher

SAMUEL M. MUSSELMAN

THE EARLY TWENTIETH CENTURY, 1901–1928

From Rhoads's time to the 1920s, powwowing continued to be practiced openly, and professional powwowers often had offices in such cities as

York and Lancaster. Some of these, including the infamous Andrew Lenhart, were suspected of crossing the line between white magic and black magic, and of casting hexes on people they perceived had wronged them. Most powwowing, however, remained within the homes and farms of the Pennsylvania Dutch.

In late 1928, a murder occurred in southern York County that cast suspicion on powwowing and those who practiced it and led to a view that anyone who believed in powwowing was deluded or, at best, ignorant. The three defendants, including a powwower, were brought to trial in York the following January, an event that drew great media attention from Baltimore, Philadelphia, and New York. Dubbed the "York Hex Murder Trial" (or the "York Witch Trial"), it is still remembered today by the older inhabitants of York and Lancaster counties and has inspired several books and a motion picture.

Katharine George

Katharine George was a powerful powwower in Berks County and was the great-grandmother (his father's maternal grandmother) of my consultant Harry Adam. She was born about 1845 and practiced at least until the 1920s. By 1938, when Harry went to see a different powwower, she had passed away. She also taught her daughter (Harry's grandmother) and grandson (Harry's father) to powwow, but his powers were more limited than hers. Harry believed that the ability ran in families and that the power decreased with each succeeding generation. All his relatives who powwowed did it part-time, even though his great-grandmother was known throughout the area. They were respected for their abilities, and everyone in the area believed in the efficacy of powwowing.

According to Harry's family's beliefs, the power to powwow comes from God, and faith in God was crucial to the healing process. All Harry's family members who were powwowers asked patients (other than infants) if they believed in God before beginning any ritual. They never asked for payment, but they could accept money when it was offered.

While his family patronized physicians, Harry said, physicians were opposed to powwowing. When his father went to see physicians and they knew he was a powwower, "They made fun of it. They made him feel small." Harry, however, expressed the opinion that medicine itself was limited. "Medicine just goes so far. [Pharmaceuticals] are made to help you but not cure you."

According to Harry, Katharine could cure anything and had a large practice. Her home address was in Reading (Berks County), but she really had no fixed home and instead went from relative to relative. She was a member of the Reformed Church (now United Church of Christ), and she used Bible verses in her practice and believed that if a powwower used books other than the Bible he or she was really practicing witchcraft. "Powwow worked for God, witchcraft worked for the devil," Harry notes. He also contrasted powwowing and hexing (which he explicitly equated with witchcraft: "[Hexing] was always sort of a secret. . . . If you knew anything about it you were hush-hush. Powwow is not secret. It may have been to some extent, but at my place it was always open. . . . It wasn't kept in the dark."

Neither Katharine nor any of her descendants used material components. She did, however, use herbal teas on occasion, such as for women who were having menstrual pain. She often powwowed for Harry.

Abram Huber

According to Abram Huber's grandson, Graybill, Abram was a "powwow doctor" with "magical powers," which he passed on to one of his daughters (Graham 1950). Abram lived "a very quiet and religious life," and Graybill did not know how Abram acquired his powers.

Abram had a large practice consisting of people who came "from miles around" to be cured of nearly anything. Most of them would come to his house the first Friday after the full moon, and people he treated between those times were "mostly emergency cases." Graybill did not know why clients came on that day, simply saying that was the day his grandfather preferred them to come.

Graybill did not know how Abram's cures worked, except that his grandfather possessed "mystical powers." However, he did witness some of the cures and was able to recall details of them (see Appendix 7, cases A14–A17).

Mrs. Knopt

Mrs. Knopt, also called "Nellie Noll," was referred to as "the Witch of Marietta," a title deriving from her residence in Marietta, Pennsylvania

(Lancaster County). Her cures were famous throughout York and Lancaster counties. She was in her nineties by the time of the York Hex Murder Trial (1929) but had come out of "retirement" to "help" John Blymire, one of the three defendants in the case. It was she who told Blymire that Nelson D. Rehmeyer had put a hex on him by having Rehmeyer's face appear in Blymire's hand. She also blamed him for hexing the other defendants. Her fee was five dollars a session.

"Doctor" Andrew Lenhart

Arthur Lewis describes "Doctor" Andrew Lenhart as a self-proclaimed powwower who operated his practice in order to extort money from his patients, typically by threatening that something dire would happen to them if they did not continue their treatments with him (Lewis 1969, 35–36). That many people feared Lenhart, including the county health authorities and the police, was, according to Lewis, one reason Lenhart was permitted to continue his practice for thirty years without interference by the authorities. According to a former reporter for the *York (Pa.) Dispatch*, "They used to say that if this fat, ugly little Dutchman put a spell on you, nobody, not even the devil himself, could remove it" (Lewis 1969, 35). Lenhart was suspected of being involved in many spousal murders because he would advise clients that they had been hexed by a spouse and that the only way to remove it was to kill the spouse. However, witnesses who knew of Lenhart's involvement were afraid to testify against him out of fear of his sorcery.

John Blymire, one of the defendants in the York Hex Murder Trial (see below), consulted Lenhart twenty times in an attempt to rid himself of a hex. Lenhart strongly suggested that Blymire's wife was to blame, causing Blymire to suspect her. Fearing for her life, she told her father, who was responsible for committing Blymire to the state hospital in Harrisburg.

Sample Cases

Case 4: Cure for a Urinary Infection (1903)

This case is reported by Lewis and derives from testimony by John Blymire, the defendant in the York Hex Murder Trial, to Dr. N. S. Yawger, a psychiatrist at Eastern State Penitentiary (Lewis 1969, 14–15).

John Blymire's grandfather Andrew, a powwower himself, was having difficulty urinating. John's father, Emanuel, also a powwower, instructed his son on how to cure the problem. First, Emanuel killed a hog, removed its bladder, and burned it. He told John to scrape up the cooled ashes with a spoon and feed them to Andrew. Once Andrew swallowed the ashes, John touched his grandfather's stomach all around the painful area and made the sign of the cross, then said the Lord's Prayer three times. When he was finished, Andrew stood up and urinated easily. He never had trouble with his bladder again.

Case 5: Cure for the Take-Off (1902–4)

This case was reported by Tom Martin, a volunteer at the Landis Valley Museum, and was relayed to him by his maternal grandmother, who used to visit his family often and tell stories about her early life. The patient was Tom's great-uncle, his grandmother's younger brother. Tom's grandmother was between six and eight years old when the events below took place. The case occurred in Cherry Hill (Lancaster County), near the Berks County border.

As an infant, Tom's great-uncle had a serious case of the wasting disease known as the "take-off" (*opnema, abmemmes*). His parents called a physician to treat him, but the physician told them there was nothing he could do and that the baby would probably die within a day. As a last resort, they called a "powwow doctor," an old Pennsylvania Dutch man, although they were "a little bit skeptical" about him. The powwow doctor "said he wasn't sure how much he could do, but he would try." Tom recounts the story:

> So what he did exactly I do not know, but as I understand, it was something to do, I think, with incantations and, of course, taking [passing] a string over top of the baby or whatever. He told them that at the stroke of midnight he [the baby] will wake up for a few seconds, he would turn his head, he'd fall asleep, and the next morning he would be fine, or he would not wake up at all and just die in his sleep. And she [Tom's grandmother] said, sure enough, at the stroke of midnight he did open his eyes for a few

FIG. 5. My informant, Tom Martin, a historical interpreter at Landis Valley Museum, Lancaster, Pa. Photo by David Kriebel.

> seconds, turned to the side, fell asleep, and the next morning he seemed to be getting much better, and he was fine.

The successful cure "pretty well convinced" Tom's great-grandparents that powwowing worked. Tom's grandmother also believed in powwowing and took Tom's mother and uncle for powwowing treatment when they were children.

Case 6: Fabrication of an Amulet (1927–29)

When Mrs. Schultz was between five and seven years old, her family took her to a "*brau* doctor" in Center Valley (Lehigh County) to have an amulet created, designed to keep her safe from harm. The *brau* doctor was an old man who lived in the woods on land that is now part of the Saucon Valley Country Club. Mrs. Schultz did not like him and at the time thought her family was wasting time by taking her there. Her opinion about him and about powwowing has since changed, however. As she told me:

> Well, that's the word right there. Powwowing. It still goes on. Lots of people think it's superstition and all that, but it's actually religion and these people had what I think they refer to today as the laying on of hands. That's the way I look at it. Of course, when I was smaller, I thought this was stupid and what have you, but they kept taking me there. I wasn't there too long, but I always had to keep wearing this little bag, and they called it a gigger [as spelled by Mrs. Schultz; however, she pronounced it "djigger"]. It was a little white bag, and they always had it pinned to my shirt, my undershirt, and I wore that to school, and I hated the darn thing. Finally, and I can't tell you if I was five or seven or what, but I know that I decided "I wonder what's in this thing," for every once in a while I'd get another one. Finally, one day I decided and I opened it. It was a little bag, no larger than a Fleischmann's yeast, you know. And I opened it and in there was just a prayer. So it couldn't have been hocus-pocus.

The "*brau* doctor" would periodically refresh the amulet: "But this man would take it and take it back into another room, and I don't know if he would write another verse—it was a Bible verse, but I don't know if it was quoted where it came from."

Mrs. Schultz didn't like wearing the "gigger," and when she was seven she simply stopped wearing it. "I just decided that I didn't need it, and I didn't tell him [the *brau* doctor], and I don't know when my mother discovered, but I didn't catch too much heck or I would have remembered."

THE YORK HEX MURDER TRIAL, 1928–29

The York Hex Murder Trial (*Commonwealth v. John Blymire*), or York Witch Trial, occupies a special position in the history of powwowing because it deeply affected both the way the practice was viewed by those within Pennsylvania Dutch culture and the way it was viewed outside. It resulted in the enactment of legislation (the Pennsylvania Medical Practices Act) and prompted a program of "scientific" education aimed at rooting out "superstition" among rural Pennsylvanians. Details of this case were published in the pulp serial *The Illustrated Detective Magazine* (April 1931) and in at least two popular books (Aurand 1929; Lewis 1969). The case also inspired the 1988 Hollywood movie *Apprentice to Murder*, starring Chad Lowe, Mia Sara, and Donald Sutherland.[13] The *York Sunday News* ran a long feature on the case on August 15, 1999, with the title "The Hex Murder: York's Crime of the Century."[14]

The Facts of the Case

The two major published accounts of the case are contained in Ammon Aurand's *Pow-Wow Book* (1929) and Arthur Lewis's *Hex* (1969). Aurand provides a more succinct summary of the crime, relying on court transcripts, and Lewis provides more background and biographical information. I use each of these in describing the case, supplemented by the actual court transcripts. However, both these accounts are heavily infused with editorial comments deriding powwowing and the people who practiced it.

Nelson D. Rehmeyer, a sixty-year-old powwower—some said he was a witch—living in Rehmeyer's Hollow, near Red Lion (York County), was murdered on November 27, 1928, by John Blymire, John Curry, and Wilbert Hess.[15] They testified that they had come to Rehmeyer's house not to kill him but to secure a lock of his hair and his copy of *The Long Lost Friend*. By burying the hair or destroying the book, they reportedly believed, they would lift a hex that Rehmeyer had placed on Blymire, Curry, and the Hess family. The trio had come armed with a rope, presumably in order to tie up Rehmeyer, a powerfully built man weighing more than two hundred pounds. However, when Rehmeyer did not get the book at once, the three attacked him, wrestling him to the ground. There was a lull when Rehmeyer promised to get the book if they let him up, but when they did, Blymire testified that Rehmeyer came at him and that the three responded by beating Rehmeyer. It is unclear who actually

13. The original working title of the film was *Long Lost Friend*.

14. I am indebted to my consultant Hazel Sauer (pseudonym) for forwarding this article to me.

15. Also spelled Blymyer or Bleimeier.

struck the fatal blow—Blymire testified that Curry did it—but eventually Rehmeyer was dead. They went upstairs to look for *The Long Lost Friend* but found nothing. Curry and Hess did find a small amount of money on a dresser, which they pocketed. They then wrapped the body in a mattress and a blanket and set fire to it and fled the house.

Background to the Murder: The Story of John Blymire

According to Lewis, John Blymire, age thirty-two at the time of the murder, was a powwower himself, following in a family tradition that stretched back three generations before him (Lewis 1969, 9). At the age of four, John began to see "visions." and at the age of seven he performed his first powwowing healing, on his grandfather Andrew (see above). However, Blymire was a sickly and reportedly homely child, and other children made fun of him. He did not start school until he was eight, when truant officers came for him, and he attended classes irregularly because of his own sickliness, his powwowing practice, and household chores. His teacher considered him "slow normal, perhaps very slow normal" (Lewis 1969, 16). After his arrest, prison psychologists measured his intelligence quotient as between 78 and 85, which they termed "dull normal." Blymire left school at the age of thirteen and went to work in a York cigar factory. His work attendance was spotty, because of his part-time powwowing practice. Those who were treated by him reported his cures as effective and long-lasting. He asked no fee for his powwowing treatments, nor was he often given any. His reputation as a competent powwower spread in the York area.

Shortly after he calmed an apparently rabid dog (see Appendix 7, case A12), however, Blymire came to believe someone had put a hex on him: "A stronger power than I had got hold of me; tormented me almost every day of my life from then on. I couldn't eat, I couldn't sleep, my skin was getting too loose on me and I had the *opnema* (take-off). I couldn't take away anybody's hex no more and I couldn't put none on" (Lewis 1969, 22–23). Blymire and his family did everything they could to remove the hex, but nothing worked. He gradually lost confidence in his ability to powwow and became so nervous that he jumped at any unexpected sound. He believed that the one who had put a hex on him was the ghost of his great-grandfather Jacob Blymire, the first powwower in the family and the seventh son of a seventh son, because one night after the kitchen clock had struck twelve, he heard a barn owl hoot seven consecutive times. After that, he moved away from home in order to get away from the family cemetery.

He continued his powwowing practice and married the daughter of one of his landlords. At that point, his symptoms abated and he began to consult a physician about his problems. The physician did not laugh at his claim that he had been hexed, but explained that Blymire's condition had been caused by his belief in the power of the hex.[16] However, Blymire suffered a relapse when his first child died in infancy and a second, premature, child lived for only three days.

The court transcript and the accounts in Lewis and in Aurand differ at this point. According to Lewis, by 1920 Blymire had consulted more than a dozen powwowers from as far away as Oley (southeastern Berks County), paying them to try to remove the hex (Lewis 1969, 33). None of them was able to help him, beyond confirming that he had been hexed. One of these was "Doctor" Andrew Lenhart (above).

However, the transcript indicates that Lenhart was the first powwower Blymire saw, and the names of the others are different from those in Lewis's and Aurand's versions. It also indicates that before he went to Lenhart, Blymire sought biomedical treatment, first with several (apparently private) physicians, including an "electric doctor" who gave him "electric treatments," then at the York Hospital.[17] There Blymire was diagnosed with "hypochondriacal melancholia" and "nervous exhaustion" and given unspecified treatment that helped "a little, not much" (court transcript, 230).

Blymire saw Lenhart twenty times, paying ten dollars for each visit. On the last visit, Lenhart told him that he had an idea who had put a hex on him and that it was someone close. This led Blymire to suspect his wife, and she began to fear for her life. That was in 1923, right after a York County woman who had been a client of Lenhart's killed her husband. When she told her father of her fear, he consulted a lawyer, who advised him to swear out a warrant for Blymire's arrest. The judge ordered a mental examination of Blymire by two court-appointed psychiatrists. On the basis of their diagnosis—"psychoneurosis, neurasthenic

16. Herbert Benson (1996) refers this as the "nocebo effect," in which belief causes real illness, the opposite of the "placebo effect."

17. There is no indication of what these treatments were, but given the psychiatric diagnoses offered, they may have been electroconvulsive therapy.

type"—he was ordered committed to the state hospital for treatment. The diagnosis was based on Blymire's admitted belief in witchcraft (Lewis 1969, 39).

According to Lewis, the staff psychiatrist at the facility was in charge of more than one thousand patients and testified that he saw three hundred patients a day, including Blymire (Lewis 1969, 39). Nor was security strict there, because forty-eight days after his commitment Blymire walked out the front gate and did not return home. Instead, he resumed his hunt for a powwower who could remove his hex. His wife had already begun divorce proceedings against him.

None of the powwowers was successful in removing the hex. Finally, one of the powwowers he had seen admitted her failure and referred Blymire to another one, an old woman in Marietta (Lancaster County) whom Aurand and Lewis refer to as Mrs. Noll but whom Blymire actually identified in his testimony as "Mrs. Knopt" (*Commonwealth v. John Blymire*, 231–32). Mrs. Knopt had ceased being an active powwower years before, but according to Lewis (1969, 46–47), she felt sorry for Blymire and agreed to take on the case. Mrs. Knopt revealed the information on the identity of the hexer in increments and charged five dollars for each session. At the first session, she confirmed that he was hexed; at the second, that the hexer was a man; at the third, that he was old; at the fourth, that the hexer lived in the country; and at the fifth, that he had known the hexer since childhood. At the sixth session, she told Blymire that the hexer was Nelson D. Rehmeyer (Lewis 1969, 47).

Rehmeyer was a family friend of the Blymires. He had actually removed a hex from John when he was a young boy and had treated him on at least two other occasions. Therefore, Blymire could not believe that he had put a hex on him. To prove that Rehmeyer was the hexer, Mrs. Knopt asked him to take out a dollar bill and lay it in his hand. When she pulled the bill away, Blymire saw Rehmeyer's head and upper body, down to the waist, in the palm of his hand; he could see the man's light-gray hair, white shirt, and dark clothing (presumably a jacket). According to the transcript, she specified that, to remove the curse, Blymire would have to either get a lock of Rehmeyer's hair and bury it six to ten feet underground, or get his copy of *The Long Lost Friend* and burn it. Once he had done that, the hex would be lifted and Blymire would be protected from any future hexes (transcript, 246).

After this revelation, which occurred three months before the murder,

Blymire continued to see Mrs. Knopt. According to his testimony, she also informed him that John Curry and the Hess family had been hexed by Rehmeyer. While he was seeing her, Blymire also saw other powwowers ("powwow doctors"), to confirm that the hexer was Rehmeyer, but they were noncommittal. At the trial, his counsel Herbert Cohen asked him why he believed Mrs. Knopt:

Cohen: Why did you believe?
Blymire: Well, because I felt just the way she told me.
Cohen: How did you feel?
Blymire: I felt nervous and restless, couldn't eat, couldn't sleep, couldn't work.

This suggests that Blymire was testing Mrs. Knopt, and because she had correctly described his symptoms as he expected a real powwower would do, Blymire believed others things she told him, too.

The Trial and Its Aftermath

At the trial, Cohen argued that Blymire was mentally incompetent and should be found not guilty by reason of insanity. The basis of this claim was Blymire's belief in witchcraft and previous diagnoses by psychiatrists, also based on this belief. The defense also argued that Blymire was feebleminded. Curry's and Hess's attorneys argued that their clients were merely Blymire's accomplices. The prosecution argued that the motive for the murder was robbery and denied that Blymire was mentally incompetent. During the trial, Blymire seemed uninterested in the proceedings and testified that he felt much better since Rehmeyer's death and the subsequent burial of his hair (with the rest of his body). He also testified that he believed he was correct in taking the actions he had (transcript, 246).

The three defendants were tried together from January 7 to January 11, 1929. The jury returned a guilty verdict on the charge of murder in the first degree for Blymire and Curry, with the penalty of life imprisonment. Blymire's attorneys filed for appeal in May, but the motion was denied. Curry's appeal was granted, but the judgment was affirmed. Hess was found not guilty of murder in the first degree, but he received a ten- to twenty-year sentence for murder in the second degree.

In 1952, Blymire's case was taken up by Philadelphia attorney Herbert

Maris, who in 1953 succeeded in having the sentence commuted so that Blymire was released from prison on ten years' parole. He secured a job as a custodian, bought his own house, and was alive in the late 1960s, having never committed another crime. Hess returned home after serving his sentence, married, and became a solid citizen. Curry was paroled in 1939, having learned to paint in prison. He returned to York, got married, and was drafted into the Army in 1943. After World War II, Curry bought a dairy farm in southern York County and sold his paintings. He passed away in 1962, shortly after requesting that some paintings he had pillaged from Germany be returned to their rightful owners.

FROM THE DEPRESSION TO 1970

Media coverage of the "witch trial" in York reinforced the "dumb Dutch" stereotype applied to the Pennsylvania Dutch and embarrassed local authorities. The remedy they adopted was to suppress all such "superstition" by introducing "scientific education" and consolidating public schools. Powwowing was consequently driven back to the more rural areas of central and southeastern Pennsylvania. Still, numerous practitioners of the art remained, as attested by Lewis's success in obtaining interviews was powwowers, some of whom maintained storefront practices late in the period (Lewis 1969). Some of these are profiled below.

Mrs. A

Mrs. A was a powwower who was referred to the Sunday family by their family physician, Dr. Stanley Brunner. She treated Elaine (Sunday) Madeira for possibly ringworm and a wasting disease, possibly the "take-off." The latter ailment also sounds like a tapeworm.

Mrs. A, whose name Elaine could not recall, lived in a one-room shack deep in the woods somewhere in the coal regions (Carbon County, she thinks). Elaine believed that Mrs. A was quite religious, because of the setting of her treatment room: "She had crosses. She had [[single]] candles lit, and it was very low lighting. . . . She had a kerosene lamp on one of those tables, like a reading table. There was a chair by the table, and I could see the sofa that I had to lay on. All the rest was dark. I looked over to the one wall, and that's where I saw all the crosses and Jesus on a cross [[a crucifix]]."

Elaine believes you had to have a setting like the woman's treatment room in order to be healed, but she later said that the back porch where I interviewed her would also be conducive to healing because it was "relaxing."

Mrs. A wore a long skirt and blouse, and her gray hair was tied back in a knot. At the time, the woman "looked like she was really old. . . . She could have been in her late sixties or early seventies." Her outfit reminded Elaine of a gypsy's clothing, but Elaine did not think she actually was a gypsy.[18] However, when she spoke her incantations, it was neither in English nor in Pennsylvania Dutch. Elaine did not think it was French, Greek, Italian, or Spanish. It could have been another German dialect, but Elaine was not sure.

Elaine described Mrs. A as looking "like a witch" and considered her to be "really spooky." I asked her why. "I think it was the way she acted," Elaine explained. "She wasn't friendly. She was a very serious person. She didn't say what she was going to do. She had me lay down and close my eyes. She said that right off, and that's what I did."

The woman's treatment session usually lasted about thirty minutes. Because her treatments succeeded, Elaine believes in the efficacy of powwowing.

David: The requirements to be powwowed are you have to believe?

Elaine: I think you do, because if I would tell an ordinary person about powwow they'd think you're not normal. To begin with, you have to go through the first session to really believe.

[[Then later:]]

David: The reason you believed powwowing worked was because you had experience with it?

Elaine: Right. I've been through it.

David: If you had just heard about it, would you believe in it?

Elaine: It would make me a little leery, but if there was something wrong with me, I would try it. But I went through it. One hundred percent I believe in it.

18. The top was dark, and the skirt was a lighter color, but neither was a "bright" color.

Elaine reports that Mrs. A "told me all the time, 'You have to believe.' And when we would go on the way out, my dad used to look back and tell me, 'Elaine, you have to believe.'"

Elaine does not recall her parents' ever paying for Mrs. A's services. "I don't know if my father and mother ever did. I don't think they did because they came from a family that was poor, and I didn't ever see them give her money. I don't know if she was charging or it was free or if they gave her something in vegetables. I don't know."

"Aunt" Sophia Bailer

"Aunt" Sophia Bailer, who sometimes signed her name "Dr. Sophia Bailer," was one of Don Yoder's principal consultants, providing a great deal of information on powwowing. As Don Yoder told me, she was a Pennsylvania Dutch woman from Tremont, Pennsylvania, and known as "the saint of the coal regions." She was exposed to powwowing and black magic as a young girl, when one of her brother John's boarders was a witch. She continued her practice until her death in 1955.

Sophia could powwow both in person and by telephone, and she did not mind revealing the incantations and rituals she used in her powwowing practice, many of which were published in Alfred Shoemaker's journal *The Pennsylvania Dutchman*. This is contrary to the practice of most powwowers.

Helen Bechtel

Helen Bechtel practiced in Jim Thorpe (Carbon County), bordering the area where I conducted my fieldwork. However, I am providing a brief description of her based on Lewis (1969, 202–5) because I discuss a few cases in which she was involved. One of these is as dramatic as Case 7, below, also from the same general area.

Lewis presents little of Bechtel's practice, other than that it appeared quite often to involve the use of holy water and the removal of hexes. Bechtel is an unusual powwower in that she is a Roman Catholic. She claims that when she told her priest about her powwowing practice, "And his answer was 'If a man has faith it must help.' He didn't tell me to stop." She never took payment for her services, not even freewill offerings. At the time of Lewis's interview (mid to late 1960s) she was in her midfifties.

"Professor" Ervin Emig

All the information on Ervin Emig derives from Lewis, who interviewed him and witnessed several healing rituals (see the cases below) (Lewis 1969, 219–18). Emig lived in the city of York (York County) and practiced out of his home, advertising his practice with a small sign. Because Lewis and Mrs. Anna Snelbecker, a stringer for the *York Dispatch*, walked in on Emig in the middle of treatment and were told to sit down, I presume the treatment room was not separated from the waiting room. The interview was conducted in 1966 or 1967.

According to Emig, he was born in 1890 in southern York County and had started powwowing ("trying") when he was twenty-one years old. He learned from a "powwow doctor" in Chambersburg (Franklin County) and then "for ten years studied the human body" (Lewis 1969, 222). Emig used in his cures a 1902 edition of *Osteopathic Practice and Psychic Research*, for which he claimed to have paid four hundred dollars.[19] Emig also drew up "letters of protection" for patients who were the victims of a hex. He claimed that all his powers came from Jesus (Lewis 1969, 224). However, Emig apparently used belief in hexing to his monetary advantage, much as a confidence man would. In Lewis's account, Emig discusses money often and charges a set fee, even asking for the money from patients, contrary to traditional powwowing practice.

Mary "Ma" Koenig

Mary Koenig was a German immigrant living in Lancaster, Pennsylvania. In 1949, two researchers performing a study of spiritualist practice visited her home to interview her (Estep and Pietchke 1949). Rather than pretend to have a disease, lest they be found out, they decided to be honest about why they were there. Mrs. Koenig (seventy-eight years old) stressed that

19. However, inside the flyleaf the number ten was circled, leading Lewis to believe that Emig had exaggerated the price by a factor of forty. Because four hundred dollars is still an extremely high price to pay for a book, it is difficult to believe that Emig could have paid that amount in the early twentieth century, when four hundred dollars was worth more than ten thousand dollars in today's currency.

she was not a doctor (the writers believe legal ramifications were behind this) and did not call herself a "pow-wow." Her daughter (fifty to fifty-five years old years old) said that they were not powwows and did not believe in powwowing: "What good can a person do with a piece of string?" They described themselves as "spiritualists." Mrs. Koenig ("Ma Koenig") had come originally from "Wurtenberg," Germany (as spelled in the 1949 article).

The two women considered their power to be a gift passed down from generation to generation. The daughter did not know all the secrets, because there were some that Ma Koenig could divulge only on her death-bed. The daughter could cure some of the minor cases, but she sometimes had to call Ma Koenig in. Ma Koenig said that an outsider could probably cure if they taught him, but that the person had to be worthy and that there was a sacred trust involved. The person had to be clean and clean-living, promise to use the power only for good, and never accept any money. Ma Koenig said that many scientific foundations, newspapermen, and others had tried to learn about her power, but she gave no information to them because she did not believe the gift should be commercialized.

Curing was effected by the practitioner doing or saying something secret that even the patient knew nothing about, in combination with the reading or recitation of prayers by the patient at certain prescribed times. The prayers were given to the patient by the practitioner. Ma Koenig said the patient did not have to believe in her power cure, that the words she used were sufficient in themselves to cure regardless of the patient's belief.

The Koenig women claimed to be able to cure only skin diseases, mainly erysipelas. They also claimed to be able to cure any kind of eczema and exterior cancers in their initial stages.

Lulu McClure

Despite her married name, Mrs. McClure was a Pennsylvania Dutch woman in New Salem (York County) who spoke the dialect. The parents of my consultant Rick Shaw took him there for treatment when he was a boy—they never went to physicians until five or six years before the death of Rick's father. His last visit happened when he was thirteen or fourteen (in 1968 or 1969). After Mrs. McClure's death, they began to see Calvin E. Rahn (see below).

Mrs. McClure's home was tidy, and she had pictures of Jesus inside.

Rick (who is now a born-again Christian) believes that she was a committed Christian. He recalls that she treated him for sore throat, mumps, measles, stomach flu, and an ulcer, but she seemed to be able to cure anything—he mentioned liver problems and migraine specifically. Her healing was conducted in a "sunroom or pantry—a sewing room attached to the main [part of the house]." Mrs. McClure had a "prayer cloth" that she would pray over while she was healing. She would never charge a fee. Rick recalls her as a very kind woman who would generally have candy on hand for the children she cured.

Rachel Rahn

Rachel Rahn was regarded as one of the most successful powwowers. Mrs. Rahn called her practice "trying," the most commonly accepted direct translation for powwowing, and "faith healing" in York County (Lewis 1969, 196–97). She learned powwowing in 1904 from her father, a veterinarian who also powwowed. As her client and housemate Hazel notes, "He was a doctor for cattle and he used to cure for them and people didn't know it." Mrs. Rahn was a practicing powwower at least until 1969, when the interview with Lewis took place.

Mrs. Rahn worked in a mill from childhood until age seventy-seven. During that period, she practiced powwowing part-time, "like most of us faith healers do." In the 1930s, however, when she shared a house with Hazel Sauer in Glenville (York County) she had a large practice. According to Hazel, she wore glasses, but after she moved to New Freedom (York County) from Glenville, "she got her second sight back" after a thunderstorm. After she left the mill, she became a full-time powwower. Hazel said that her husband worked at a feed mill in Glenville and that they had an adopted daughter. It is unclear whether this was the same mill that employed Mrs. Rahn. Mrs. Rahn was a member of "Leshish Church," located off Route 116 near Spring Grove (York County). Hazel described the Rahn family as nice people: "They would do anything for me."

One had to be born with the power, Mrs. Rahn believed, but that power had to be trained in order to be effective. The only ability that could not be taught and that required no training was stopping hemorrhage. In fact, that was a litmus test for whether one was worth training. "I always say to them, 'If you can't stop the blood, you'll never be a powwower, so don't waste your time'" (Lewis 1969, 197). According to Hazel, Mrs. Rahn informed her that she was able to learn, but Hazel declined, out of fear that she would inadvertently become involved with evil powers. She told me that Mrs. Rahn had explained the use of incantation manuals: "One book is for the devil, one is for God." Hazel added, "I didn't want to get the wrong book. The devil's loose as it is. I don't want to get mixed up with him!"

While I have no reason to doubt Hazel's account, this training could not have been directly from Mrs. Rahn to Hazel, because Mrs. Rahn believed in the orthodox theory of cross-gender transmission, that is, that women can teach men only, and vice versa. This apparent conflict in stories can be resolved if a male (such as Hazel's husband, who also patronized Mrs. Rahn and other powwowers) could have acted as the intermediate link. That was how Daisy Dietrich was able to learn from Ruth Strickland Frey.

"Professor" Howard Resh

I interviewed two clients of Howard Resh, a York County powwower who is also described by Lewis (1969, 187–96). One was Rick Shaw, who recalls going to see Resh until the late 1960s. Rick describes Resh as older, large, and possessing a deep voice with a heavy Pennsylvania Dutch inflection.[20] He found Resh nice but "very intimidating," probably because of his imposing stature. Resh had a "junky" house, and he would treat people at his kitchen table and sit there with bare feet.

Rick cannot remember what Resh treated him for, but he recalls that Resh could heal nervous conditions, stomach trouble, corns, and toothache. He could also get blood flowing better and remove curses. Once, Resh removed a curse on Rick's Uncle Kurt, supposedly from a witch in Windsor Township, York County. The curse was on five hundred dollars that Uncle Kurt received from a trust fund. Resh instructed him to bury it in his backyard and was able to remove the curse.[21] According to Rick, Resh kept a copy of *The Long Lost Friend*, along with other books of

20. Rick describes him as "a big man . . . about six feet, three inches" in height. However, Lewis called him "a fat wheezy little man" (Lewis 1969, 191).

21. I recently viewed a television program in which a woman who had worked as a "psychic reader and advisor" admitted using a similar technique to con a woman out of the buried money. I do not accuse Resh of being a con man, but I believe that fraud is a problem that must be dealt with in connection with *Brauche*.

powwowing recipes, and his Uncle Kurt had a copy of *The Sixth and Seventh Books of Moses*. In his cures, he remembers how Resh would "wave a thread around" and blow air on areas requiring healing.

According to Lewis, Resh was eighty-two years old in the late 1960s (Lewis 1969, 191). His age notwithstanding, Resh saw patients six days a week, fifty-two weeks a year. His office hours were from two to four o'clock in the afternoon and six to eight o'clock in the evening, on weekdays and Sundays. Resh had been powwowing since he was seventeen years old (roughly 1904) but claims he gained a great deal more power after 1948, when he had a vision. After that, he never raised, ate, or touched pork (Lewis 1969, 192). Part of Resh's practice was the fabrication of *Himmelsbriefe*, or letters of protection. Resh credited his cures to Jesus—according to Lewis, he had pictures of Jesus on his wall—and was a practicing nondenominational Christian.

But some of Resh's behavior does not reflect the pious or even saintly image of many powwowers. For instance, he strongly hinted to Lewis that he had put a hex on someone, a county health officer who had demanded that Resh take down the sign advertising his services, which Resh refused to do: "I fixed that county officer, all right; made him let me alone" (Lewis 1969, 193). Resh also bragged that he could obtain the sexual favors of any woman he wanted. It is likely that Resh believed that the latter effect (if true) was also due to his power. This suggests that Resh was one of those powwowers who at times engaged in black magic and functioned as a witch.[22]

Resh indicated a strong dislike of the biomedical professions, mainly because of the use of pharmaceuticals and the tendency to keep people in hospitals. He believed physicians were greedy and incompetent: "They don't know what they're doin' half the time." In keeping with custom, Resh never asked for money; patients left any money next to the Bible. Resh even refused Lewis's offer of a freewill offering after the interview, because he had not done anything for him (Lewis 1969, 195).

Mr. Sunday

Mr. Sunday was the father of my consultant Elaine Madeira. He was Pennsylvania Dutch and appears to have been a powwower of the nonpro-

22. In fact, Lewis calls him a "hexer" (Lewis 1969, 187), but I am reluctant to place too much

fessional type, treating only members of his immediate family and refusing to treat others. He used a number of home remedies, some augmented by the use of whispered incantations, but he referred to only one of his practices—passing a child around table legs to cure livergrown—as "powwow."

Elaine describes her immediate family as "big believers" who went to church every week. Perhaps this explains why she sees nothing wrong with powwowing and believes it is perfectly acceptable for a Christian to be treated by a powwower and to practice powwowing. She thinks being a "believer" and a churchgoer helped her to accept the idea of going to a professional powwower as a young girl, as below. However, she is convinced that powwowing works, because "I've been through it, so 100 percent I believe in it." She does not, however, share her father's belief in hexes: "My father was a strong believer in that. When we had bad luck with kids, they would say, 'Oh, this person is hexing us.' And then my father would put salt in front of the doorstep. I never believed in it. He was raised to believe in it."

Her father treated his immediate family and grandchildren, as well as his farm animals, on whom he sometimes used a special salve. As a result, "we seldom had need of a [medical] doctor." But he restricted his practice to the family.

Elaine: He didn't treat nobody else, no. If one of the boys would have called and say "We have problems with one of the kids" he would have run back. I had a lot of trouble with Dani. He thought she was colicky. He believed in riding back from the hospital that she could have livergrown that's why we did the table business [passing her around a table leg three times]. Also, he believed Dani was constipated. We didn't have all those things in the soaps. He would shape a suppository and put it up her and said words. Then within half an hour she went.

David: So he thought the suppository itself would not work unless he said something?

Elaine: Yes. He used to say words.

David: You couldn't make out what he said?

Elaine: No.

---

weight on this designation because Lewis is free with his terminology throughout the book, often using the term "necromancer" to refer to a powwower. Whatever powwowing is, it is not necromancy.

Some of his home remedies, while not necessarily deriving from powwowing, were reminiscent of material components used in powwowing. One of these involved using a sock filled with onions and a red beet to cure a fever. Elaine describes it in response to a question by William Donner, the Kutztown University anthropologist who helped arrange the interview at his house:

Elaine: My kids had a lot of problems when they were young. Not my oldest daughter, but my son and my daughter, Stephanie here, they were always sick when they were small. My son would get temperatures of 100 degrees and 101 degrees. My father would come up, get a sock. We'd put an onion in there, a red beet, and we'd put this on his foot. Within an hour, the temperature was down. So, I think my father himself knew pretty much about powwowing.

The onion had to be soft, not cooked through and through. Onion is supposed to draw out the fever, and the red beet is supposed to protect them from dehydrating. He would put it in a sock. He would put his foot in the sock and put a loose rubber band or a string around it, and his fever would drop.

David: Did he ever give you any theories as to why this worked?

Elaine: No. My father—I trusted him with everything. He knew what he was doing. I'm not going to question him, why did he do this or why did he do that.

Because Elaine was so sickly as a child, her father was concerned about her, and the two developed a close relationship. She said he was always ready to render healing assistance with her own children :

> I think my dad was more concerned about me compared to the boys. They were okay. They had no problems. I think my daddy was worried about me, when I was a kid. Since I had problems when I was first born. I think my dad felt very close to me like I was close to him compared to the boys. I don't remember the boys going along up there. My mom went along just like I was with my boys. He'd come running more than my mother. I could call my dad anytime and say, "Hey, Daddy, I'm having trouble with Blaine with his ears again," and he'd say "Try to get his

urine and drop it in," and I'd say, "I don't know if I can do this," and he'd say, "Don't worry, I'll come up and help you."

Sample Cases

Case 7: Healing a Man Near Death (late 1920s–early 1930s)

This dramatic case was reported by Michelle Burch, a thirty-seven-year-old Pottstown woman. It involves her maternal grandparents and took place in Summit Hill (Carbon County) on the periphery of the culture area. The story was passed down from her mother. The case, which involves a mysterious "powwow man," appears to have made a great impression on her, judging from her reaction when I walked into the Spring Valley Inn (Lehigh County) and asked about powwow. She told me that I was the only nonfamily member who had ever mentioned the word "powwow" to her, and she believed it was some kind of sign.

Michelle's grandfather Raymond, who went by the nickname "Ramie," was a Pennsylvania Dutch coal miner who had married an Irish-Catholic woman, Lizzie (her grandmother). Once, Ramie got into a terrible accident at the coal mines and was brought home to her grandmother unable to walk and suffering from pneumonia. Michelle's grandmother was told Ramie would die. That evening, it was dark and rainy, and a stranger came to the house carrying a satchel.

The man, known to the family as the "powwow man," said he had come to heal Ramie. But if it were to happen, her grandmother had to do exactly as the man instructed. The man handed her grandmother something from his satchel—Michelle thought it was a piece of clothing—and went upstairs to see Ramie. "Why they even entrusted this man—that was the oddest thing," said Michelle.

I have included a long excerpt from Michelle's account, which includes the incident and her family's reaction to it. Some of it is repetitive:

Michelle: [My mother's] daddy worked in the coal mines. So it had to be in the 1920s–30s. I don't know. When she was a little girl, her dad got sick. He was so sick. He was paralyzed and, I forget—It was a bad accident at the mine.

David: Did it collapse or something like that?

Michelle: Yeah. He was, like, they didn't think he was going to live. He was in bed paralyzed. They went through really hard times and stuff, and the kids were just little, and my mom said that there was a knock at the door one day, and this man came, this man with a real thick accent. Now they had a funny Irish accent. Her mother was Irish, and her father was German [from other information, Pennsylvania Dutch]. They talked with an Irish twang up there.

Anyway, when she was a little girl, her dad was really, really sick and there was a knock at the door, and a strange man was standing there. They always picture him, the way she described it, with a big hat. It was scary. It scared the kids. They were scared to death. And he had this thick accent and he said, "Is Ramie there? Ramie?"

They got their mom, and, you know, "Who are you?"

"I've come to see Ramie. I've come very far. I've walked through the valleys from far, far away."

He just appeared. Nobody sent him there. He never said anyone sent him. He just came to see Ramie, and he's sick.

For whatever reason, my grandmom let him in the house, and she was taking him up to the room to see Ramie, and the conversation went on that they didn't know him. He was just there to see him.

David: Ramie is your grandfather, right?

Michelle: Yes. He was just there to see Ramie. He had a thick Dutch accent.

David: So the powwow man was Dutch?

Michelle: Yeah. Real thick German Dutch accent. A scary man with a big black hat on and dark clothes. Real scary to little kids.

David: Did he show up at night? Or was it during the day that he came?

Michelle: You know, I think it was at night. They were so frightened. Everything about this man scared these little kids, and my grandmother, for whatever reason, let him go up.

He said, "I need to talk to Ramie, and I need to be alone with him. You stay downstairs and make some hot tea or whatever. But whatever you do, don't come up and don't go in that room." And the man went in and was there for long, long time, and then screams came from the room. And she [Michelle's grandmother] went to run upstairs and was crying and [the powwow man] said, "No, no. You go downstairs. Raymond's going to get up in the middle of the night tonight, and he's going to call your name, and you don't go to him. He's going to cry and he's going to scream and cry for you. And you're gonna want to help him. Don't go to him. Let him be. Ramie will be okay."

Whatever went on in that room—when you would hear my mother describe this, it was just like this—these little kids were scared to death. They didn't know if this man was up there—this strange man came and he was killing their dad, or what. Everyone went to bed. In the middle of the night my mom remembers hearing all this. The rooms are connected, the doors and stuff. He called for Lizzie. She wanted to go so bad and she just sat there and cried and cried.

And the man told her, "Whatever you do, do not do this. If you want Raymond to be well, don't go to him. He's going to call you three times."

He called. My mom said she never saw her dad cry—that night he was screaming and crying. The next morning he got out of bed. She wasn't to go in the room. He got out of bed and, so help me God, was healed and walked again. He was healthy, fine. That man went back to work again. And he was dying. I mean he was dying. I don't know if he fell in the mine shaft or some big collapse, or something like that. But it was really weird. Just a real weird story that my mom told me, and I used to love to hear it because she told me in detail.

It was like—I could just sit there and picture these things happening. But it's so bizarre that you came there asking for a powwow—The man left. He wasn't a mean man, just frightening. Very scary. He left. No one ever saw him again, heard of him, but he came from far, far, far away. He traveled and he walked through valleys to come there. And nobody ever sent him there. Do you know what I mean?

David: None of your grandfather's friends mentioned that they mentioned anything to this guy?

Michelle: No. He was from far, far away. He just appeared there from nowhere, and that was a strange thing. A stranger coming to the door with that thick accent and dark and mysterious. They didn't know what he was going to do to him [Ramie]. The next day he got out of bed. And during the night, when he was screaming and crying, he was begging her, "Please, please, Lizzie come and help me. Please, please, dear God help me." And she sat there and cried and cried. This man told her, "If you want him to get better, you do not go to him."

And whatever went on in that room with the screaming and the loud noises and the banging—I mean, who knows? But he appeared well. Nobody ever heard. None of the family sent him. It was just some stranger that appeared out of nowhere. Never to be seen again.

The doctors—there's no explanation for what had happened. I mean, he was never ever to walk again, ever. He was like completely paralyzed on one side and stuff, and I think her dad tried dragging himself out of bed and falling and dragging and screaming for help, and everybody was forbidden to go to him and help him.

David: And the doctors had seen him and said he was not going to walk?

Michelle: Oh, no. And he was sick. I guess he had gotten pneumonia and all kinds of things. He was able to raise his kids and take care of his family. Everyone was grown when he had passed away. Why we trusted this man to go up there. That was really bizarre. I never heard anyone say powwow before in my life.

David: Never heard it till me?

Michelle: No, no, no.

David: Most powwowers say their power comes from God.

Michelle: Well, it would have to, it would have to. There was no evil about that. Whatever praying and the banging and the noise and the screaming in that room that went on, who knows, but this man was healed the next morning. I would think that he was up there praying, like, with such a vengeance or who knows? The whole thing is so bizarre—Who sent him? And you have to think that this was a good man that came that was sent from far away by someone. Who? God? I don't know. No

> one ever knew. Here's this funny man coming in a small little coal-mining town in the middle of nowhere. As my mother would explain the story, he came from very, very far, and he walked. But he just appeared, and nobody in the town knew. It's a small little town. Dad never knew him, never saw him again.

Michelle considers this incident to be a miracle. She thinks about the man often. "Always I could just picture this man traveling through the mountains. . . . Through his power of prayer or whatever, he healed my grandfather. It was miraculous." She says the powwow man "definitely was a good, spiritual man."

Michelle's family members, apparently under the guidance of her grandmother, have visited faith healers, not always with success. The grandmother stressed to Michelle's aunt on one such trip that she had to believe in order for the cure to work. Her grandmother also always had all kinds of religious items around and prayed regularly. Michelle herself has a strong faith in God, although she is not a regular churchgoer, and she believes faith heals. She and her brother have each had near-death experiences. I believe this subsequent history of faith was influenced by the visit of the "powwow man."

Case 8: Using a Hex to Kill (1940–42)

Dr. Albert Mattern, a retired physician living in Berks County, used to have a practice in Reading. There he learned of a group of elderly women called "The Committee" who attempted to use hexing to kill other elderly people. "The Committee believed that as long as they could push another old person over the rim, they would never die, they would have life eternal." Dr. Mattern reports that The Committee also did not like their relatives visiting him and would attempt to stop this by hexing the patient:

> The people who were part of the Committee thought that if they would put a hex on somebody they would have eternal life. A man asked me how he could get rid of water running under his skin. I treated him for alcoholic neuritis, and it went away. One

> Saturday I saw him and asked him how he was doing. He said, "Fine," but he found out what caused it. He found his mother-in-law running water on his picture, and that's what caused the feeling in his arms. He said as soon as he found it out, her spell was gone. At the same time I was treating his wife and would give her an envelope with pills. Your fee at that time was not for your diagnosis; it was for the medicine you gave them. Most doctors dispensed medicine. She asked me to change to plain envelopes without my name or address, because if her mother finds out where she's was going, she'll put a hex on the medicine, and it won't do any good. I was about the fourteenth doctor she had been to.

I asked Dr. Mattern about a recent article in the *Reading Eagle* in which they were called "hexer-eye doctors," and he replied,[23] "It's actually 'hex doctor.' They put a hex on her [the woman just mentioned]. This is why you go around Pennsylvania—in Berks County you see the signs on the barn. That's to keep the hex away from the animals. In fact, I put one on my barn. I often had patients in the Reading Hospital. They'll have hex doctors come into the hospital to treat them. I didn't care if they treated them, as long as they took my medicine." Dr. Mattern indicated that the "hex doctors" stopped coming into the hospitals around 1942. He equated these "hex doctors with powwowers":

David: Were the hex doctors also called powwows?
Dr. Mattern: Powwowing, yes. When they did the powwowing, they took some hair and put it under the back of the barn in the full of the moon. They had all kinds of ideas to take the spell off themselves.
David: Do you see powwowers as equivalent to hex doctors?
Dr. Mattern: The same thing.

Dr. Mattern reports that two of his patients died after were being "worked on" by The Committee. This helped convince him to leave Read-

23. Likely a misspelling of *hexerei* (witchcraft).

ing. "I said to Vicky, 'We better move out of this neighborhood before The Committee starts working on us.'"

Case 9: Countering a Hex (1940s)

This case derives from Susan Stewart's 1976 study of powwowing in rural York County. It, and others in Appendix 7, concerns a family (identified as the Xs) living near Stewart's consultant's family when she was a girl. This family believed in and practiced "powwowing." The consultant's family considered the Xs ignorant and a throwback to older times, because most powwowers had disappeared from the area after the York Hex Murder Trial. The consultant credits her mother with saving the lives of the neighbor children by telling their mother to "stop that powwowing business and get those children to a doctor" (Stewart 1976, 12).

The case concerns a witch who had already plagued the family once before. This time she tried to put a spell on Mrs. X's sister, so her mother called a powwow doctor in York. The powwow doctor, a woman, said she knew they were coming and also knew what the visit was all about. The powwow doctor took the sister's hand in hers and "said some things." When she was finished, she told the mother, "If you know this person [the witch], when I take my hand off hers you'll know her." When Mrs. X's mother looked at her sister's palm, she saw a picture of the witch there. This is just like the event that precipitated the "Hex Murder."

The powwow instructed Mrs. X's mother to take the girl home and predicted that the witch would come to the door and ask to borrow something. She told the mother to take off the girl's undershirt and hide it in a dresser drawer. The mother was not to let the witch in the house but to "cuss her to the four highest words in the Bible," although Mrs. X could not recall just what those words were. The mother did all this, and when the witch came her mother told her to go away or she'd use the broom on her. The weather was terrible that night—raining, snowing, and hailing—and some men were working on the road. The witch told the men that Mrs. X's mother had been talking about her. Mrs. X seemed to think that this was meant to get back at her mother because the spell had been broken and because "bad witches have to work on someone all the time or they don't feel well."

According to Mrs. X, a witch could hex someone by pulling a string from the victim's slip, taking a piece of clothing or lock of hair from the victim, or knowing the victim's full name. She also said witches do not like children, that they have witch books that they read backward and that they "sell their self to the devil." Witches were mainly women, but could also be men who lived by themselves without a wife or children.

Case 10: Cure for Ringworm (1947–50)

When Elaine was a small child, from five to eight years old, she had a serious case of ringworm on her face. "Because I was raised on a farm," she said, "I got close to ringworms and the animals. I had powwowing done for that." Her family physician, Dr. Stanley Brunner, actually referred her to Mrs. A, the powwower.

David: Did you go to see any medical doctors?
Elaine: I have seen Dr. Stanley Brunner. He's no longer living. He used to live at Krumville. I was being treated then for a while with all my problems I had, and nothing worked. So he was the one that sent my parents and I to this woman.
David: So the doctor referred you to her?
Elaine: Yes.
David: Did he say "I want you to see a powwow"? That's how he said it?
Elaine: Yes.

When they went to see Mrs. A, her parents would go in with her and discuss the problem. Then she sent them outside and began the treatment.

Elaine: She would make them go out, and it was dark in there. She had a kerosene lamp—she had everything dark, and then she'd have a few candles setting around. She'd make me lie down on a sofa. First I would sit there. One of my problems—like the ringworm situation—she would make me close my eyes, and she'd put something over my face like a powder or some kind of medicine, and then she would talk in her language—you know, mumble things and pray for me. She usually took about half an hour. Then after that we went home, and I usually went back for another treatment, and by that time it was gone.

David: So you had two treatments total?

Elaine: Yes.

David: Was she a Dutch lady?

Elaine: I don't think she was. She looked—She reminded me of the witch type, you know, years ago. She was really spooky looking. She was not Pennsylvania Dutch.

David: What was her accent? You said she spoke in her language.

Elaine: She spoke in English, but not very well. When she did the powwowing over me, she prayed and then she would talk like m-m-m, aak-aak-aak, and did things to me like that. That's the way she done it.

David: Did she call it powwow?

Elaine: Yes.

Elaine found the first visit frightening for a number of reasons. First there was the strangeness of the mountain shack and the fact that her parents had to remain outside during treatment. The room was "really dark," lit only by candles, and Mrs. A was not friendly, reminding her of a witch. Elaine also didn't like having to keep her eyes closed. But after the first visit, she wasn't afraid anymore, "because I felt better after, like a couple of days later, and then we had to go back up again and get re-treated."

Case 11: Cure for Sleeplessness (unsuccessful) (1950)

In 1950, Robert Graham, a student at Franklin and Marshall College, investigated Lancaster powwower Mary Koenig, whom he called a "powwow doctor" (Graham 1951). He decided that the best way to learn about her practice "would be to have something wrong with me that she might be able to cure." He decided that this "something wrong" would be his habit of sleeping in the afternoons and staying up working late into the night. Graham told his fraternity brothers about this, and they wanted to go. He advised them that they should have something wrong with them too, if they were to go. One had a wart on his hand and accompanied Graham to see Mrs. Koenig (see Appendix 7, case A53).

Mrs. Koenig was "about seventy-five" at that time but appeared (from her face) to have a youthful spirit. She was watching a baseball game from Philadelphia on a sixteen-inch television set, which Graham found surprising. After watching television for ninety minutes and discussing various players and professional wrestlers (which she evaluated as "clean" or "dirty"), she called him over to the other side of the room and asked what his trouble was. After Graham told her in great detail, she sat "perfectly still for a minute and thought." Graham describes the rest:

> She then put her hand in the opening of my shirt and felt around for almost a minute. Finally when she seemed satisfied with one particular spot, she held her hand there, closed her eyes, and mumbled something under her breath that lasted two or three minutes. When this was over, I asked her if this was all there was to it. She told me that it was not all. She gave me explicit instructions that when I was ready to go to bed at night, I was to rub olive oil around the area of my liver and then say the Lord's Prayer three times. This was to be done for nine nights in a row, and at the end of that time, if I followed the instructions, I would be over my malady.

Graham followed Mrs. Koenig's instructions, but two weeks later, he was still sleepless at night.

Case 12: Cure for Erysipelas (1952)

This case is from Don Yoder's consultant "Aunt" Sophia Bailer of Tremont, Pennsylvania, based on letters to Yoder and interviews conducted by him that were published in *The Pennsylvania Dutchman* in the summer of 1952. In each of these cases, the relevant section is reproduced verbatim, with errors of punctuation, capitalization, and spelling corrected. The original is run together without any punctuation or capitalization other than commas in the expression "By, by, by," capitalization of the names Mother, God, and Lord, and the words capitalized in the incantations. I have left the incantations unchanged. She signed the letter "Dr. Sophia Bailer" and refers to the practice as "pow vowing," almost certainly reflecting her pronunciation of English.

I will tell you what I say when I go down over their body as good as I can in Dutch for erysipelas. You take a red thread of wool, hold it in your two hands, and stretch it across the person. The string must be wider than the person. Take your two hands with the ends, one end in your right hand, the other in your other hand, then say, "Wild fire" or, in English, "Erysipelas, move out of this person [body]. Mention full name. The red string will chase you by, by, by." You throw your arm with the red strings as if you were throwing the wild fire away. But I do not want them to eat salty meat until it is gone away and you smoke the string with smoke. You light a stick, blow it out, and let the smoke fly out at the string and hang the string near the stove. It is falls on the floor, sweep it with your broom and throw it in the stove. And my Mother told me when someone has erysipelas they have inflammation in it and then you should pow vow for rode *laufa* [note variant spelling for *rote laufa*]. This is what I say:

rode laufa rode laufa
feeler du denier hits
vet der froma Toby seina farva
wu er unser leva Heiland
betroen hut.

In English:

inflammation
lose thy color and heat
like Judas lost his color
when he betrayed
Jesus Christ
God the Father
God the Son
God the holy Ghost
help to this amen.

[The Pennsylvania Dutch version she provides omits the trinitarian formula and the concluding line.]

You use these holy words at everything you pow vow and ask them to help to it amen.

I made it pretty plain as good as I can take notice you ask for God to help to it and when you are done, then blow your breath three times over the body of the person you pow vow. Don't get tired reading this. Some of it is God's work. The Bible don't say what he said when he called a blessing on the people. Best regards to all of yous. May God bless yous.

Case 13: Curing Livergrown (early 1960s)

Elaine Madeira's eldest daughter was diagnosed with livergrown by her father, Mr. Sunday, who "powwowed" for it by passing her around table legs, a common remedy for this illness. Elaine describes the process:

Elaine: Another thing, my oldest daughter, when she was born she was colicky, and them children, they cried all the time mostly and would get really severe stomach aches. So my father would come up and we'd pass her around the table leg. Nobody could be in the room but my father and I. Daddy and I used to do that. We'd pass her around one way, then pass her around the other way, and then he would say something. I couldn't remember what it was.
David: Was he speaking in Dutch?
Elaine: Yes. He'd say something. He believed when children were small like that and they were colicky from riding home in the car, they'd get livergrown.
David: When you passed her around the table leg, how did you hold her?
Elaine: Like that [demonstrating holding the infant].
David: Would you crawl around the table with her?
Elaine: No. We weren't allowed to get underneath the table. If Daddy was going around one side, I'd have to reach under and he'd pass her to me on her back, and then we'd go to the next table leg and I'd pass her through, and he would take her. And that's the way we did it around the whole table.
David: How many legs did the table have?
Elaine: Four.

David: Do you know if the number four was special, or was it just however many legs it happened to be?
Elaine: I think it was just how many legs it happened to be.
David: If there were six, they'd do six?
Elaine: Yes. It was like a weaving thing though. It wasn't like pass her through and catch her on one side then take her to the other side.
David: You would make one circle of the table. He would say something. Would he lay hands on her?
Elaine: He would put his hands on her stomach and say something.

After this "powwow" treatment, the daughter got well and ceased being colicky. Elaine would not hesitate to go to a powwower today.

Case 14: Hex Removal and Casting out the Devil (mid-1960s)

Helen Bechtel, of Jim Thorpe (Carbon County), relayed this account to Arthur Lewis (1969, 202–4). During the interview, she and two other women who knew the story seemed excited.

Mrs. Bechtel was called to the house of Walter Miller, a sick man who believed he had a hex on him that was causing his suffering. He could not eat or sleep "and was wasting away like the abnehme [['the take-off']]." He had been to see a string of powwowers, paying each of them, but received no relief. After listening to his story, Mrs. Bechtel agreed that he was hexed and was pretty certain the witch who placed the hex on him was someone in his own house. That night, she had a dream, and in it "I seen someone with three fingers off'n her hand, and right away I know'd that had to be the witch that put the spell on Walter."

The next night Mrs. Bechtel went to Walter's house. Because the experience began as soon as she walked in the door, I shall quote the account recorded by Lewis in its entirety, leaving out only Lewis's remarks and replacing them with ellipses. The speaker quoted by Lewis is Mrs. Bechtel.

> Next night I went over to Walter's house and tole him. I could feel somethin' pullin' at me the minute I walked in. I wasn't afraid; I had my holy water along.
>
> I took Walter with me and together we went through every

room in that big ole house. Walter lives alone since his mother died. . . . Finally we climb up the attic steps and all the while that feelin' I had is gettin' stronger and stronger.

I led the way up that dark flight of steps, Walter right behind me. I pushed open the attic door. It was pitch black, and I don't mind tellin' you the feelin's I was gettin' then was strong. Walter was really scared.

I pushed him back of me and I tole him, "Walter," I says, "don't be afraid. I'll protect you no matter who or what's in this room." I pulled the stopper out of my holy-water bottle and got it ready.

Just then the feelin' I had grow'd unbearably strong. The light of the moon shined through a window covered with cobwebs, but you could see somethin' anyway; the rays shined down on the center of the attic and rested on a floorboard. Somethin' was pullin' and pullin' at me, makin' me move there.

It was terrible powerful on one spot, and I whispered to Walter, "Lift up that floorboard. Whatever it is or whoever it is put the hex on you is under there."

I stood aside . . . and he tugged and tugged at the board and finally raised it up. Underneath it right in the middle was an old doll.

"My God! Helen." he says. "It's a doll I used to play with when I was a little boy. I ain't seen it for fifty years. How'd it get here?"

Walter was afraid to pick it up, but I wasn't. I held it up to the moonlight so's I could get a good look at the thing. Even though it was hid for fifty years or longer, it was in good condition, a little dusty maybe, but otherwise perfect. Then I looked at the thing's left hand. So help me, there was three fingers missin'!

Right at that moment there was a weird howl that sent the blood curdlin' through my veins. I could feel somethin' tryin' to get at Walter. He was shakin' all over. I stepped in front of him to protect him. I could see what I thought was a beast ready to leap. But it wasn't no beast; it was the devil hisself.

The devil grabbed holt of me and pinched my behind so hard I screamed with pain—Squeezed me so tight the marks was there

> for days. Kept tryin' to shove me aside and reach Walter, but I wouldn't let him. I kept pushin' him back.
>
> Then I got my right arm free and sprinkled holy water all over the devil. At the same time, I called out, "Stop in the name of the Father, the Son, and the Holy Ghost!" and the devil rushed out of the room through the window as fast as he could. His power over Walter was destroyed and he was free of the hex.

Walter offered to pay her a large sum of money after that, but she refused. Mrs. Bechtel never took any money for her powwowing services, not even freewill offerings.

FROM 1970 TO THE PRESENT

It is during the period of 1970 to the present that powwowing assumed the form it has today—a secretive practice carried out away from population centers but with a strongly religious cast. At the same time, academics and local historians, the caretakers of Pennsylvania Dutch culture, began to believe that powwowing was no longer practiced at all. For instance, in 1999 one well-known local historian in northwestern Montgomery County told me that he believed powwowing was last practiced in southeastern Pennsylvania in the late 1970s.

Yet, during the latter part of this period (1990s), a new type of practitioner has begun to emerge: the New Age powwower. It is in this form that powwowing has been introduced to a non–Pennsylvania Dutch audience that is interested in magic and neo-paganism. Silver RavenWolf, a neo-pagan writer, has written a book, *HexCraft: Dutch Country Magick* (1997), later reissued as *American Folk Magick*, in which she claims to have been taught powwow by Preston Zerbe (a traditional York County powwower). RavenWolf, however, writes that Zerbe was wrong in believing that powwowing was Christian in origin. Rather, she locates its origin in pagan magical practices that subsequently were given Christian trappings to protect their practitioners from persecution.

RavenWolf's book represents an attempt to popularize powwowing as a form of "magick" (the typical pagan spelling of the word, to distinguish it from stage magic) and teach powwowing to her readers. RavenWolf describes herself as a practicing "Pow-Wow artist" and teaches it to both

Wiccan and Christian students, including her daughter. She uses all the various "magickal" traditions and books and makes no distinction between powwowing and black magic. She also freely "experiments" with various "chants," claiming that they work just as well substituting "Maiden, Mother, and Crone" (the Wiccan "Triple Goddess") for the names of the Christian Trinity. RavenWolf acknowledges that other "Pow-Wow artists" may not consider what she does to be "Pow-Wow" "because it is not exactly the way they practice" (RavenWolf 1997, xix). This is the attitude taken by Tom Barone, a newly trained traditional powwower who is aware of RavenWolf's writings and highly critical of them.

Ironically, efforts by neo-pagans to show that powwowing is not a Christian practice reinforce similar claims by the Eastern Mennonites and other indigenous opponents of powwowing, who suspect that it is at best a psychological crutch and at worst the work of the devil. Hostility toward powwowing and powwowers by various groups remains powerful and is a major factor in the practice's going underground during this period.

Ruth Strickland Frey

Ruth Strickland Frey was the instructor of Julius and Daisy Dietrich (Schuylkill County) and the powwower for another consultant, Harriet Miller (Berks County). According to Harriet, Mrs. Frey lived in Fogelsville (Lehigh County) and was a registered nurse who powwowed in the Allentown hospital. Her method was to have her patients sit down and hold the Bible in front of them, and then she would run her hands over the patient's body. This was also the method used by Daisy Dietrich when she powwowed me for arthritis. According to Harriet, Mrs. Frey's brother was supposed to learn it, but he did not want to. She did, however, teach Julius Dietrich, and he taught his wife Daisy in 1978. According to Harriet Miller and Daisy Dietrich, she also passed her ability on to her nephew, but Daisy had not heard that the nephew had done any powwowing as of 1999. Although she practiced into the 1990s and passed away in 1998, the latest case I have of a powwow ritual conducted by Mrs. Frey is from 1981.

Gertie Guise

My consultant Sarah, in eastern Adams County, a client of Gertie Guise[24] and took her children to be powwowed by her. Mrs. Guise was also the instructor of Preston Zerbe, another powwower patronized by Sarah. Mrs. Guise, who lived in York Springs in eastern Adams County, reportedly had a "very large" clientele and saw patients who called ahead "when [they] were in the area." She conducted her treatments on her sun porch. Sarah recalls that Mrs. Guise was a gentle woman who kept to herself. She always gave any children who came to see her a piece of candy after the treatment session and had a candy man deliver the sweets to her door. Mrs. Guise (and Preston Zerbe) accepted payment: "You gave money. You gave what you wanted, and sometimes they gave coins. I did not always give coins."

Maude Kreisher

Maude Kreisher was a part-time professional powwower and "spiritual healer" who lived in a brick rowhouse in Reading. She was featured in an article in the *Philadelphia Inquirer* (Schreiber 1976). Although she admitted to performing powwowing, she considered herself primarily a spiritual healer. When she powwowed, she did so only in High German. She was eighty-one years old at the time the article was written.

As a young girl, Maude had visions of spirits and believed that others could see them too. When she told her mother about it, she called the family physician, who ordered Maude to stay home from school, so in order to be allowed to return to classes, Maude stopped telling her mother about her visions. Although both her grandfathers were powwowers, Maude's first healing experience did not occur until she was forty-five (see Appendix 7, case A38) because it took that long for her "guides" to get through. She had been healing ever since, first on evenings and weekends, then after retirement by appointment on any day of the week. "I'm booked heavy," she said.

Judy McMullin

Judy was featured in the same *Philadelphia Inquirer* article as Maude Kreisher. She was only thirty years old when the article was printed,

24. Pronounced like "Geiss."

which would make her sixty or sixty-one years old now. She was born in Reading and at the time of the article lived in Denver, Pennsylvania (Lancaster County).

Judy had become a powwower at the age of twenty-seven after healing her son's blisters, and she began to participate in church healing services and to teach classes in her home. It was apparently after this experience that her grandfather presented her with a copy of *The Long Lost Friend*. She carried the book everywhere because of its self-proclaimed amuletic property, which supposedly keeps the bearer from harm.

Calvin E. Rahn

Calvin E. Rahn (no relation to Rachel Rahn) was a Lancaster County gunsmith who treated the mother of Rick Shaw, one of my consultants, in 1970 or 1971 for a sore arm, possible arthritis, and a sore throat.[25] He may have been active through most of the 1970s and into the early 1980s, as well, because he reportedly died in 1981 at sixty-five years of age (Beissel 1998, 53). Calvin E. is the father of Calvin M. Rahn and father-in-law of Anita Rahn. He was interviewed by Arthur Lewis, the source for much of the following information (Lewis 1969, 176–78).

Calvin claimed that he had had the power to heal and fight the devil since his birth and that this power came from Jesus. He believed he acquired this divine power because he was the seventh son of a seventh son.[26] Unlike Rachel Rahn, who believed witches were becoming "dumber" and had lost much of their power, Calvin felt that they were stronger in the 1960s than they had been previously: "Make no mistake about the devil's presence; he's everywhere. He puts strength into witches; they're all around us" (Lewis 1969, 177). Calvin claimed that there were eighteen witches in the small southwest Lancaster County town where he and the other members of his family lived. He also

25. Rick remembers little about the sessions. His mother went to Calvin Rahn after their regular family powwower had passed away.

26. An alternate version of how Calvin became a powwower appears in Beissel's *Powwow Power* (1998), a self-published book that contains a hodgepodge of stories about Calvin's son (also named Calvin) and the author's great-uncle, the Northumberland County powwower William Wilson Beissel. In this version, Calvin (the elder) learned powwowing in 1952 from a woman named Mamie, in Clay or Lebanon, Pennsylvania. In my opinion, however, this "Mamie" is identical with Lewis's "Amy" and refers only to the additional training Calvin received in the early 1950s. I consider the Lewis account more authoritative because it is based on an actual interview with Calvin and is a more coherent and continuous narrative.

recounted stories of how he struggled with witches, describing two in particular.

Calvin powwowed only for immediate and extended family members (wife, son, aunts, uncles, cousins) until he was thirty-eight years old (in 1954). He powwowed to cure illness, remove hexes, and help farm animals, such as cows that were not giving milk, and hens that were not laying eggs. When others heard about his power, they wanted him to help them, too. Calvin believed that he needed to increase his power in order to handle the many additional clients, so he went to see an ancient woman named Amy (or Mamie), who lived on a shack on Garrett Mountain, near Carlisle. It was under her guidance that he underwent what resembles an Amerindian vision quest, at the end of which he met five "Indian" spirit guides.

Calvin treated patients from as far away as Youngstown, Ohio, and reported "emptying" his waiting room three or four times a night. His office hours were from approximately six o'clock in the evening to after midnight. He claimed that physicians often sent patients to him when biomedical procedures were ineffective, and he cites a case in which he cured a boy of leukemia. He was frequently called on to render emergency treatment, particularly for burn victims. Calvin could even powwow over the telephone in cases requiring immediate treatment. He considered powwowing to be physically exhausting.

As is typical for powwowers, Calvin never requested payment, but patients frequently placed money either in his hand or on his living-room table beside a large family Bible. He also apparently conducted a form of experimental research in healing, because he informed Lewis that he was working on a cure for cancer and believed he was "getting someplace": "Pretty soon I believe I might be able to cure it, in the early stages at least." He was also attempting to find ways to make a salve he had acquired in Florida that was supposed to cure cancer safe for use on his patients. This was necessary because after purchasing the supposed healing salve he had taken it to a pharmacist to be analyzed and discovered that it contained three deadly poisons (Lewis 1969, 187). This action is an example of the widespread belief, contra Howard Resh (above), that biomedicine and powwowing can work together.

Calvin M. Rahn

Calvin M. Rahn was the son of Calvin E. Rahn and the husband of Anita Rahn. He was a retired engineer when he died in 1999 at the age of sixty-one, two weeks before I arrived in the area.

Calvin M. learned powwowing from his father, a violation of the customary cross-gender mode of transmission. He reports that his father trained him because he had no sisters and his mother was not a powwower (Beissel 1998, 54).[27] According to his father, Calvin M. had fifteen "Indian" spirit guides who worked with his father's spirit guides when the two consulted on a case (Lewis 1969, 179). However, at the time of Lewis's interview (in the late 1960s) his father indicated that Calvin M. was not interested in powwowing, even though he was born with the power.

In his practice, Calvin M. reported that he never used notes, booklets, or literature, and he claimed not to use the same ritual each time because repeated use tended to negatively affect the ritual's results (Beissel 1998, 24). He claimed to be able to cure anything and to have worked on the following ailments (no mention is made of the degree of success achieved): abrasions, arthritis, back problems, bellyache, bleeding, bowel obstruction, breast inflammation, broken bones, burns, cancer, "cardiology," colic, corns, ear problems, erysipelas, eye problems, fever, goiter, headache, heart problems, hex cures, hips out of joint, infections, inflammation, insomnia, jaundice, crooked limbs, lumps, menstruation, nervous problems, new rupture, pain in limbs, paralysis, pleurisy, pneumonia, poison ivy, proud flesh, rheumatism, rupture, seizures, shingles, "sick," skin disorders, sprain, sunsickness, surgery, swelling, sweeney, throat pain, toothache, unknown illnesses, and warts. He also claimed to be able to find stolen goods and generate letters of protection (Beissel 1998, 67).

Ruth Stoner

Ruth Stoner, a Lancaster County powwower, also appears in the *Philadelphia Inquirer* article on powwowing (Schreiber 1976). At the time the article was published, she worked in a factory and saw patients at night, and she believed she was the only powwower still practicing: "If the art's dying out, it's because the young people don't want to be tied down."

The writer, who visited Ruth to have a wart removed (see sample case 16, below), describes her as having a "kind, grandmotherly air" and seem-

27. Of course, Calvin E. could have trained his wife, who then could have trained the son, but it is possible that he did not train her because of a belief that one must be born with the power in order to be able to learn.

ing genuinely concerned about her patient. She did not accept money after treatment.

Preston Zerbe

I first learned of Preston Zerbe in Silver RavenWolf's *HexCraft: Dutch Country Magick* (1997), a book that purports to instruct anyone on how to practice powwowing. presented as having its origins in the "Old Religion."[28] I was skeptical that he was a real person because much of the "information" in RavenWolf's book is contrary to what I learned from consultants and documentary sources.[29] However, his name also came up in my interview with Sarah, where I learned that he was Sarah's powwower after Gertie Guise. Sarah recounts, "Preston Zerbe at one time had a very good job, and he owned a little drug store. Generally, you would find these people do this after they retire." He lived in York Springs, in eastern Adams County.

According to both Sarah and RavenWolf, Zerbe learned powwowing from Mrs. Guise (above). RavenWolf says that he did not use the Bible in his practice, although he read it often and used memorized Bible passages from an out-of-print book published around 1860, *Lessons in Sympathy*.[30] She claims to have noticed that Zerbe "used Bible verses mixed with Heathen charms" and that "he used Psalm magick," that is, used the songs in the Hebrew Bible's Book of Psalms to accomplish certain specific purposes, which varied from psalm to psalm (RavenWolf 1997, 261).

Zerbe did not hold the belief of some powwowers that the illness of a patient was temporarily transferred to his body after a healing ritual. RavenWolf claims that he used what she called a "Divinity stone" to remove pain from the bodies of patients, human or animal. It was round, smooth, deep brown in color, and about three inches in diameter. RavenWolf describes it as looking "like a potato" (RavenWolf 1997, 54). According to RavenWolf, Zerbe believed anything a powwower touched would retain power. She quotes him on this point: "The Indian Pow-Wows believed this more than us faith healers. They had wolf skins, snake

28. This is a "Craft name," a designation employed by some pagans (such as RavenWolf) to hide their identity. However, RavenWolf herself has not been particularly careful in her publications to hide her legal name, Jenine Trayer.

29. This book is discussed in greater detail below.

30. Possibly related to William Beissel's *Secrets of Sympathy* (1938).

skins, you name it. They also used lots of plants and were big on salves. Rattlesnake was a favorite. Likewise, there was a belief that the elements provided by God, if used properly, would bring sympathy for healing. If you added emotion to it and concentrated real hard, the Pow-Wow could not be stopped" (RavenWolf 1997, 42).

Zerbe stressed the role of the patient's faith, citing the example of a man who had been to see Gertie Guise eighteen times without success, yet on the nineteenth visit he was cured. Zerbe said he asked everyone who came for treatment if he or she believed in the Holy Trinity, and he claimed that he could tell if they really believed in it or not (RavenWolf 1997, 74).[31] At the end of each session, he would say, "Don't thank me, thank God in your prayers tonight."

RavenWolf claims that Zerbe taught her how to powwow and that he also instructed another woman, Wilma Clark. RavenWolf claims to have been in communication with Zerbe and received more information on powwowing after his death (mid-1990s). According to Sarah, Zerbe also wanted her to learn, but she was afraid to complete her training because she was concerned about the "dark side" of the practice and worried that she might be led into black magic.

Sample Cases

Case 15: Cure for the Take-Off (probably late 1960s to early 1970s)

Sarah went to take her infant to Gertie Guise to cure the baby of "the take-off." She describes the procedure for curing this malady but uses the generic term "the powwow" to refer to Mrs. Guise. It was only later in the interview that I learned her identity. The procedure described below is a form of the folk custom of measuring.

Sarah: As a child, my mother used to take me to the powwow. Then when I had my children, I knew what the powwow did; however, it was not as prevalent as when I was a child.

So I took my children to the powwow, and one of the main

31. RavenWolf, as a Wiccan, substitutes "Maiden, Mother, and Crone" for "Father, Son, and Holy Spirit" in the cures that Zerbe taught her.

things the powwow did is what they call the "take-off." The take-off is done with a string and many times this string is red. I don't know why. And this string, they take the bottom of your feet, and they take it from the heel to the toe. It would have to be barefooted, and seven times they fold this string. But first of all, it's seven times the foot, but they put it around your waist or you could do the foot, and then mark it, and then you would put it around your waist. If you [[the circumference of the patient's waist]] were more than the seven times [[the length of the foot]], that was something. It was called flesh decay. And if you were less than the seven times, I don't know about that. I know that was the test for flesh decay. So then this powwow would tie this string together so it would be a loop. I don't know how it was, but they would make it go up over your head and bring it down through your body and up through the other side, and then they would make an X in between it,[32] rub your chest and rub your back. In other words, you were surrounded by that string.

David: And that healed it?

Sarah: Well, my babies, their tummy would be distended. Then the next day or so, they would be crying, and the reason they were crying is because their stomachs hurt.

David: And when their stomachs went down they would stop crying?

Sarah: Exactly.

Sarah, who at one time considered becoming a powwower (and now practices her own form of energy healing and other therapeutic procedures), described this as a normal procedure to cure the take-off. A similar account is preserved in a 1955 letter from Anna Smucker in Smithville, Ohio, to her grandson, a Mennonite pastor in Vernfield, Pennsylvania (Montgomery County), although in that case the height, rather than waist circumference, is measured against the length of the foot.

Case 16: Wart Removal (unsuccessful) (1975–76)

A writer for the *Philadelphia Inquirer*, Karen Schreiber, whose cousin was powwowed for warts at age three, decided to visit Ruth Stoner to have

32. I believe this refers to tying the loop of string in such a way that it has four lobes, at right angles to one another, looking like an "X."

her wart removed (Schreiber 1976). Ruth asked her patient if she were sleeping well, where she lived, and what she did. Then she asked Schreiber her name, wrote it on a slip of paper, sprinkled the paper with Johnson's Baby Powder, and folded it. Schreiber describes the rest of the ritual in the article:

> Then she sat me down sideways on a wooden chair with my back toward her . . . she stroked my back firmly. Then she stroked my head and neck, stopping to draw crosses with her fingers on my forehead and cheeks. As she made crosses just below my collar bone, she explained, "I know that some don't go over your whole body for warts. But I think it's necessary to get all your healing power to work for you." Then she went down my arms, ending each stroke with a light shake of her hands. Again the crosses, this time on my wart. Finally she went down my legs, and then was done.

At the end, Ruth expressed skepticism about whether it would work: "Usually you do warts two or three days before the full moon. You're a little late. . . . But with all the cloudy weather we've been having, you couldn't even see the moon. So that's why I went ahead with it. It may work anyway." As it turned out, Schreiber still had the wart at the time of writing the article.

Schreiber's account is very similar to what I experienced when I was treated by Daisy Dietrich and Anita Rahn.

Case 17: Curing a Skin Disease (1976)

Joyce Doxtater and her husband took their son to Mrs. May to have their son "powwowed" for dry, scaly skin, diagnosed by a dermatologist as atopic dermatitis. Before seeing Mrs. May, she said, "We always had a skin doctor, dermatologist, every month. We put cream on, try this medicine, that medicine, use no soap or special soap, whatever. It didn't help. And it got, you know, he was scratching and itching and, you know, you felt embarrassed when you were out in public."

At Nora Gearhart's urging, they took their son in to see Mrs. May. Joyce describes her as "very nice," but she wanted thirty dollars to cure

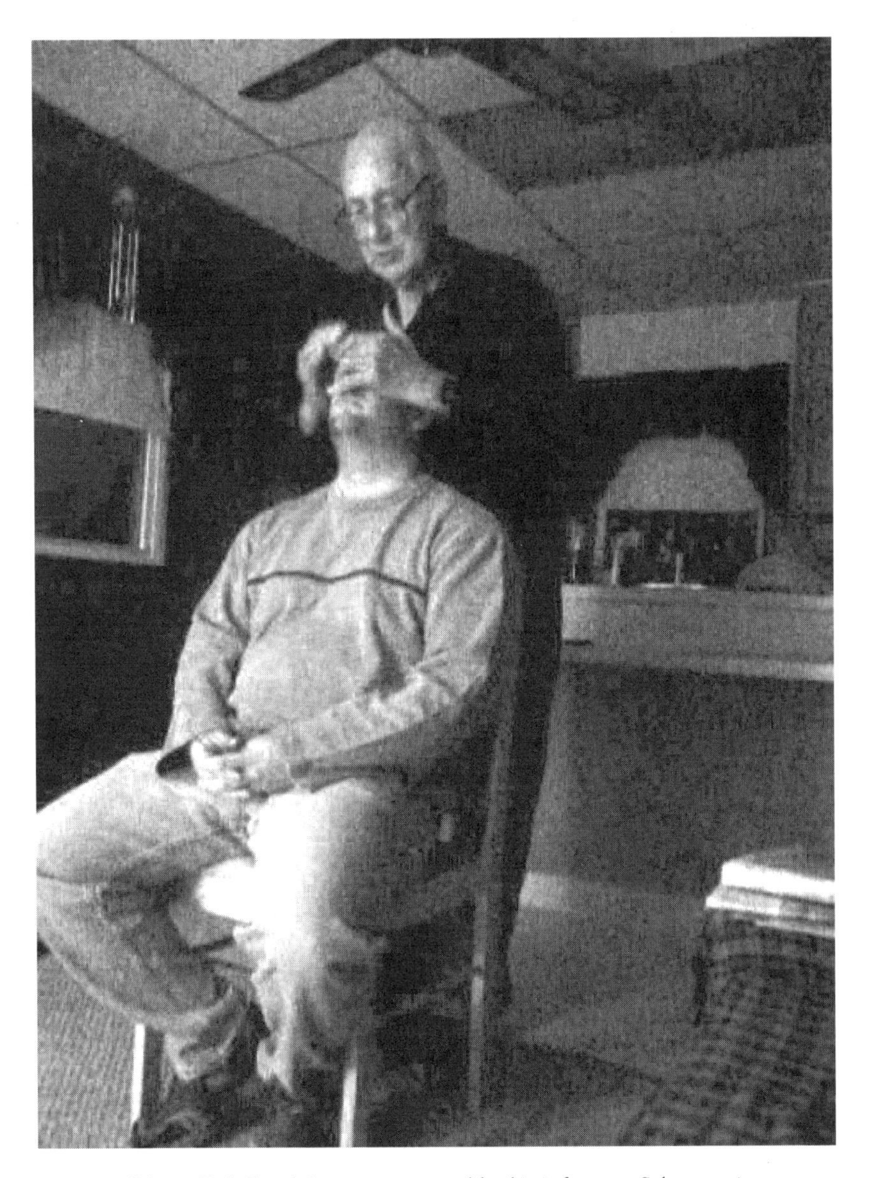

FIG. 6. Folklorist Erik Fasick being powwowed by his informant Sal, an active powwower today. This ritual resembles the one I underwent with Daisy Dietrich. Video capture by Danielle Fasick. Collection of Erik Fasick.

him. Joyce's husband, Stan, told her they would pay ten dollars at the time of the treatment and the rest later. Joyce describes the treatment, which only lasted one or two minutes:

Joyce: So we went into this room, I went in with my son and she had candles lit, it just seemed like she touched him, arms and legs.

David: When she ran her hands over his arms and legs, did she say anything at all?

Joyce: I didn't . . . it was low and I didn't understand a word she said. Sort of muttering, you know. . . . She said, now he might scratch once or twice that day, so—that was on a Friday—and we would have come back Monday and she said maybe another time or two after that. He did not scratch, we went for dinner, we had other shopping to do. Once on the way home and once that evening he scratched. Monday I took him back in again, she did much the same thing—it only lasted a minute or two, and I think Wednesday we went again, and I had given her at that time the thirty dollars and he was supposed to come back Friday. Well, my son was a little balky. He did not want to go. So we never went back for the last time. But that seemed to help.

David: It helped.

Joyce: Did it! I quit going to the dermatologist. Now I won't say he's 100 percent cured, because he does have sometimes dry scaly things on his ear. But this used to be . . . it'd get rashy and itchy and so forth. So I think in that instance it really helped.

Case 18: Remote Cure for Pain and Intestinal Bleeding (1999)

This case is from a series of e-mails sent to Daisy Dietrich (via Julius Dietrich's account) from the husband of a patient whom Daisy treated remotely (about a thousand miles away). The wife tried biomedical treatment before resorting to powwowing and continued seeing a physician and taking pharmaceuticals during the treatment.

The husband provided Julius with a series of progress reports on his wife's condition via e-mail over a period of twenty-two days. I have reproduced excerpts from his reports. Some of them have questions that are not answered, because Julius did not save his own responses.

> Day 1:
>
> She said that while she was facing east, she felt drowsy and really relaxed and felt heat across her shoulders.
>
> I think what you can do is so good for her. She won't listen to me when I tell her to see other doctors or take her pain pills when she hurts. She believes you can help her and wants to quit taking her medication. I told her not to quit but if she wants to cut back on some of them that would be OK. Do you agree?
>
> Day 2 (written early morning of Day 3):
>
> Carol had a good experience [with a healing session by Daisy] yesterday. She said she felt so relaxed; like she was floating. She is feeling better and in a good mood.
>
> Day 3:
>
> Carol had another good session. She said she could feel when you started your Pow Wow. She said she was sitting there getting ready and all of a sudden she felt like something happened and she went into her relaxed state. Felt real good. Like she was in a daze.
>
> Another thing, she had a real bad backache and was going to take some pills for it but she thought she would wait until the session was over. At the end of the session, she got up and her backache was gone and here it is 2:45 P.M. and her back is fine. No pain.
>
> Day 7:
>
> Carol is really feeling your prayers. While she is in there concentrating, she feels like she is in another world. Relaxed and calm.
>
> She has been feeling real good for the last three days. She really looks forward to your session.

Day 8:

This one [session] was a really strong one. Carol said she felt like she was floating. Had to open her eyes to make sure. She was dizzy when you got through with her. She is feeling fine now. Real relaxed. Did you take her somewhere?

You are doing her a lot of good. She hasn't felt this good for a long time.

Day 9:

Carol had another good sitting. She said it wasn't as strong as it was yesterday. She has a minimal amount of bleeding and her back pain has not come back at all since yesterday morning. She seems like a different person since she is not hurting as she was before.

I'm taking her to see her doctor and will let you know how things are going.

Day 11:

Carol's exam showed quite an improvement except for the last fifteen centimeters of her colon. The doctor said the new medicine that he is prescribing should take care of that and the bleeding. She goes back to see him next week to check the results of the new medicine.

I think Daisy's treatment had more to do with the improvement than the medicine. Carol's spirit is up so things are looking good. Thanks to Daisy.

Day 12:

Carol is still on a good run. Feels good. Not even a backache. Thanks to Daisy.

Day 18:

I haven't given Daisy a progress report on Carol's condition. She has had no pain since the next to last session. She is really feeling very good and easier to live with. She still has a little bleeding

> that is from her hemroid [*sic*], but as far as internal bleeding; none, nada, nothing. The thing she likes about this is that she doesn't have to take any pain pills.
>
> Day 20:
>
> Carol had a real backache when she returned from her hairdresser. After the session was over, her backache was gone and has not come back. She said she still has some irritation in her bowel area, but the internal bleeding has subsided quite a bit.
>
> She does feel much better and she claims that her improvement is due to Daisy and not the medicines she takes. They didn't work before so she doesn't see where they would be working now.
>
> Day 22:
>
> For Daisy—Carol is feeling good. She doesn't get her backache hardly ever. Then it only lasts a short time. Her bleeding is almost gone. No internal bleeding. She is feeling much better, thanks to you.
>
> [Later that day:]
>
> To Daisy: Carol's session went real good today. She said she knows when you start praying and when you stop. She feels like she is floating during the whole time and comes back to earth at the end. She is feeling real good. She is proud that she hasn't taken any pain pills in such a long time. No pain and she is sleeping better. More like her old self. Thanks, Daisy.

I have been able to obtain biographical information on seven living powwowers who practice in the traditional way. Many people still believe it works and would see a powwower if a visit could be arranged, and at my talks I am often approached by listeners wanting powwow referrals.

Once I actually tried some powwowing myself. During the summer of 1999 I was in Elizabethtown (northwestern Lancaster County), parking my car before interviewing the owner of a herbal medicine shop, when I noticed that the skin all over my left palm was peeling. I had never experienced this sort of episode, and it was mildly disconcerting. I recalled some of my information on powwowing and decided to try it out. I took some saliva and applied it to my palm, making the sign of the cross and saying: "I powwow this in the name of the Father and of the Son and of the Holy Ghost. Help to this, Amen." A minute afterward, it was all gone and my palm was normal. The problem has never recurred.

SIX

SOME CONTEMPORARY POWWOWERS

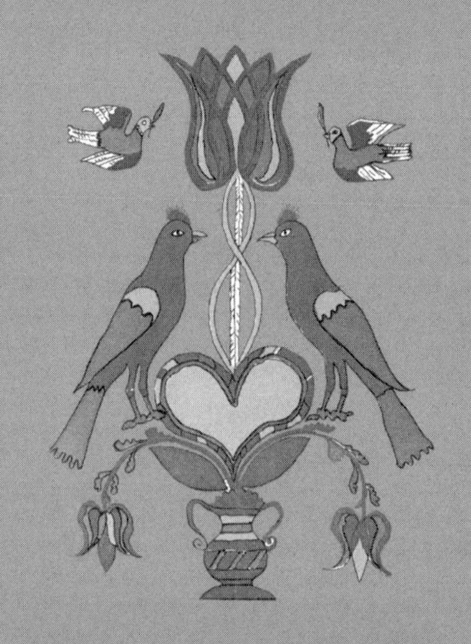

Through my research I have learned of the existence of at least eighteen living powwowers, and I have sufficient material to present a biographical sketch for six of them.[1] I have been unable to reach the others because I learned of them through consultants who were unwilling to provide their names, probably due to the controversy still surrounding the practice, particularly in more rural parts of the culture area. I have interviewed six of the eight living powwowers whose identity I was able to learn and who are described below. The six I interviewed are Tom Barone, Aaron Boehm, Daisy Dietrich, Julius Dietrich, Anita Rahn, and Leah Stoltzfus.[2]

TOM BARONE

Tom Barone[3] is an Italian-American from northeastern Pennsylvania who has long had an interest in powwowing and who considers himself to have a strong spiritual affinity with the Pennsylvania Dutch. He has strong Pietist leanings and, although he joined the Eastern Orthodox Church in 2005, has long been interested in the teachings of Conrad Beissel, founder of the Ephrata Cloisters. Tom is a scholar of religion, magic, and mysticism, but he also takes those subjects seriously. Unlike other powwowers, he does not reject the label of "magic" for powwowing, but he resents the neo-pagan revisionist stance taken by Silver RavenWolf and believes that powwowing must be practiced in its traditional—and firmly Christian—manner.

In 2004 he learned to powwow from Daisy Dietrich (below) after reading one of my articles on powwowing and asking to be in touch with her.

1. This may seem to be a low number, but considering that most consultants (including those who had done research on *powwowing*) believed that no one practiced powwowing anymore, it actually is surprisingly high.

2. I have attempted to reach the other two (Mrs. May and Jenine Trayer) but have not received a response. Mrs. May was arrested for fortune-telling in 1998, and I called and visited her place of business but found it closed. Jenine Trayer is a nationally published neo-pagan writer. Her published e-mail address proved to be incorrect, and I received no response from her publisher. It is worth noting that these two are of the "entrepreneurial" type and have enjoyed significant financial benefit from their practice relative to other "professional" powwowers. Many of my other consultants who have been powwowed would not consider them to be "real" powwowers.

3. Pseudonym.

He consults with Daisy to gain additional knowledge of the practice, and he maintains a friendship with her. Powwowing reminds Tom of traditional Italian healing techniques that he observed being practiced by his older relatives while he was growing up. At age thirty-seven, he is the youngest practicing powwower I have been able to interview.

AARON BOEHM

Aaron is a "professional" powwower of the "traditional" type, but his practice departs from the "professional" model in several respects. He has no separate treatment area because of the nature of the rituals he performs—they must take place outside. Moreover, because certain atmospheric and astronomical conditions must be met—it must be a clear night, with the moon in its third quarter—he does not perform treatments on a regular basis. He does not advertise his services, and he maintains secrecy about his clients, although he has mentioned that he trained between six and ten of them to be powwowers themselves. He neither requests nor accepts payment for his services. His practice is located at his home, in rural Berks County, outside Kutztown.

Aaron, who is originally from Lehigh County, is seventy-five years old. His first language was Pennsylvania Dutch, and he still speaks with a pronounced accent. He is a member of the United Church of Christ (UCC) and was previously a member of the Reformed Church, before it merged into the UCC. He is a retired supermarket owner and a grandfather. I have met his grandchildren, both of whom are prepubescent and seem quite intelligent. When asked, his grandson said he was curious about powwowing and might want to learn it some day. Aaron himself learned from his mother-in-law, now deceased.

Aaron's treatments are limited to what he can see—mainly skin diseases and varicose veins. His procedure is as follows:

1. He and his client stand outside (or sit, if it's more appropriate).
2. They face the moon.
3. He rubs the affected area while speaking an incantation in Pennsylvania Dutch.

The effect of this is to send whatever ailment is afflicting the client to the moon. The importance of the moon was also stressed by Samuel Musselman (see sample case 3) more than a century ago.

DAISY DIETRICH

Daisy Dietrich is a "professional" powwower of the "traditional" type in her early sixties who lives in southern Schuylkill County. Her late husband Julius was also a powwower and Daisy's instructor in the art. Julius passed away in 2005. As is typical of consultants whose first language is English, Daisy describes her practice as "powwow" rather than *brauche*. She sees patients on her enclosed front porch and has no waiting room. She has been practicing for more than twenty years and sees patients Monday through Friday. Because Daisy appears to be the best example of a professional powwower that I have encountered in my fieldwork, I have devoted more space to her and have quoted her extensively.

Daisy did not fit the stereotype of a "grandmotherly" female powwower, although she is, in fact, a grandmother. She is young-looking and blond, and when I first met her she was dressed in shorts and a blouse. She was active, frequently going boating with her husband. She has lived in the same village her entire life and considers herself Pennsylvania Dutch. She is able to understand the dialect, because her parents always spoke it around her, but she speaks very little of it. A high school graduate, she has taken some business courses to help her husband in his construction business, but she has always been a housewife.

Daisy is a very religious woman, wears a cross, and prays frequently. Many members of her United Church of Christ congregation come to her for powwow treatment. Even a UCC minister comes for powwow, although not the minister of her church. She has never encountered any opposition to her practice from religious leaders.

Daisy can cure nearly anything and can powwow remotely. Patients who are not physically present, however, must give her their name and ailment and agree with her on a time when the treatment will take place. This last requirement is because all patients, whether powwowed in person or remotely, must sit in a chair facing east and hold a Bible in their hands.

As she works, Daisy uses complicated hand movements and murmurs incantations under her breath. Each treatment has three segments, which are identical as nearly as I can tell, each of which lasts about fifteen minutes. At the end of each segment she does "the blessing," which I take to mean invoking the names of the Trinity. "And it's always done in threes," she says. "Everything's done in threes. They have a session today, I go over them three times today. It usually takes at least forty-five minutes to an hour, depending on what is involved. If they have heart problems, if they have a lot of pain there, if they have lung problems—you know, I can't just pinpoint something now for you."

She believes that the symptoms of an ailment, if not the ailment itself, are transferred from the patient's body to hers; during the "breaks" between segments and at the end of the treatment session, she shakes her hands and brushes her arms to minimize contagion. In order to be effective, she requires that three treatments be given, one each week. More details of her treatment technique are provided below.

Daisy and Julius both have powwowers in their family—Julius's mother and sister do it, although only for the immediate family. Daisy's uncle had a large practice: "The farmers knew he did this. He was quite busy at times."

Daisy began to learn powwow after her first grandchild received a terrible burn on her hand after touching her mother's curling iron. They took her to their neighbor for powwow treatment:

Daisy: [My uncle] could do certain parts of powwowing. I had gone to him. You could just see the heat rising. This child was barely a year old, and that started me right then and there. I said, well, I have to go further.

David: And he taught you how to do that?

Daisy: No. He didn't know everything, so he in turn referred me to someone else. And at that point the woman told me she could not give me the words because it has to be passed from a man to a woman, and a woman to a man. So it had taken me several months then until I had finally come across someone.

The woman to whom the neighbor referred her was Ida Wagner, a well-known powwower who lived in Strausstown (Berks County) on Old Route 22, the "Hex Highway," and who died in 1995. She had treated the mother of another of my consultants, Shirley Lesher. Many people went to her from the Hamburg and Bernville/Strausstown areas. By the time Daisy was able to see her, Ida said, "I'm too old. I don't remember everything, either." She referred her to Ruth (Strickland) Frey.

Because Ruth could pass the ability only to a man, she had to teach Julius first. Once he had learned to powwow, he taught Daisy:

> In fact, my husband learned first. Then he was stricken with Agent Orange. So while he was studying I said to him I'm interested in doing this now. "Well," he said, "let me see if you are to do it." So, he started me in the beginning, because it's not up to an individual to say whether a person is to do it or not. You start off by saying certain parts of it, and if you can come back to that individual and repeat what he has given to you, you are meant to go forth.
>
> So then you keep going further and further until you know it completely. Now, you do not tape-record. You do not write. It's all done by memory while we are sitting across the table from one another.

Once Daisy had learned, Ruth Frey referred all her patients to Daisy and gave them Daisy's telephone number. She also passed on a recipe for a home remedy for gallstones.[4] Currently, Daisy's patients come from Quakertown, Lenhartsville, Quarryville, Illinois, Indiana, Florida, and

4. An account of the remedy as used by Daisy follows:

> I had a nurse here a couple of weeks ago. She thought the problem was with her stomach. She thought it was her stomach and it wasn't. It was her gall bladder. So I said, "You have gall stones. When I'm finished with you, I'll check to see if it's inflamed. If it's inflamed you can't do the process I want to give you." She was fine. The process is to drink a quart of apple juice per day between breakfast, lunch and dinner for four days. You can eat your regular meals. On the fourth day, you can only have your breakfast. At lunch time you can have your apple juice again. Around supper time you have to take disodium phosphate with a glass of warm water. That is to drink twice. When you go to bed you have to drink six to eight ounces warm olive oil. Now if that doesn't want to stay down, always have a small portion of grapefruit juice and that will cut the grease. Then you bring your knees up as far as you can to your chest and lay on your right side for half an hour. The following morning you'll pass it. You don't have to have any surgery. Hardly any pain is involved. So now that was a recent one, and she is doing fine. She is a young woman. In fact, she just had a baby.

Philadelphia. In addition to her powwowing practice, Daisy also prescribes herbs and practices ear candling.[5]

Daisy believes she can cure anything as long as God wills it. The healing time varies according to the individual. Cancer, however, is a special case:

Daisy: Well, all you can do is try, because it is not up to me, it's up to the One above. You can always try, because there is always hope.

David: And you can try for anything?

Daisy: Yes. Now, the majority of the time the individual, if they're stricken with cancer, it usually helps relieve their pain, but it doesn't cure it. But it will go into remission. Now that has been the case with several of the people that I've gone over. So it has given them several years.

David: So you have given them several years through powwowing. It doesn't just take away the pain; it also can give them extra time?

Daisy: Correct.

Knowing the full name of the patient is crucial. In my case, that meant supplying my middle name, and in the case of a married female patient it would mean including her maiden name. The name must always be as it appeared on the birth certificate. The only exception was if the patient was adopted. In such cases, Daisy would merely say, as she powwowed, "one of God's children."

She uses certain Bible verses in the healing process, mentioning Ezekiel 16:6, which is used to stop blood. But she would not mention any other verses to me unless she were training me herself. As for those verses and the other incantations necessary, some were in English, some were in High German (such as the concluding blessing), and some were in Pennsylvania Dutch. If a person was meant to learn, they'd be able to pronounce the words regardless of their linguistic proficiency: "This is where it comes in if you are meant to do it, it will come right to you. Because I never had German."

Daisy uses no other books besides the Bible, nor does any other pow-

5. She describes this therapy as follows: "It's done with pure cotton. This is rolled and dipped in hot wax. They have to be kept in the freezer until you actually use them. So a person lies on the table. I put this candle in their ear and light it, and you can feel the wax coming out. No pain. So many people get relief that way. That's an old, old remedy—ancient times, really."

wower she has ever known. "I only believe in one, and you can only serve one—cannot serve both." Her comment evokes the New Testament injunction that one cannot serve both God and Mammon, a false idol. I believe she means that other charm books contain material that is not from God and may in some cases be from the devil. In that case, the "both" would refer to God and the devil. Her comment also signals the change that powwowing has undergone in the minds of its native practitioners, from an eclectic form of "white magic" interpreted through a Christian lens, to a form of spiritual healing coming directly from God.

Daisy accepts no payment other than a freewill offering. Clients must place the payment under the Bible, and she cannot touch it until the client leaves. Otherwise, she says, "That would be saying I'm the one doing the healing, and by no means; I'm not. So it's God."

Daisy is the only powwower I have interviewed who performs hex removal, a process she is often called on to perform. Because our conversation provides details on this aspect of powwowing that are not available from other consultants, I quote it at length:

David: When you use this to heal people, has anyone come to you saying that they were *ferhext* [that they have been hexed] or anything?

Daisy: Yes.

David: And do you remove the hex from them also?

Daisy: Yes. You can actually tell when you go over them. You can tell if they've been possessed.

David: First of all, how do you tell? Do you get a feeling in your hands or something?

Daisy: You can just feel it in my body. Just a certain feeling you get, and then I have to keep going over that individual until I feel that it has lightened up somewhat. Now if that doesn't help, then I might have to write sayings down. And this has to be on a triangle parchment paper. Now, that has to be folded into a triangle too.

David: So the paper starts out triangular, and then you fold it up into a triangle?

Daisy: I mean it starts out as a square and is folded into a triangle.

David: And you write sayings on those things?

Daisy: Yes, I write the verse on these, what is to help them. And then they keep that on their person at all times in their wallet.

David: Have you ever written letters of protection for people, or is that what this is, sort of?

Daisy: Pardon?

David: Letters of protection at all? *Himmelsbriefs*, or anything like that?

Daisy: No. I have blessings like for a car I can give an individual to protect them that way.

David: So you can give them this piece of parchment that will protect them from auto accidents?

Daisy: Correct—or any harm to them whatsoever. And then, of course, the blessing to remove the possession—whatever that individual was trying to get on that person at that time. A lot of times it's all through jealousy. This is normally what it is.

David: That's why people put a hex on people, because they're jealous of them?

Daisy: Right. And normally what they do is they give that individual a gift, and as that gift is given to them as a gift, it is given to them out of remorse, really. So that stays with them. They actually have a hold on them.

David: So the gift helps them to have a hold on the person?

Daisy: Right.

David: The gift is not to make up for what they did to the person, or is it? For instance, suppose someone puts a hex on someone else, and then they say, "Well, I'll give you this gift." But they're giving the gift because they feel guilty about putting the hex on, or is the gift meant as a way of controlling the person?

Daisy: Of controlling.

David: So it's not a real gift?

Daisy: No.

David: Do you recommend to the people that they throw this out?

Daisy: Yes, I do.

Daisy's discussion reveals a belief that material objects can be imbued with the power to harm or to cure, depending on the source. It also suggests that hexes are caused by the possession of an object, letting the hex into the victim's personal space and possessing him or her, much as intrusions of objects are believed to cause disease in some healing traditions. The blessed objects (the amulets Daisy and other powwowers create) prevent this. Such amulets can also protect structures from evil influences by guarding points of entry, as can be seen in the following exchange regarding a rash of barn fires believed to have been caused by a witch.

David: All the barns were on fire, and someone called you to protect their barn?

Daisy: Right. And their home and their garage—whatever possession they had outside they asked me if I would bless it. I said, "Most certainly." Now, in that case I had to put a blessing over every opening—windows, doors—because I was taught that no matter where there is an opening the devil can come in. So as long as that phrase is left there—

David: The devil can't come in through those openings?

Daisy: Right.

David: What was the blessing you said? [[It is actually written on paper and inserted in the windows.]] Is it in the Bible, or is it common, or is it a secret that you know?

Daisy: It's secretive, yes. It's only passed on to an individual if they're going to learn. Now, that's in High German.

David: They caught the arsonist after you did this?

Daisy: Yes. How I found out about that was that individual that I did the blessings for, they called me and told me that they had caught that individual.

Daisy has a large practice, but she notes: "It goes in cycles. Some weeks I might be really busy. It all depends. Now this year I had a lot of people that had shingles. That was very bad this year. And of course, allergies." She reports that people used to have erysipelas more in the past, but it is relatively rare now.

Her clientele is restricted, however, in that she cannot help her parents ("those I came from") or her children, although she can powwow herself. She can also treat her grandchildren, "because the bloodline was broken."

She can powwow remotely, by going through the entire procedure, including running her hands over the outline of the person's body, as if they were sitting in front of her. All she needs is their full name, where they are—if in a hospital, the room number—and an agreed-on time. There's no need to use a telephone, as Aunt Sophia Bailer did. Daisy describes a typical remote session:

Daisy: Like this woman Carol from Florida, she would face east in Florida holding her Bible, and I tell her to sit in that position for forty-five to sixty minutes. And she always knew the minute I started, and when I finished, because she always got a sensation. That's what everyone will tell me. They know when I start, and they know when I finish.

David: What kind of sensation do they report?

Daisy: They usually might get a tingling sensation, a chilling sensation, or they might get very, very warm. Everyone's different. I had people here. They're sitting there while I'm going over them, and they say they can actually see, like, a white flash.

David: Do they have their eyes closed?

Daisy: Yes. After I'm finished, I ask them what they felt. After they have given me their words, I can tell them that that was the Lord touching them.

Daisy makes house calls, sometimes traveling as much as a hundred miles, and has visited hospitals. She has never had any problem with any of the physicians there. None of them refers any patients to her, "because I don't know the doctors." Daisy has nothing against biomedicine and notes that her father has been in the hospital, but she never uses it because she has no need—she cures herself. She believes that some of the physicians, even though they don't know her personally, "might tell a patient to look out for a powwow."

Her family supports her powwow practice. One granddaughter imitates her when she powwows remotely, by moving her hands and mumbling nonsense words. She thinks maybe one day the girl will want to learn to powwow.

As mentioned earlier, Daisy uses no charm books, and the only material component she has ever used is a penny, to remove warts. Her procedure is a classic example of divestiture, in which the penny serves as a *Zwischentrager*: "The wart has to be done after the first full moon—the first Friday after the full moon. Then you take the penny over the wart, say your verse, give the blessing, that you do three times. Give the penny back to that individual and they must spend it."

She believed there were few powwowers left in the area and considered it "a dying trade." Fortunately, she also believed that fewer and fewer people were throwing hexes on other people, and she typically handles only one hex case a year. She used to consult with Ruth Frey on cases, but now that she is gone, there was no one left with whom to discuss cases. She very much wanted to consult with other powwowers and was interested to know whether I had found others.[6] She also said I could mention her real name to people who needed powwowing treatment, and explained that word of mouth was her sole source of patients: "I can't advertise—word of mouth only."

Daisy finds powwowing a somewhat draining experience, mainly after she has had two sessions in a row, and she has to rest up to recover. However, she performs it whenever people need her services:

David: Do you plan to do this permanently?
Daisy: It all depends—whatever is needed. I've had several times when I'm sound asleep and I'm awakened, and I'm told that I have to pray for that certain individual, so I get up and pray for that man or woman, and then I can go back to bed and I can sleep again.
David: Did those people know that you're praying for them?
Daisy: I'm sure, because a lot of people will call me and say, "You prayed for me at such and such a time."

The people in the area know that Daisy can help them and recognize her as a person of special powers. Once, the fire police called her to ask if she could find a lost girl. They brought her a picture of the girl, but she told them all she could do was pray: "I don't have that knowledge, as to actually see where she is. That was never given to me." However, she knows that there are people who could find a missing person using supernatural powers. Ruth Frey could do it "at certain times." Daisy also has a client, a man, who "can see visions that way," she says. "He can see a wrongdoing."

When she can help, it provides Daisy with a great deal of satisfaction: "It gives me such easement to know that God has helped that individual." She cites a healing experience in which a patient suffering back problems saw an angel while Daisy was healing her.

Daisy: One woman who sat there thought she had seen an angel. She

6. Unfortunately, none of the other traditional powwowers I know wants to meet fellow practitioners, but since that time I have introduced Daisy to Tom Barone, who learned from her and became a practicing powwower himself. He now consults with her.

thought a light was on 'cause she opened her eyes and then she realized it wasn't.

David: Do you believe in angels?

Daisy: Oh, yes. To this day that woman hasn't come back, but other people who know her say that she feels great, and this has been years and years. She couldn't get any relief whatsoever.

JULIUS DIETRICH

Julius Dietrich, like Daisy, was a "professional" powwower of the traditional type in his sixties when he passed away in 2005. He learned to *brauch* (powwow) from Ruth Strickland Frey and passed it on to his wife, Daisy. He preferred to work on children and animals rather than adults. According to one of Daisy's patients, Tom Clemens, "Her husband was better than Daisy at one time, but he forgot everything. He's a little funny too." Julius supplied the herbal preparations that both he and Daisy used. According to Daisy, he studied herbology in New Jersey.

Julius was also a retired Navy lieutenant and Army warrant officer who flew helicopters in combat. Until 1999, he owned and managed a Schuylkill County construction business. An avid sportsman, he owned a boat named after his wife, and together they often took it out on the Susquehanna. He was computer literate—his computer sits on a desk in the treatment area, right next to the chair where patients sit during treatments.

Julius's methods of healing were similar to Daisy's. He also claimed that he could powwow remotely, and he provided me with a series of e-mails with a Florida client who had been healed that way. During the interview I had with the couple, Julius was reluctant to speak and sat far away, on the opposite side of the sun porch. They allowed me to tape the interview (although not on video), with the understanding that I would turn the tape recorder off at certain points, including the period when she performed the powwow ritual on me. Daisy did most of the talking, but at certain points she would stop explaining. I had two other observers present (to observe my healing session), and they noticed that she became quiet or altered her speech in response to a gesture from him. He also controlled when the tape recorder was to be turned off; he would come over and make a throat-cutting motion with his hand to her, and she would then request that I turn off the recorder for a moment. Later, I asked him if he, being her instructor, had some control over Daisy's healing practice, but he responded in the negative.

ANITA RAHN

Anita Rahn is the widow of powwower Calvin M. Rahn, from whom she learned the art. She is a "professional" powwower of the traditional type, although she performs powwowing on a part-time basis and works for a large accounting firm until three in the afternoon every day. Anita sees individuals one at a time in her small enclosed porch and has yet to turn anyone away. She is about seventy and originally from Indiana. While her husband was Pennsylvania Dutch, she is not, and she does not understand the dialect.

Although she can powwow for any illness, Anita does not guarantee results. "Some of the older people call it 'trying,'" she notes. She believes her healing power comes from God and that the patient must believe in Anita's ability and in God in order to be healed. The person does not need to be a Christian in the sense of someone who believes in Jesus Christ as the Son of God; for instance, Anita believes that a Jewish person could be treated successfully with powwowing. She does not charge for her services, but people may leave money if they desire.

Like her husband and his father, Anita believes that not everyone can learn powwowing. She plans to teach her son, now in his mid-forties, to powwow, but she does not plan to teach anyone else. She agreed with the orthodox belief in cross-gender transmission, but confirmed that her husband learned it from his father. When I asked how long it takes to learn powwowing, she indicated there was no set period of time.

Anita was reluctant to answer questions and refused to be taped. I contacted her by phone originally, and she agreed to meet me to perform healing but not to answer any more questions. She accepted a copy of my survey but would not promise to return it. She was not interested in meeting other powwowers, but agreed that I could refer other patients to her if I wanted.

LEAH STOLTZFUS

Leah Stoltzfus is an Old Order Amish woman who is the wife of an Amish clergyman—the local bishop, according to Rebecca Yoder[7]—in a part of Lancaster County that is still rural yet caters to tourists. Her husband is the first cousin (father's sister's son) of Rebecca Yoder, who identifies herself as a "Conservative" Mennonite. At the time of my second interview (January 1999), Leah was fifty-seven years old and had thirteen children and twenty-three grandchildren. I first learned of her powwowing practice in a newspaper article about "Amish Voodoo" on the Internet. Because she is the only Plain powwower I have been able to interview, I have provided more background information on Leah than on the others. Her practice resembles that of other Amish powwowers in that she uses vitamins and herbs, believes she has a special gift for healing, experiences a sense of electricity in her hands, and does not employ charm books (Studer 1980).

Leah lives with her large family in a large red-brick house backed by a barn and two garages—a large one containing three gray carriages ("buggies") and a smaller one with one carriage. There is also a chicken coop and clothesline. No telephone was in evidence, nor did I see any evidence of electricity. Inside the portion of the house I was in, I noticed oil lamps and that she dries her clothes on the line. The house is actually two houses side by side, which I at first perceived as two sections. The larger one contains the family's main living space, including a meeting room for community religious services. The smaller one contains her treatment room, an herb kitchen, and a waiting room. It also has its own front door and back door, the former giving onto the large front porch, the latter onto a small, recently built deck. According to Rebecca, her aunt (Leah's mother-in-law) used to live in this smaller adjoining house. She referred to it as the "*daadi* house," almost certainly a shortened form of the term *Grossdaadi Haus*, which refers to a grandparents' dwelling adjoining an Amish family's main farmhouse (Hostetler 1993, 168–69). There are cows in the pasture behind the house and barn, and Rottweilers—which they raise—trotting around the yard. The family sells quilts and wishing wells.

Leah is a powwower of the entrepreneurial type. She easily qualifies as a "professional"—she has a large clientele from outside her immediate fam-

7. Pseudonym.

ily, has separate treatment and waiting rooms, and accepts money. She claims that she has treated many bishops, denying that Amish and Mennonite bishops frown on the practice.

I class Leah as an entrepreneur not because she advertises openly—although many in the local Amish and Mennonite communities know of her practice through word of mouth—but because she specifies a fee rather than merely accepting a freewill offering. However, she claims she sets a fee, which she describes as "not full price, not near." "I just have a low rate," she says. "It makes it a little nicer for them if they know what to give."

Like other Amish powwowers, Leah avoids the terms "powwowing" and "powwow," even though her practice fits the description of powwowing as practiced among Plain populations (Hostetler 1993, 337–38; Miller 1981, 158; Schlabach 1978; Studer 1980). "I say reflexology,[8] I don't say powwow," she said during my first interview with her. On the second interview, I asked her why she didn't call what she did "powwow." She replied that it was because of people's reactions to the word. "It's their lack of knowledge. Some people would say it comes from the devil's work. I had a couple of complaints, ⟦that⟧ this could be a New Age thing, you know."

In fact, Leah does practice reflexology, but she also has a practice that fits the laying-on-hands model of powwowing. Moreover, whenever I asked local Amish or Mennonite people about powwowing, those who would answer me honestly would refer me to Leah. As Hostetler (1993) and others have noted, most Amish powwowers view powwowing as only one of a number of healing methods they might use, including reflexology, massage, and chiropractic. Leah shares this view. However, her fear of disclosure is also real. Her fear is justified by the reactions of others in her community. Rebecca Yoder, Leah's first cousin by marriage, believes that what Leah does comes from the devil, and an Amish man who knew her, told me, "She'd better not be ⟦powwowing⟧." When I asked him why, he said, as if stating an obvious truth, "Because the ⟦Amish⟧ church forbids it." According to Rebecca, Leah's mother-in-law also disapproved of her powwowing.

8. Reflexology is an alternative healing practice based on the assumption that the proper massaging of the nerves in the toes has beneficial effects on the head, neck, spine, stomach, digestive system, and other parts of the body (Hostetler 1976, 252).

Setting and Background

My first contact with Leah occurred when she was outside taking down clothes. She is about five feet two inches tall and plump. She has gray hair but a young face. She speaks with a pronounced "dutchy" accent and sometimes seemed not to follow my English. (I later discovered that she had learned English and German in school.) When I approached her, she was suspicious and reluctant to talk with me. When I asked whether I could ask her a few questions about her healing practice, she replied, "I don't know you." She asked where I had heard about her, and I told her the quilt shop at a local tourist shopping area. Several times she asked me where I was from. I told her I was a student and showed her my Penn I.D. card to demonstrate that I really was a student. She said, "I don't want any publicity." I reassured her that I wasn't a reporter, that I wanted to interview her for academic reasons, and that I just wanted to learn about what she did. She asked whether I wanted to learn how to do what she does, and I responded that I was indeed interested in learning because my great-grandmother was able to powwow, but that my primary reason for coming to see her was to learn about her practice.

I also mentioned the article on the Internet. At the time, Leah appeared surprised and wanted to know who wrote the article. I could not remember the name of the writer. She asked how the writer had gotten the information, and I replied that he said he had interviewed her. When we arranged a date for a more in-depth interview, I offered to bring a copy of the article, and she said she wanted to see it. I came away thinking the article had been bogus, but later, Leah recalled the reporter's interview and seemed to be familiar with the article.

Leah allowed me to interview her on the spot as she stood outside with her wash, her children, and the Rottweilers coming and going, and she discussed her healing practice. I believe that the fact that my mother was in the car and that I pointed my mother out to her was helpful in gaining her trust. For the second interview, held in her house, she requested that my mother be present, saying she would feel better about it. As a later, non-Amish consultant who was familiar and friendly with local Amish families told me, "To her, a son and his mother could do no harm."

At the second interview, six weeks later, I was a little nervous; because she did not have a telephone, I was unable to contact her to confirm my appointment. We were also later than I had hoped, due to traffic and bad weather and because we had a late start from Baltimore. I came to the front door, noticed that there was no answer after knocking a number of times, and started to go around to the back to see whether anyone would answer there, when Leah appeared at the door. We had already glimpsed a woman moving in another room. In the front room there were chairs set up in rows—an irregular assortment, but mostly folding chairs. It looked as if it had been set up for a church service, and indeed that proved to be the case.

Leah smiled and waved us around to a side door, located off a professionally constructed wood deck with a swing. She ushered us in to what at first looked like a kitchen because there were sinks and drain boards. On the drain boards were numerous little bottles neatly crammed together. These, Leah said later, were herbal concoctions of her own manufacture. The room opened up, and we saw a corner china cabinet crammed with store-bought vitamins and herbal remedies. She later informed us that this was the waiting room for her clients.

Over the sofa, the wall was paneled in wood. There was an oil stove burning, behind which I later noticed a green wood bathroom-type sink affixed to the wall. Across from the window was a long sofa with a large afghan draped over it with three points down, arranged symmetrically. Leah, however, ushered us to chairs. I at first sat in a rocker and started to write in the dim light. She had politely declined my request to tape the interview—"I'm not much of a talker"—so I was required to write rapidly.

Shortly after that, however, Leah offered to light a lamp and suggested that I sit at the table by the window, offering a different rocker to my mother. Leah claimed that the other rocker (the one I had been sitting in) would be more comfortable, but my mother remarked later that it had been less comfortable. Both women mentioned their bad backs. Leah chose a straight chair and, once seated there, lit a gas lamp and another heating element lit up as brightly as a lightbulb. I later learned that this was an arc light, but the technology was unfamiliar to me and I did not ask. I was anxious to complete the interview before dinner, particularly because two of Leah's daughters came in later, one speaking Pennsylvania Dutch, the other accented English. Leah told the English-speaking girl to start getting dinner ready.

From the table, I could see more of the room. Above me was a small, wood pendulum wall clock decorated with black lacquer borders with a flower design thereon. The clock "sings to me" every hour, Leah said. My mother noted the musical melody of the clock when it chimed, but I did not, being too engrossed in framing the questions appropriately and recording the responses.

Below the clock on a small table was a framed poem on colored paper titled "A Mother's Love," similar to the kind sold in card shops. It had black letters on multicolored paper and certainly looked store-bought. Above the sofa on the wall were three plaques. On the left was a small white one with tiny (from my distance, about eight feet) lettering, and I could not read it. On the right was a small decorative wood-burned plaque saying "The Stoltzfus's." Between them, but closer to the wooden plaque, was a large (perhaps eighteen by fourteen inches) white plaque with brown lettering and flourishes, emblazoned with the words:

> ATTENTION
>
> Stretch your
> toes and
> rotate your
> ankles daily!!!
> for better health

This saying likely refers to her reflexology practice, which holds that the feet are connected to other areas of the body and that manipulations of the feet can cure many other ailments. More generally, it serves as an emblem of Leah's authority as a healer.

As we started with the interview, Leah warned me that she wasn't sure how well she would be able to understand and answer my questions—"I think in Dutch," she explained. Before I moved to the table, I began with a few background questions to learn her age and the number of children she had. Of her thirteen children, eight are girls and five of them are married. She mentioned something about the children preaching, so I asked whether her husband was a preacher. She looked at me sharply and said, "How'd you know my husband was a preacher?" I responded that she had just said something about her children preaching and that I thought she had said her husband had preached too. She accepted this and confirmed that her husband is an "ordained" minister. Her response suggests that she does not want it to be known that he is a bishop, and she probably suspects that Rebecca had told me.

Leah described her education as "eighth grade plus."[9] After eighth grade she continued with a program of supervised reading at home until she was fifteen. She said that this was normal for Amish people.

Leah's Healing Procedure

Leah's healing practice includes several methods of healing in addition to powwowing, including reflexology, massage, acupressure (which she referred to as "pressure points"), chiropractic (which she referred to as "adjustments"), herbalism, and (formerly) medical dowsing.[10] Such treatments are popular among the Amish and Mennonite populations of the area, who view them as less-invasive alternatives to biomedicine. Powwowing can be practiced with all of them. Traditionally, powwowers, like many nineteenth-century physicians, grew and prescribed their own herbal preparations, although the use of such homemade medicines is an adjunct to powwowing and not a defining feature of the practice.

Her powwowing ritual is of the kind I term "laying on hands." She begins by feeling all over the patient's body until she finds "the sore spot." She believes she can detect pain, either directly through her hands or through an object such as a battery-operated massager (she demonstrated the latter on me).[11] After she senses pain, she explains, "I let it out, shake a little, blink my eyes." When she sensed my pain with the massager, however, her reaction was more dramatic: she threw her head around, her eyes rolled in her head, and she emitted a series of staccato popping sounds. This is probably what the newspaper article describes—citing one of her patients—as "yapping" (Canon 1996).

Leah describes the qualifications one must have to detect pain: "I can feel pain in my hands. . . . I have a lot of electricity in my body. My

9. Completing eighth grade and then moving on to some form of less formal, "on-the-job" education is a normal pattern for Amish children (Hostetler 1993, 178).

10. I use the term "massage" because Leah uses both her hands and her "massager" to soothe muscles, although she does not practice an established form of therapeutic massage, such as "Swedish" or "deep tissue" massage. I use the term "herbalism" to denote the prescription, manufacture, and sale of vitamins and herbal substances. "Medical dowsing" refers to her former practice of choosing which vitamins or herbal medicines to give a patient by having the patient hold bottles of pills while she dangles a pendulum over them and notes whether the pendulum appears to be attracted to any particular bottle. Leah purchases vitamins wholesale and also manufactures herbal pills and teas at a sink in her waiting room.

11. It was home-made, wrapped in tape with a circular ring at the end.

youngest one has more electricity than anybody. He has a 'W' in his hand. They say if you have a 'W' in your hand you can sense pain."

At that point she held up her hand to show me the "W" in her palm, but I could not see it. She also looked at my mother's palm and mine to see if she could see one there. She did not.

Once she detects pain, she uses one of her healing practices, including powwowing, to remove the pain. The latter involves holding her hands on that area and concentrating, a process that can take hours. Leah does not like to powwow, however: "I don't like to do that too much because it takes too much out of me."

Leah believes that it is natural to rub a hurt with hands and believes her powwowing is merely an extension of a mother's care for her children. In the first interview, she said she does not actually heal anyone, but rather allows the patient's blood to flow freely so that the patient's body can then heal itself. "Blood is life," she noted. She compared the blood of a sick person and the blood of a healthy person, claiming that the blood of a sick person is "blocked" and that the blood of a healthy person flows freely.[12] She compared it to two streams—one muddy (sick) and one clear (healthy). "That's the way your blood should be—clear" and free-flowing.

Leah uses her ability to heal her children and grandchildren. "Whenever my grandchildren get hurt, you hold their hand. If you hold it for a couple of hours, they'll be healed." She believes that all parents can and should do this with their children. She also recalls her mother healing in that way: "When we were sick, my mother rubbed us. It's my instinct to do that." She described how she healed one of her sons who was cut on the leg. "I laid him on the couch and stroked [his leg] for two hours. Then I told him to get up and walk, and he did. . . . It's a gift from God. I can feel when I'm helping somebody." Seeing other patients who are not family members is a burden to Leah. "It's sometimes more than I prefer. I like to have my days off. There's so many people who need help these days."

She finds her practice draining, and it takes a lot of time away from her family. News of her gift spread "by word of mouth" among the Amish. Because it takes up time, she treats only "our people," which she then explained meant other Amish people. She said she wouldn't have time to treat "the English."[13] That's one reason she doesn't want publicity.

12. I supplied the term "blocked," as she seemed to be searching for one, and she then used it herself.

13. "The English" is the Amish term for all non-Amish people, including other Pennsylvania Dutch people.

Another reason is that she said she does not want "to get above anyone else" by having something "special" that others don't have, because it wouldn't be "humble." Humility is a character trait that the Amish consider essential to life in a redemptive community (Hostetler 1993, 389).

How Leah Acquired the Power

Leah provided what appear to be two separate accounts of how she first learned she could heal. In the first, she told how when one of her children fell down and hurt her arm, Leah grasped the arm in her hand, "as is natural to do," and the pain went away. Her second account is more involved and is detailed below. I do not think that Leah was attempting to mislead me in giving two accounts. Rather, I believe the first story is an instance of healing that occurred after the second one and that she relayed it either because it was the first one that came to mind or because I had not made myself clear to her.

In the second account, Leah first learned that she could heal ten years ago, when one of her grandsons bumped his head on the corner of a stand. They took him to a hospital, where he stayed for about four days. "He had a busted blood vessel. At first they thought they had to operate. Then they gave him strong medicine.[14] He was restless, and they let him go home before they should have. He had seizures. We took him to the hospital again, but he passed out on the way so we stopped at another reflexologist for help."

The reflexologist instructed Leah to put one hand at the boy's neck, and the other on his spine, to get the circulation going. "I felt this thump, thump, thump through my body. I stayed there for hours. He was paralyzed, but a couple of hours later he moved his hand. The reflexologist said, 'You have healing hands.'"

Leah maintains that the "circulation healed his body. . . . It's the blood flow that heals." Once the boy recovered, the reflexologist gave additional instructions on how to heal. "Then people found this out. That's how I got started." Then some people started bringing their babies to her, and she began her practice. She now sees patients three days a week.

Her husband takes care of the business end of the practice: "He counts

14. "Strong medicine" is how Amish refer to pharmaceuticals. A saying of some Amish is "Too many pills and strong medicine are not good for a person" (Hostetler 1993, 325).

my money for me." Leah explained that she charges only a small, set amount so that people do not feel awkward about deciding what to give. It is customary for a powwower to refrain from accepting money, because God is the source of the healing, although freewill offerings may be accepted. Her husband's handling of the money may be analogous to Daisy's practice of having customers place whatever they choose under the Bible instead of into her hands.

Leah strives to improve her healing power by studying books and through practice: "I got all my education through books and experiences." She has consulted with other powwowers ("people who have the gift of healing"), and she knows two people who are learning it but would not supply their names. She said she can feel whether others can do it: "They'd have to have a warmth in their hands." She does not think a woman of child-bearing age could learn, probably because of the drain the healing places on the practitioner.[15]

Attitude Toward the Power and Health

While Leah believes her healing power is a gift from God, she also repeatedly and strongly stressed "I never asked for this. I never wanted this." Still, she uses her healing power, in addition to her other treatments, and never turns anyone away. She plans to continue her practice as long as she can and believes she and her patients have received supernatural guidance: "I have had many leadings. . . . The angels have sent me to people, or people to me at the right time." She believes people have more need of healing today than previously and wishes there were more people who could do it.

"There's so much sickness today," Leah laments, "so many viruses and plagues." She believes physical sickness causes mental sickness and that that is why she never looks down on people with mental problems because "it's not their fault that they have something physically wrong with them." She also believes that physical sickness causes stress and is even resulting in the decline of the United States: "Our country is going down because of all these viruses, plagues, and diseases." She commented on how so many young people are getting sick[16] and believes that antibiotics

15. She also believes that mothers are generally not as healthy today as they once were: "I don't think they could have thirteen babies."

16. Possibly a reference to AIDS.

do not work. She uses herbs and has an herbalist who grows herbs supply them to her. She asked me whether I knew anything about herbs, and I told her I knew people who did.[17] She also blames poor nutrition for people's poor health, believing that the milk, eggs, corn, and other agricultural products lack the vitamins they once had. Power lines are an additional worry to her; she believes they cause thyroid problems. In her opinion, each generation of humans is getting weaker: "We did more muscle work and less head work." This laziness has resulted in a reliance on pesticides that pollute our food. She also blamed then President Bill Clinton for much of the country's troubles.

I asked her whether she believed that the Bible was the inerrant word of God, and she reacted with surprise that such a self-evident assertion should even be questioned. She believes we are living in the end times predicted in the Book of Revelation.

17. I had in mind some of my pagan consultants from previous research, but I did not reveal that.

SEVEN

A PENNSYLVANIA DUTCH MODEL OF POWWOWING

To understand powwowing's place within Pennsylvania Dutch culture, it is necessary to examine the cultural assumptions that undergird powwowing. These assumptions can be expressed in the form of a cultural model or as a set of propositions that all members of the society share.[1] Cultural models allow us to process experiences (information) and make sense of them. They shape social and personal identity and give significance to the world. Indeed, cultural models can be viewed as theories of reality, the mechanism through which humans create the social world.

The cultural model of powwowing represents how the culture explains the practice. As I discovered, powwowing can be accommodated within the Pennsylvania Dutch worldview as part of a larger model of healing. However, this model is only an abstraction from interview and survey data and should not be construed as a rule predicting how individuals will react to powwowing. It simply elucidates the cultural context in which powwowing exists. Within that context, a variety of beliefs can and do exist, ranging from enthusiastic belief to disbelief to outright opposition and condemnation.[2]

1. Cognitive anthropologist Roy D'Andrade (1987, 112) defines a cultural model as "a cognitive schema that is intersubjectively shared by a social group." In describing the Pennsylvania Dutch cultural model of powwowing as a subset of a larger cultural model of healing, I have had to draw on schema theory, which originated with cognitive theorists in psychology. These theorists proposed that learning produced schemas in the brain, which could be inferred from performance and verbal report (Wallace 1970, 75). However, I prefer to hold the question of the precise biological basis of cognition in abeyance, so I use the term "mind" rather than "brain" throughout this book. For a longer discussion of schema theory and cognitive anthropology, please see Appendix 1.

2. My attempt to construct a cultural model for healing in Pennsylvania Dutch culture was inspired by D'Andrade's "folk model" of the mind (1987, 112), but my procedure differs in one important respect. D'Andrade began by constructing the propositions of his model based on his own perceptions and then tested it by interviewing five students. As an American, D'Andrade was part of the group that supposedly shared the cultural model he wanted to test, so he could justify using his own insights to generate that model.

I had to proceed somewhat differently. Although I grew up at the margins of Pennsylvania Dutch culture, consider myself part Pennsylvania Dutch, and value that part of my heritage (that is, it forms part of my personal identity), I cannot consider myself a full member of that culture. I am, as Yoder might say, an "Old American" who has selected multiple ethnicities, including "Pennsylvania Dutch" but also "Irish," "English," and general "Celtic (Welsh and Scots)." While a few of my consultants are "Old Americans" (of mixed European ancestry), they have uniformly selected "Pennsylvania Dutch (or German)" as their ethnic affiliation. Because I did not trust my own perceptions of powwowing enough to construct a cultural model on my own, I waited to construct the model until I had done preliminary documentary research and interviewed a dozen Pennsylvania Dutch individuals, building and refining my model with successive interviews as I went along.

To make relationships among elements of the model quantifiable, I distributed a survey questionnaire to my consultants and others in southeastern and south-central Pennsylvania, asking respondents to indicate their reactions to each along a five-point scale ranging from "strongly agree" to "strongly disagree." In the survey, no order was consciously imposed on the questions, although the survey order was not strictly random. Aggregate scores were from −74 (strongest possible disagreement) to +74 (strongest possible agreement). All responses tallied were from individuals who identified themselves as "Pennsylvania Dutch" or "Pennsylvania German" and who had heard of powwowing or *brauche* before participating in the study.

CHARACTERISTICS OF THE CULTURAL MODEL

Any postulated cultural model for healing that applies to powwowing must be one that is shared by powwowers, their clients, and other Pennsylvania Dutch people who know of powwowing as a result of growing up within that subculture. Accordingly, the model presented below was constructed through interviews with field consultants and documentary sources citing testimony by others for whom powwowing is a part of their culture, and tested through survey material. Its purpose is to situate powwowing specifically as a health-care choice for these individuals. These propositions are beliefs, so this model can be considered an attempt to elucidate the structure of belief behind the practice of powwowing. There may, of course, be other models that adequately describe the belief structure.

The model is linked to other cultural models through shared propositions. For instance, the proposition "I believe in God" states a cosmological belief that may also be an element in a cultural model of the religion. It is hierarchical, covering a variety of healing practices. This hierarchical structure is characteristic of schemas in general and cultural models in particular. Thus, there can be embedded models and schemas that function in a manner analogous to a subroutine in a computer program. The proposition "Powwowing can work cures" is also part of a cultural model of powwowing, and the proposition "Physicians are [[free]] agents who control the use of their skill" is part of a cultural model of biomedicine. Note, however, that these cultural models exist specifically within the *Pennsylvania Dutch* model of healing and that therefore their cultural model of biomedicine may not be (and probably would not be) the same as a model of medicine found in another subculture (such as American academic culture) or American culture as a whole. Because my focus here is powwowing, I shall pay special attention to the embedded cultural model of powwowing.

A CULTURAL MODEL OF HEALING AMONG THE PENNSYLVANIA DUTCH

The process of constructing a cultural model revealed that some beliefs are more strongly held than others. For instance, beliefs specifically about powwowing are not as strongly held as their enabling beliefs (such as "God exists"). Beliefs about biomedicine are held more strongly than those about powwowing, perhaps because biomedicine is now the treatment of choice among Pennsylvania Dutch populations. It is also notable that hexing is not a viable theory of disease causation; its decisive rejection at the end of the century contrasts with reports that suggest that belief in hexing was rampant in the culture area at the time of the York Hex Murder Trial (see Aurand 1929, Lewis 1969). This finding is also in accord with my interview results.[3] As Cowen has noted, the Pennsylvania Dutch generally perceive illness to be due to the will of God rather than to the actions of men (Cowen 1987, 95).

One explanation not supported by the responses is that relatively weak belief in the efficacy of powwowing is due to a drop in supernatural belief in general. Supernatural beliefs, such as "God exists" and "God can exert influence in the world," are still strongly held. Thus, if there is little cultural support for a belief in the efficacy of powwowing, it is not because of any pervasive skepticism concerning the supernatural. Doubting powwowing does not equate to doubting God.

Some responses were surprising, given what I had learned in interviews before distributing the survey. For instance, the proposition that "powwowing works because the patient believes it will," suggesting a native "placebo effect" theory, showed more agreement than expected, because I had been told by many consultants that powwowing works because of

3. This is not to suggest that the belief is extinct—hex removal is still being practiced (Daisy Dietrich does it about once a year)—but belief in hexing definitely appears to be not as widespread as previously.

the power of God *and* the faith of practitioner and patient. The contradiction between these two explanations may only be apparent, however, because the term "belief" may be considered coterminous with "faith" in consultants' minds.

Another surprise was the perception shown in this survey that powwowing is not dying out. Based on my interviews, I had come to believe that most people in the culture area thought the practice had ceased, even though other evidence suggested that powwowing, while practiced more infrequently than in the past, was in fact not totally disappearing. Correcting and clarifying my own perceptions was a valuable feature of the survey.

In the model presented below, I have included propositions for which the aggregate response was either "agree" or "strongly agree" (aggregate scores 14.8 to 74.0). Responses with an aggregate response of "no opinion," "disagree," or "strongly disagree" were discarded, because they cannot be considered part of the cultural model.

The model's propositions are classified into "primary," "secondary," and "tertiary" beliefs in decreasing level of generality. All tertiary beliefs must be consistent with secondary beliefs, which in turn must be consistent with primary beliefs. As mentioned above, this kind of hierarchical ordering is characteristic of cultural models. In the survey, primary beliefs are distinguished from lower-order beliefs by the level of agreement; all beliefs in which the aggregate response was "strongly agree" are classified as "primary." Aggregate scores are given following each proposition in the model.

The model of healing, including powwowing, is presented in four parts:

A. Primary beliefs related to healing, most of which may be considered general, or background, information
B. Secondary beliefs, more specifically focused on healing
C. Tertiary beliefs about healing, which also constitute a cultural model of powwowing
D. Tertiary beliefs about healing, which are also part of a cultural model of biomedicine

A. Primary beliefs
   1. God exists [[I believe in God]]: aggregate score 72 (STRONGLY AGREE)

2. Jesus is the Son of God [I believe that Jesus Christ is the Son of God]: 66 (STRONGLY AGREE)
3. The Holy Spirit exists [I believe in the Holy Spirit]: 65 (STRONGLY AGREE)
4. The Christian Trinity exists [I believe in the Christian doctrine of the Holy Trinity]: 56 (STRONGLY AGREE)
5. God can exert influence in the world: 56 (STRONGLY AGREE)
6. Prayer has the power to heal: 52 (STRONGLY AGREE)
7. God is the source of all healing, including powwowing and healing by physicians: 46 (STRONGLY AGREE)

B. Secondary beliefs (healing in general)

1. Illnesses are caused by natural factors (bacteria, viruses, etc.): aggregate score 42 (AGREE) (plus 1 respondent who circled "agree" and wrote in "yes and no")
2. The devil, or Satan, exists [I believe in the devil, or Satan, a being in opposition to God]: 40 (AGREE)
3. Those with healing power are channels for God's power: 34 (AGREE)
4. The devil can exert influence in the world: 31 (AGREE)
5. People can recover from illnesses spontaneously: 31 (AGREE)
6. God gives healing power to certain chosen people: 19 (AGREE)
7. Something harmful is removed from the body when a person is healed: 18 (AGREE)
8. A person who believes in God will get better faster than a person who does not believe in God: 18 (AGREE)
9. Because they are channels for God's healing power, those with healing power may not ask for payment: 15 (AGREE) (Marginal; within 1 point of "no opinion")

C. Tertiary beliefs (a cultural model of powwowing)

Powwowing and curing

1. Powwowing can work cures: aggregate score 20 (AGREE)
2. Powwowers are people given healing power by God: 17 (AGREE)

Role of belief

1. Powwowing works because the patient believes it will: 32 (AGREE)
2. A person must believe in God to practice powwowing: 27 (AGREE)
3. A person must believe in God to be powwowed: 19 (AGREE)

Training of powwowers

1. You don't have to be Pennsylvania Dutch to be able to powwow: 29 (AGREE)
2. Only a woman can teach a man to powwow, and only a man can teach a woman: 25 (AGREE)
3. Ability to powwow is passed down through families: 16 (AGREE)

Powwowing and hexing

1. Hexing is the opposite of powwowing: 25 (AGREE)

Powwowing and biomedicine

1. It is okay to visit both a powwower and a physician: 23 (AGREE)

D. A cultural model of biomedicine

1. God gives skill to physicians: aggregate score 41 (AGREE)
2. Because they control their own skill, physicians are paid directly, as anyone performing a service for hire would be: 34 (AGREE)
3. Physicians are free agents who control the use of their skill: 25 (AGREE)
4. It is okay to visit both a powwower and a physician: 23 (AGREE)

The Significance of "Primary Beliefs"

The beliefs labeled "primary" are held more strongly than any of the other beliefs, so strongly that they are not actually part of the cultural model of healing but rather are elements of the "worldview," the level above cultural model. As such, they define the taken-for-granted reality that is the product of world construction and that Berger identifies as "culture" (Berger 1969, 6). Certain primary beliefs, which are part of the worldview, also link that worldview to a specific cultural model. In the case of the cultural model of healing, these "linking beliefs" are "Prayer has the power to heal" and "God is the source of all healing, including powwowing and healing by physicians."

Secondary, tertiary, and lower-order beliefs need not be derived from primary beliefs, but they must not contradict them. This includes the (tertiary) beliefs that belong to the cultural models of powwowing and biomedicine. Thus, the secondary belief "People can recover from illnesses spontaneously" must be interpreted in light of the primary belief "God is the source of all healing." Spontaneous healing still comes from God, as does healing by physicians, powwowers, or other human intermediary.

When contradiction occurs because beliefs from a source outside the worldview begin to be widely accepted, the culture may begin to change. Culture change is seen in any shift in worldviews, the set of defining elements of that culture, analogous to the "paradigm shifts," that are characteristic of scientific development (Kuhn 1962, 110).[4] When worldviews shift, subordinate cultural models, like scientific theories, must be revised or discarded. One major source of such change is experience.

Beliefs that result in culture change may do so directly or indirectly. For instance, the belief that the world is round, once accepted based on Columbus's reports of his experience, directly changed European culture. Indirect changes result not from immediate changes in the worldview but from instabilities introduced in subordinate cultural models. When new beliefs introduce multiple or partial contradictions in such models, the worldview must explain them. If it cannot do so, the worldview itself is revised. Direct change may be conceptualized as "top-down" change, and indirect change as "bottom-up" change.

LOGICAL RELATIONSHIPS OF LOWER-ORDER BELIEFS

Certain lower-order beliefs have a logical relationship to one another. For instance, the belief "Powwowers are people given healing power by God" places powwowers within the subset of others who have been given healing power by God. Therefore, the propositions "Those with healing power are channels for God's power," "God gives healing power to certain chosen people," and "Because they are channels for God's healing power, those with healing power may not ask for payment" also apply to powwowers. These last three propositions, in the case of powwowing, may be transformed into the following:

- Powwowers are channels for God's power.
- God chooses to give healing power to powwowers.
- Powwowers may not ask for payment.

These propositions may be considered valid beliefs about powwowing because they may be deduced from propositions that were tested. Because

4. As Kuhn (1962) noted, just as when there is a shift in a scientific paradigm all theories must be revised or discarded, so must all cultural models when there is a shift in the worldview of a culture.

these beliefs are entailed by other beliefs, they are called *entailed beliefs*.[5] As such, empirical evidence for the existence of these beliefs (deriving from field interviews) implied the beliefs from which they were entailed. That is the reason those other beliefs were included in the preliminary cultural model.

Folklorist David Hufford distinguishes entailment from another logical relationship of beliefs in this model: enablement. Entailed beliefs may be deduced from other beliefs, but enabled beliefs are permitted by (but not deducible from) other beliefs. For instance, the proposition "Powwowers are people given healing power by God" is not deducible from the proposition "God gives healing power to certain chosen people." However, it is enabled by that proposition: if God has chosen to give some people healing power, *maybe* God has given healing power to powwowers. However, as with entailment, if the second proposition is true, the first is as well (assuming that a gift is always a choice).

A GRAPHIC DEPICTION OF THE CULTURAL MODEL

The diagram depicts the principal features of the cultural model for healing among the Pennsylvania Dutch, including aspects of the cultural models for powwowing and biomedicine that are directly related to worldview. Other elements, such as the belief in "crossways" transmission of powwowing, listed above, are not included, because at this time they have no identifiable connection with worldview. However, they do form part of the model, because they do not conflict with the worldview.

A NARRATIVE DESCRIPTION OF THE CULTURAL MODEL

Among believers in powwowing, in this (revised) model, the triune Christian God is ultimately responsible for all healing, whether by the intervention of powwowers or physicians, or by the spontaneous remission of symptoms. Human practitioners and antibodies, then, are all under God's control. There is a devil who can act in the world, just as God can, but neither he nor his evil spirits cause most disease. Thus, the Pennsylva-

5. This is the term used by folklorist David Hufford, who has drawn on the work of philosopher Carolyn Franks-Davis.

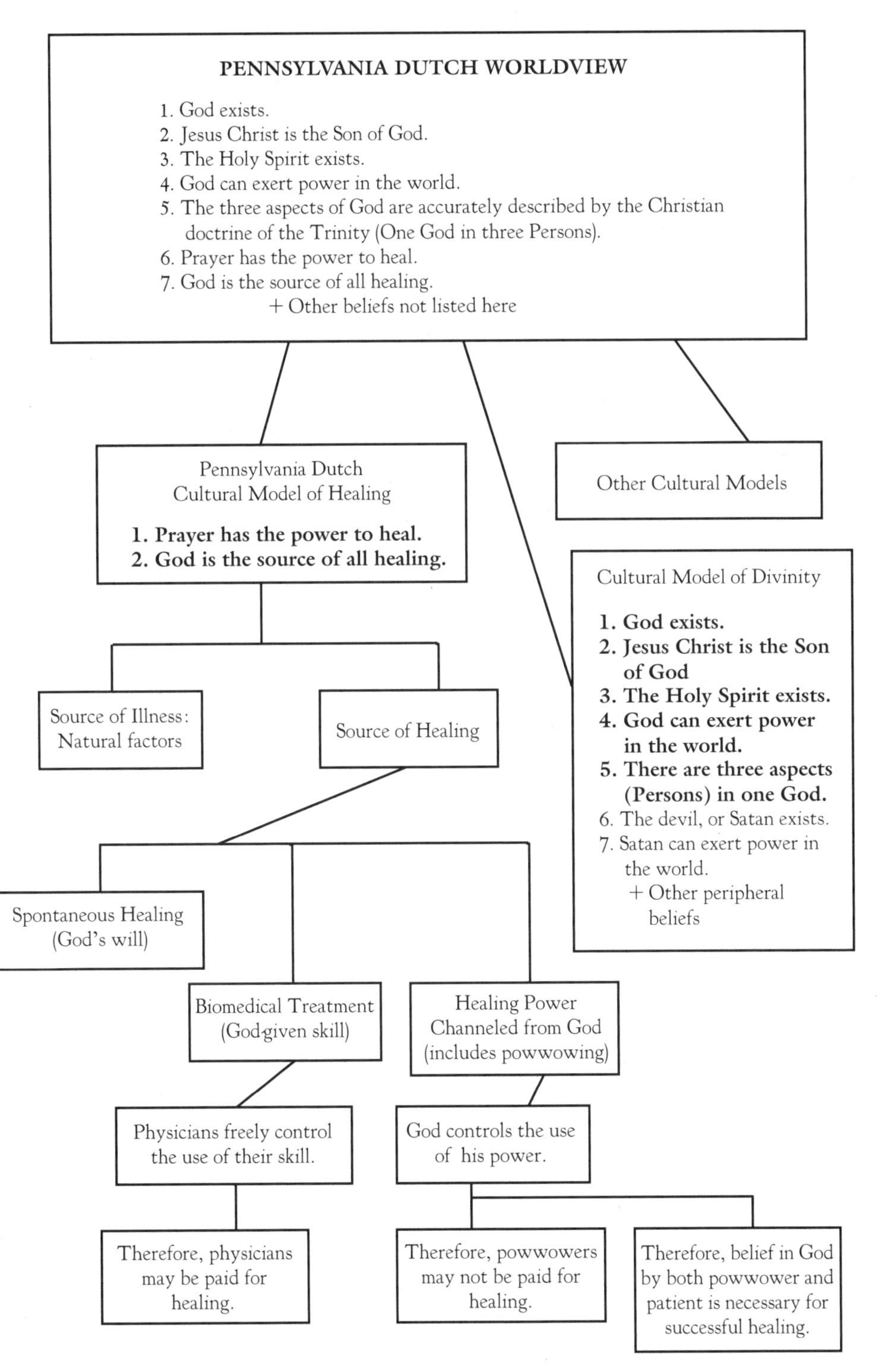

A Pennsylvania Dutch cultural model of healing

nia Dutch have a generally "naturalistic" system of disease causation, meaning that diseases are ascribed to "natural" causes, such as infections or being shaken while riding in a carriage, rather than to "personalistic" causes, such as evil spirits or sorcery. However, there are personalistic elements in the form of hexing.

Yet, God can act more directly, in some cases using people of faith as channels of divine healing power. Such individuals, including powwowers, cannot be paid because they are not using their own power (or skill) to perform the healing. A physician may, however, be paid because he chooses how he uses his skill (this implies a belief in human free will), even though the skill itself is God-given. God also answers prayers, by which anyone can obtain healing.

Because the dominant disease etiology is naturalistic, physicians are able to cope with most diseases. However, powwowing (the exercise of direct divine power through humans) is needed[6] to deal with hexes (the exercise of direct demonic power). The faith of the patient is not required for biomedicine to function effectively, but it is required for powwowing. In both cases, something harmful is removed from the body when healing takes place, whether that be a disease or a hex. The powwower is generally a respected member of the community, but his status is somewhat ambivalent. This may be attributed to the significant power that the powwower wields, and to the powwower's status as a person chosen by God.

Opposition and Secrecy

Because powwowing can be accommodated within a Pennsylvania Dutch cultural model of healing, why should it be secret, more so than any other nonbiomedical healing practice? Why is there such controversy about it? In this section I shall first describe some of the difficulties I faced in conducting my fieldwork, then address the sources of the controversy over

6. As indicated above, there is less perceived need now for powwowers to remove hexes than in years past. I realize that the theory of hexing needs further development, but I believe that hexing requires its own study to adequately understand it. For now, I speculate that one key difference is that powwowing is undertaken in the *hope* that God will respond by sending healing power to the patient through the powwower, whereas hexing is undertaken in the *expectation* that the hex (spell) will be effective in bringing direct demonic power (from the devil or other demonic beings) to bear against another human, animal, or object. In powwowing, God uses divine power (with the powwower as channel), but in black magic (witchcraft), the witch uses demonic power (the source of which is the devil or other evil spiritual beings).

the practice and the nature of the secrecy that surrounds it. I shall argue that opposition to powwowing stems in part from "antibeliefs" that can also be accommodated within the cultural model of healing and the wider Pennsylvania Dutch worldview.

During the course of my fieldwork, my inquiries were often met with suspicion, and I encountered a number of potential consultants who I believe lied to me about their knowledge of the practice. In one case, my consultant Sarah (Adams County) recommended that I stop by an herb shop where, she claimed, the owners practiced powwowing, but she insisted that I not give her name or approach them openly with the purpose of my research.[7] She herself agreed to be interviewed only if I gave her a pseudonym (which she selected) and signed a paper with her that read "I will not be responsible for anything said or wrote."

On another occasion, I called a reflexologist in Lebanon County with a pronounced "dutchy" accent and broached the subject. An excerpt of the conversation (from my July 1999 field notes), follows.

David: I'm doing some research on an alternative form of folk medicine called "powwowing" and I thought you might know someone who does it.
Woman: (*silence*) That depends how you define powwow.
David: I mean a traditional form of healing. It's called *Brauche* in the dialect. It's a form of faith healing.[8]
Woman: Well, that's very controversial, isn't it?
David: I'm not trying to debunk it or anything. I just want to learn about it for my research project. It would be totally confidential.
Woman: I'm not interested in that.
David: You don't know anyone who does it?
Woman: I don't know anything about that.

On another occasion, I noticed an African-American woman, about sixty-five to seventy years old, in Plain dress at a Lancaster County market sitting on a bench by the exit. She remained there from at least the time I entered until I stopped on my way out and asked whether she was a Mennonite. She replied yes. I explained my research project and asked

7. "Sarah" is the pseudonym she chose.

8. I am not drawing any specific comparison with "faith healing" at this time; the phrase was simply a convenient shorthand that I used to help introduce the subject of powwowing.

whether she knew anything about powwowing. She said, "Oh, no, I'm not connected with that." I then asked if she'd ever heard of it and she said "No." I left the store, then went to my car near the exit and looked in the rearview mirror. She was hurrying out of the store into a plain black van.[9] I happened to have glanced at my watch on the way out and was able to time her. This senior citizen with orthopedic shoes was in her car and driving away within thirty-five seconds of the time I asked her about powwowing!

I believe the widespread reticence about discussing powwowing has two principal causes. First, many consultants expressed a concern that "modern" people might think belief in powwowing is evidence of ignorance and backwardness—the "dumb Dutch" stereotype invoked in coverage of the York Hex Murder Trial. Some, such as my York County consultant Hazel Sauer and the Reading woman who sought powwow treatment to remove a hex, would not even reveal their belief in powwowing to their family members for fear of being ridiculed. A second factor is the significant opposition to the practice by local churches (particularly Eastern or Conservative Mennonites) and religious figures, who fear that powwow cures, to the extent that they work, come from the devil. One Conservative Mennonite, who was related to Leah Stoltzfus by marriage, expressed this opinion and requested that I report back to her the results of my interview with Leah.[10] An Amish man who knew Leah but did not know of her powwowing practice said "she'd better not be" powwowing because "the church forbids it."[11] It is worth noting that powwowers themselves are hesitant to discuss their practice, out of a concern that those who are not properly trained to powwow might use spell books or incantations improperly and thereby be drawn into black magic.

Science and Satan: The Roots of Controversy

The embarrassment that many of my informants expressed at having their belief in the efficacy of powwowing exposed, and their insistence on the use of pseudonyms, derives largely from the program of scientific educa-

9. Many Plain Mennonites drive black vans or cars without chrome showing. These are the so-called "black bumper" Mennonites.

10. Needless to say, I chose not to become involved in this kind of "espionage."

11. Another consultant had suggested to him, in my presence, that she might be a powwower.

tion imposed on schools following the York Hex Murder Trial. At the same time, many parents began to teach their children English, rather than the Pennsylvania Dutch dialect of German, as a first language, so that many who were born after 1930 do not speak the dialect. This amounted to a suppression of traditional Pennsylvania Dutch culture.

This is not to suggest that "scientific education" attempted to disprove the existence of powwowing by scientific arguments or experiments, or that it involved any discussion of powwowing whatsoever. The intent behind such programs was not scientific but political. The image of the region had suffered as a result of the "witch trial" (the York Hex Murder Trial) and it had to be rehabilitated. The "dumb Dutch" had to come into the modern age, the era of automobiles, electricity, radio, airplanes. They had to put away quaint "superstitions," such as powwowing, and they had to speak English, like "normal" Americans.

The success of this approach was mixed. Such programs did indeed diminish the use of the Pennsylvania Dutch dialect and reduce the number of people who believe in powwowing. The fear of some of my consultants that their friends or relatives would think they were "crazy" if they admitted belief in powwowing demonstrates the at least perceived existence of a "culture of disbelief" in the area now. Some consultants opposed the practice because they believed that it was unscientific, or did not work, or both.

Mr. F is an example of someone who objects to powwowing on scientific grounds. He has many ancestors and relatives who were involved in powwowing as practitioners or as clients. He does hold some supernatural beliefs (for example, he believes in ghosts because he has witnessed "apparitions"), but he considers powwowing to be a superstition that modern, educated people should not believe in.

> My father only had a fifth-grade education. He was taken out of school to farm as a child. And he believed in some superstitions. I went to school and found out that superstitions and things like that are not based on scientific facts. We tried to explain to my father that these things are no longer being done and shouldn't be expressed like this, and he got kind of disturbed as he said, "When I was a little boy—"
>
> I said, well things are different now. We're in a different age and a different time.

Furthermore, when I sent Mr. F a copy of the survey to complete, he sent back the following note, written in large letters:

> Mr. Kriebel,
>
> What was in the Past—
> Will Remain in the Past.
>
> Respectfully,
> [initials]

Dr. Robert Kline, a retired physician in Lebanon County who has studied powwowing and has an active interest in Pennsylvania Dutch culture, is also strongly opposed to powwowing and believes that no one should see a powwower, because it could delay seeking biomedical treatment. He would refuse to see a powwower under any conditions, even if he were terminally ill. He believes powwowing cures work because of the placebo effect but have no intrinsic value. He also believes that Christians heal faster than nonbelievers and that prayer works because of a biological placebo effect ("It stimulates the production of endorphins").[12]

Not raised to believe in powwowing, Dr. Kline associates disbelief with higher education. His grandparents took his mother to be "powwowed" as a girl, but "she was a high school graduate and didn't believe." He believes that powwowing once had a vital role to play in community health, because, "Don't forget, the local physician didn't know much," before the twentieth century. Now, however, he believed that powwowing was dying out—he last heard about it in the 1960s.

Dr. Kline would refuse to take on any patient who was also being treated by a powwower, a chiropractor, or other alternative practitioner. "I would say, 'You'd better see him full-time.'"

Geraldine, a Pennsylvania Dutch local historian, believes the York Hex Murder Trial is the basis for opposition to powwowing. She also believes that it has colored outsiders' perceptions of the Pennsylvania Dutch: "I think an awful lot of the opposition to *Braucherei* came after the hex trials in York County. The 'Witch Trial [York Hex Murder Trial]' and *Braucherei* tended to go underground, because . . . it was an international

12. Dr. Kline is a Christian himself (he belongs to the United Church of Christ) but does not accept all Christian doctrine. For example, he is skeptical about the existence of the Holy Spirit.

incident. We had reporters here from London and all over Europe. And all of a sudden, the 'dumb Dutchman.' And it's like any other incident—one unfortunate incident colors an entire culture."

However, a survey of my consultants fails to show that higher education diminishes actual belief (as opposed to admitted belief) in the efficacy of powwowing. Nor can it be shown that higher education plays a role in the decision to seek powwow treatment. These conclusions were consistent with McGuire's findings in her study of a range of spiritual healing practices in the contemporary United States (McGuire and Kantor 1988). Older people, however, may be more likely to believe in powwowing than younger people, which suggests that powwowing may be dying out. It is significant that the use of Pennsylvania Dutch as a first language seems to indicate a greater interest in powwowing but not necessarily a higher level of belief. Further study is necessary to confirm these tentative conclusions.

Religiously based opposition to powwowing has an even longer history. Its source lies in the Pennsylvania Dutch churches. An early opponent was the nineteenth-century Reformed minister Daniel Weiser, who preached against powwowing and collected a number of cases in which powwowing was used with harmful effect. The Amish man in the holistic healer's shop who said that the church forbade powwowing is a more modern manifestation, as was Leah Stoltzfus's relative and the Mennonite man at Good's Store in Schaefferstown. When I began my research on powwowing in 1998 at the Schwenkfelder Heritage Center in Montgomery County, a gentleman there opined, "I think people should go to the church for that," meaning spiritual healing.

This statement is, I believe, the key to understanding religious opposition to the practice. The churches seek to monopolize and authorize the use of supernatural power. Any unauthorized use of such power must either be useless or else under the control of another supernatural power—"the second highest power," in the Mennonite man's words.

However, there is variation among congregations. For instance, Hazel Sauer reports that Rachel Rahn, the powwower with whom she shared a house in the 1930s, had many wives of ministers among her clients, and there are even reports of ministers who engaged in the practice themselves (Hostetler 1992, 109). Leah Stoltzfus is the wife of an Amish bishop who, at least in the opinion of Rebecca Yoder, approves of her practice: "She wouldn't do it if he didn't want her to."

Furthermore, there is a long-established tradition that religious faith is an essential ingredient in the making of a successful powwower. My parents describe my great-grandmother, who practiced powwowing, as "a very religious person." Hazel Sauer describes Mrs. Rahn as very religious also and notes that she was an active member of a (probably Lutheran) church in Maryland. According to Mrs. Lenhart, who also knew her, Mrs. Rahn insisted that a powwower had to be a person of excellent character: "She said you daren't swear." This position was echoed by many other consultants and published interviews.

The hostility of the organized and overwhelmingly Protestant Pennsylvania Dutch clergy is muted at the present time, probably because the practice of powwowing is at least perceived as dying out. Many ministers know little about the practice, and those who do seem to regard it as more a curious, even charming, relic from the past than a threat to the church or the Christian faith. However, as the Schwenkfelder official's reaction shows, opposition is still found. A minister from Germany recently toured Pennsylvania, preaching against powwowing.[13] Don Yoder identifies Protestant opposition to powwowing with a desire to separate "religion" from "superstition," thereby suppressing folk-healing traditions that had hitherto found a religious basis in Roman Catholicism (Yoder 1967, 39). Opposition, when it is articulated, stems from a belief that powwowers accomplish their feats with the aid of evil spirits. Jacob J. Hershberger, an Amish minister, wrote in a 1961 newspaper column:

> We do not deny that cures, even miracles, are often worked by those who use enchantment, powwow, etc. After all, there are many evil spirits in the world, and like Pharaoh's magicians who turned water into blood and dust into lice with their witchcraft and sorcery, the same evil spirits can work wonders today. It is even quite possible that there are those today who practice these "curious arts" and don't realize that the source of their power is the devil rather than God. (Hostetler 1992, 107)

That column did not go unanswered. Four individuals wrote in and denied that powwowing was harmful or had anything to do with evil spirits or black magic. In fact, the relationship between powwowing and black magic has long been a matter of contention. Some powwowers, such

13. David Hufford, personal conversation.

as Mr. A of rural Berks County, says: "In no way do I believe in anything of the hex. That has nothing to do with powwowing. Because powwowing is more or less faith-healing. You have to believe" (Westkott 1969–70, 4). Every powwower I have encountered, heard about, or read about has claimed that the power he or she uses comes from God.

On the other hand, witchcraft and powwowing are connected in the minds of many nonpractitioners. For instance, the York Hex Murder Trial involved the murder of a man who supposedly placed hexes on people but also offered powwow treatment. An article by folklorist Alfred Shoemaker in *The Pennsylvania Dutchman* tells a story about an old woman who could powwow and throw hexes (Shoemaker 1951, 2). As Reimensnyder notes concerning powwowers who claim to be able to remove hexes, some "believe that what a powwow doctor can take off he can also put on" (Reimensnyder 1982, 21).[14] The use of various books also blurred the distinction between powwowing and hexing. For instance, *The Sixth and Seventh Books of Moses* have been used by some powwowers but are held by others to be evil because they contain information on ritual magic and summoning spirits (Snellenburg 1969, 44). As a little girl, Mrs. Schultz had a neighbor who was rumored to be a witch and who possessed a copy of this book, which Mrs. Schultz's grandmother claimed was a book of the devil. When Hazel Sauer's daughter was cured by Mrs. Rahn, she asked her how she might learn to powwow herself. Mrs. Rahn offered to teach her but cautioned that "you had to be careful not to mix the bad with the good" and that dire consequences could ensue if one tried to learn from the wrong book. This dissuaded Hazel from trying to learn to powwow at all.

Some lay Pennsylvania Dutch disapprove of powwowing in the strongest terms. For instance, Rebecca Yoder believes that Leah Stoltzfus's activities are either ineffective or due to the power of the devil. She also accepted the term "magic" as describing Leah's activities and said she would not be surprised if "New Age" people tried to do powwowing themselves. When asked if it was ever all right for a Christian to do what Leah does, she replied "No." However, she believes in healing by prayer and laying on hands. In both cases, she believes it is the prayer that effects cures, and she herself keeps a prayer list. Over and over again she identi-

14. A good example of such a person is Don Yoder's consultant, Aunt Sophie Bailer of Schuylkill County (Bailer 1952b, 8).

fied the main part of Leah's practice that she found disturbing, namely, her use of medical dowsing to identify the medicines her patients should take.

Eastern Mennonite members (who dress plain, use entirely black automobiles, and speak English) have been particularly active in opposing powwowing. I have already mentioned the opposition to Mrs. May's various occult practices from Mennonites in Lebanon County. Chris Wine, a twenty-nine-year-old Eastern Mennonite farmer outside Kleinfeltersville in southeastern Lebanon County, believed he was speaking for the Eastern Pennsylvania Mennonite Church in condemning powwowing, along with such other practices as dowsing ("water-witching" or "water-smelling"), aura reading, use of Ouija boards, "weighing vitamins," "black boxes,"[15] massage therapy, therapeutic touch, and healing by laying on hands or oil (unless used with prayer). He also was leery of chiropractors who would not refer patients to physicians when necessary. His primary point was that any reliance on "things" leads to "fear and bondage," creating dependence on magical spells, charms, amulets, and the like. "The devil's power is bondage, not liberty," he noted. Like Rebecca Yoder and the man at Good's Store in Schaefferstown, he believed that powwowing worked, but "it's a power of darkness."

Chris Wine indicated that some Old Order Amish and Old Order Mennonites (including some of his relatives) practiced powwowing, but he said he wanted to believe they were not deliberately doing evil but were simply misinformed. Tom Martin, of the Landis Valley Museum north of Lancaster, stated that the Old Order Amish and Mennonites he knows, including many of his relatives, generally approve of powwowing and patronize "various powwow doctors of sorts . . . and go to reflexologists and all these sort of things." However, he noted that the "more progressive" Mennonites of the Lancaster Conference "seem to think that it's black magic and related to the devil and just don't think it's very good." Dean Hochstetler, an Indiana Mennonite minister and exorcist raised in an Amish community, agreed with this sentiment, saying, "[Powwowing] does one thing well, brings people under bondage to Satan." He claimed that 90 percent of Amish people practiced powwowing and 40 percent of

15. "Weighing vitamins," may refer to "medical dowsing" (see Chapter 6, note 11, above). "Black boxes" contained pieces of metal that supposedly collected electricity from weather vanes turning the wrong way.

Mennonites were "involved, one way or another" with powwowing (Hochstetler 1978).

Gerald Studer, a Mennonite who performed ethnographic research and collected documents on powwowing in the 1970s, considered powwowing to be "white magic" rather than "black magic." However, he agreed that even use of white magic was incompatible with the Christian life, and he urged that charm books intended for instruction and use rather than scholarly study be burned (Studer 1980, 23).

Antipowwowing sentiments have found their way into other church bodies not traditionally associated with the Pennsylvania Dutch. For instance, the daughter of Harry and Erma Adam, who believe in powwowing and who see powwowers (like Harry's father, grandmother, and great-grandmother) as good, religious people, now strongly opposes the practice after joining a new church that Harry and Erma consider "a cult." The church preaches against powwowing and sees it as the work of the devil.

My consultant Mr. F also opposed powwowing on religious as well as scientific grounds, but his position is more nuanced:

David: Is it morally okay for a Christian to powwow or to be powwowed?

F: For me I would not do it, but each person has to be subject to their maker. So if they do it, they'll have to answer why they did it. All I can see in her case it was desperation.

David: If you were in a desperate position and wanted something badly, or whatever, you would never even resort to it?

F: I believe in my faith and maybe when I had Alzheimer's or something, I don't know.

David: But only if something like that were to happen—you wouldn't do it in your right mind?

F: I would not do it.

In my experience, many of those who oppose the practice of powwowing do so on both religious and "scientific" grounds, and the two forms of opposition are mutually reinforcing. Mr. F reports that his grandfather (Northampton County) opposed powwowing because he did not believe in it and that his grandfather once physically threw a powwower out of his house. That caused a rift in the family that lasted for decades:

F: My grandmother was dying from a fibroid tumor, and her maiden name was Saylor, and her relatives which were Saylors brought in an old powwow doctor from the Hellertown area.[16] When my grandfather discovered him in the house, he physically picked up the powwow doctor and removed him from the house, and he told my mother's brothers and sisters, "Please do not return with this individual because I do not believe in witchcraft or powwowing."

David: He saw the two as being synonymous—witchcraft and powwowing?

F: I think he was referring to all aspects of magic—saying words, doing things, bringing odd objects into your religion.

David: You said your mother's father threw this powwow out of the house.

F: Yeah, physically, because he said the man was not washed or shaven. He was concerned about his wife, who was gravely ill, and he was concerned that he might give her something that might hasten her demise. So he asked her relatives not to come back. They weren't welcome in the house.

David: So they never came back?

F: No, they didn't. There was a rift in the family up until 1985, when I started to do genealogy, and started talking.

In fact, much in the history of powwowing supports the contention that there is a fine line indeed between powwowing and hexing, white magic and black magic. Powwowers such as Howard Resh and Andrew Lenhart were known for hexing people who offended them and even bragged that they could do it. John Blymire complained when he believed that he himself had been hexed, that his power to remove and bestow hexes had been taken away. Powwowers who did not engage in black magic themselves warned that one could easily be led astray, particularly if they read "the wrong book," as Hazel Sauer put it. Preston Zerbe's student Sarah ended her powwow training because she worried about the dangers of being involved with cases of demonic possession and feared that she might inadvertently be led into black magic. And then there is the old Pennsylvania Dutch saying from Lehigh County, "En *braucher* hot

16. The Saylor family was a prominent family in the area associated with *Brauche* practice.

en hadder Dod. Er is dem Deiwel ergewwe"(A powwower has a hard death. He has given himself over to the devil).[17]

ASSESSING THE CASE AGAINST POWWOWING

Is any of this opposition justified? That is, is there any good reason to think that the practice of powwowing is actually harmful? Because of the dual nature of the opposition to powwowing, the question is more complicated than it first appears. Those advocates of "scientific education," whom I shall call skeptics, are really concerned with belief in the efficacy of powwowing, not with the putative effects of powwowing itself. Those who fear the supernatural power of powwowing, whom I shall call "hostile believers," worry that powwowing derives from the devil. It is possible to be both a skeptic and a hostile believer, so that one can believe (with the Eastern Mennonites) that powwowing fosters magical thinking, which may become a psychological crutch, but does occasionally work with the assistance of Satan.

The skeptical concern that belief in powwowing is harmful has two aspects. One is the notion that powwowing creates compulsive behaviors or delusional beliefs that can cause people to fear doing anything without the appropriate charm or incantation. Few people I interviewed revealed this kind of behavior or expressed this kind of belief. Patients saw powwowing as one healing modality among others and generally did not rely on magical assistance as a routine part of daily living. The only two exceptions I observed were Sarah, the apprentice powwower who claimed she needed a divinatory pendulum to decide matters for her, and Carrie, who believed she was possessed by the spirit of her deceased mother, who had been a witch. Both women said they had dealt with evil spirits—Sarah as an assistant exorcist, Carrie as a victim of possession.

The second aspect of skeptical concern is the question of whether belief in powwowing creates an inaccurate picture of the world, as against the supposedly accurate picture supplied by "modern science." This is not a major concern of most Pennsylvania Dutch people or, indeed, of most Americans. But it is a concern of people I shall call "science advocates,"

17. Collected by Thomas R. Brendle from Mrs. Mary Koch, Egypt, Pennsylvania (Beam 1995, 100).

individuals who may or may not be scientists, and it has been a concern of local education authorities, albeit for different reasons. Many science advocates subscribe to a philosophical materialism that denies the possibility of an order of existence beyond the material. But this is not the place to analyze the motivations and influence of such individuals. It is sufficient to say that to the extent that belief in powwowing entails a belief in a nonmaterial order of existence containing supernatural entities such as God, angels, and evil spirits, it represents a necessary target for materialists.

Local education authorities have also been concerned about powwowing since the York Hex Murder Trial, not because they oppose all supernatural beliefs on a philosophical basis, but because they oppose only beliefs that cannot be squared with the "modern" worldview. Belief in powwowing is such a belief, and was at the time of the trial (1929) a highly visible belief that was deeply held by many in the culture area. That such an outlandish belief could be held by moderns was inconceivable, and so, popular and press accounts of the proceedings depicted those who believed in powwowing as throwbacks to an earlier time, fourteenth-century people living in the twentieth century. The local authorities were both embarrassed by this portrayal of the "dumb Dutch" and at the same time seemed to believe that it represented an accurate description. The solution, clearly, was to change people's beliefs so that medievalists would become moderns. The mechanism was public education. While it is true that widespread belief in powwowing besmirched the public image of York County and the Pennsylvania Dutch heartland in general, it is doubtful that such a "medieval" belief prevented individuals from functioning in the modern world of the twentieth century. Contemporary powwowers and their clients have no difficulty participating in the wider society, nor do they eschew "modern" medical practices when needed.

Turning to the question of religious objections to the practice, we find that such objections are even more problematic than those raised by skeptics. The religious argument against powwowing, like the materialist argument, rests on highly contestable premises. For one thing, it assumes that the power wielded by powwowers does not derive from God, an assertion that flatly contradicts the claims of powwowers. Today, all the powwowers I interviewed gave all the credit to God. If powwowers knowingly invoked diabolical power, it is unlikely they would make a statement that might be expected to support faith in God. Nor would the devil as described in Christian literature be likely to perform an act that would enhance the prestige of his adversary.

However, a second objection might be raised. Perhaps powwowers do not knowingly invoke the devil, but their use of magical spells is itself proscribed by the Gospels and should therefore be regarded as unchristian. This raises anew the question of how much of powwowing is magic and how much is religion. Certainly powwowers have used formulae that resemble magic spells and continue to use such spells today. Christians have used such spells almost since the beginning of the faith, particularly in Egypt; and in the Middle Ages, some—including such clerics as Marsilio Ficino—argued for a distinction between "natural magic" (which used astral and elemental forces) and "spirit magic" (which invoked demons). According to Ficino, natural magic could be used by Christians without fear of divine punishment, although spirit magic was another matter. The Albertus Magnus book, historically used by a number of powwowers, was careful to label its incantations and recipes "natural," though there are incantations in that book that do involve binding spirits, even demons, for specific tasks, albeit using the power of God to do so,

But are the powwowing formulae magic at all? Social scientists have long wrestled with drawing definitional lines between magic and religion. Some suggest that magic spells differ from religious rituals and petitionary prayers in that the former compel the supernatural entity addressed to fulfill the wishes of the magician, while the latter merely request such assistance. Under this system, published powwowing spells appear to be magical in that they are expected to work. However, the expectation is generally claimed to be based on experience, not on some invariant power in the spells themselves. Moreover, powwowers acknowledge that God does all the healing and that without God they can do nothing. Conversely, the Catholic Church holds that religious sacraments such as baptism and the Eucharist are effective in all cases, no matter the circumstances under which they are performed. The distinction between magic and religion in such cases becomes blurry indeed.

A second criterion that social scientists have proposed to distinguish magic from religion is that the former is done individually and the latter is done collectively. Certainly this distinction applied in Hellenistic culture, in which the sorcerer was viewed as a solitary figure, usually suspected of all sorts of evils, whereas the priest (who also performed spells to mobilize supernatural power) did so in the context of a community. This distinction has also been used to separate shamans from witches. If we accept it, as representatives of official Pennsylvania Dutch churches appear to, then powwowing is certainly magic, because it is a solitary method of mobilizing supernatural power without the explicit sanction of the church. However, prayer is also often performed in a solitary fashion and may be done without church sanction (such as praying for victory in war or sports). Is such prayer a magical rather than religious activity? Some would say yes, but the question is far from settled.

The third distinction to be considered is whether magic is aimed at achieving an empirical result (such as catching fish), whereas religion has goals that are nonempirical (such as salvation).[18] Leaving aside the questionable use of the term "empirical" (rather than "material") in this definition, it is clear that powwowing can be viewed as magical, because it is indeed aimed at achieving an observable result. Yet, again, there is some question. If one defines powwowing as magical using this standard, then all petitionary prayer must be seen as magical as well. And then there is the question of intent. If the purpose of spiritual healing is simply to help restore a person or animal to health, the case for labeling it "magic" is stronger than if healing has some higher purpose, such as glorifying God. Indeed, that is the reason Jesus ("the first powwower") gives for performing miracles of healing.

It is clear that powwowing cannot be definitively classified as exclusively "magic" or "religion." It has qualities in common with both. Therefore, religious criticisms of powwowing on the grounds that it is an unauthorized magical practice forbidden by the Scriptures cannot be sustained on the basis of the evidence.

REACTIONS OF POWWOWERS AND THEIR PATIENTS

Given these hostile attitudes toward powwowing, many practitioners today try not to draw undue attention to themselves. Even those with a relatively large clientele do not often advertise, but instead attract patients through word of mouth. Sometimes they will perform powwowing along with reflexology or some other more acceptable alternative therapy.

The reasons for secrecy are several. Former patients keep their belief in

18. This was the distinction that Bronislaw Malinowski (1954) proposed in his essay "Magic, Science, and Religion," although some (Tambiah 1993) have pointed out that the distinction is not particularly well defined.

the efficacy of powwowing secret out of fear of being ridiculed by their more "modern" children, relatives, or neighbors. Powwowers hide their practice out of fear of condemnation by religious people (such as ministers and neighbors). They also guard their rituals, but for a very different reason: such things are for the initiated only and should not be lightly made known to those who could misuse them. Methods for passing on the ability to powwow differ, as do the qualifications for becoming a powwower, but all would agree that the ritual knowledge is reserved for properly trained individuals. That is why incantations are pronounced subvocally, so that patients even a few inches away cannot hear what the powwower is saying.

The secrecy surrounding powwowing rituals is similar to the secrecy surrounding any means of utilizing supernatural power in which the power is not seen as accessible to everyone. In my research on neo-paganism, for instance, I was not allowed to read spell books (Books of Shadows) or to witness certain rituals. The ancient mystery cults and Gnostics likewise restricted knowledge of their rites to initiates.

The secrecy that results from fear of ridicule by skeptics derives from a clash of worldviews. The dominant worldview, in which God acts rarely, if at all, in the world, leaves little room for the intrusion of supernatural power. Biomedicine is the only legitimate form of healing, in this view. My research suggests that the Pennsylvania Dutch worldview is quite different, accommodating both biomedicine and powwowing under the sovereignty of God.

It is possible to share the cultural model of healing articulated above and yet oppose the practice of powwowing. The issue is not so much that of competing worldviews, but more one of competing views of the source of power behind powwowing or of the legitimacy of supernatural power by individuals not holding church office. The first concern is whether the power comes from God or the devil. The second, related to the first, is whether powwowing is a religious practice (authorized by the Scriptures) or a magical practice (proscribed by the Scriptures). If the practice is both effective and magical, then it must be from the devil. If ineffective and magical, then it is a psychological crutch. As the Eastern Mennonites point out, both are to be avoided. Of course, powwowers and their patients see matters quite differently, but they adopt secrecy out of a desire to avoid the notoriety that is sure to follow exposure in a climate that they perceive as hostile to the practice.

EIGHT

THE PERSISTENCE OF POWWOWING

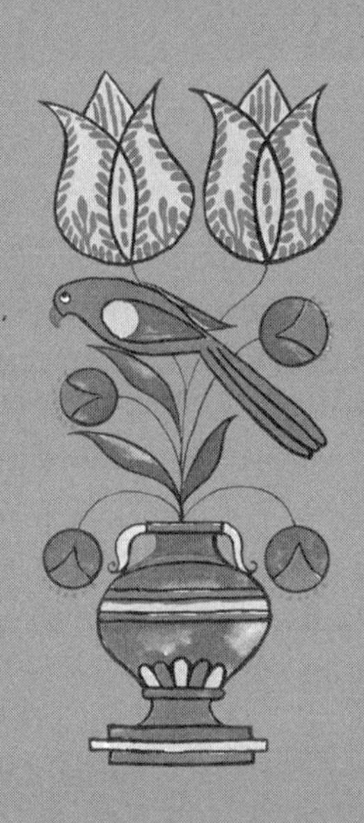

It is clear that powwowing, far from being an extinct esoteric practice, is still a part of Pennsylvania Dutch culture, even if it has retreated into the shadows in the face of scientific and religious opposition. In closing, it is worthwhile to examine the persistence of powwowing and to hazard a little fortune-telling to see how the practice might develop in the future. In this chapter, then, we shall look at the reasons that people have patronized powwowers, assess whether powwowing is in decline, speculate on how the practice might survive and change, and consider future directions for research.

Why do people continue to seek powwow treatment, particularly when effective biomedical treatments are now so readily available? One possible explanation is that there is a nostalgic desire by older members of the society to continue traditional practices in order to support the local culture. To be sure, the Pennsylvania Dutch culture has a strong element of self-consciousness about it, and it does appear that the indigenous population wants to maintain its distinctiveness. However, I find it implausible that people who have real health problems would patronize a practitioner purely out of nostalgia when they know perfectly well that a physician has an office a few miles away.

A second possible explanation is that there are some ailments that are either culturally defined as treatable only by powwowing (for example, livergrown, take-off, hexing); some diseases against which biomedicine either has no effective treatment (for example, erysipelas before the 1960s) or require a treatment that is painful or otherwise unpleasant (for example, warts); or emergency cases in which there is not time to reach a biomedical facility. This explanation would account for the primacy of biomedicine as a health-care choice and does appear to apply to nearly all cases involving nonprofessional powwowers. This explanation is supported by the fact that powwowing was used significantly more frequently for culturally defined ailments and skin conditions than for other medical problems. However, professional powwowers typically treat a much broader range of ailments than those mentioned above, and there are ailments against which biomedicine has no effective cure (for example, many forms of cancer) that are nonetheless rarely treated by powwowers.

A third explanation, suggested by Susan Stewart, is that people tend to use treatments with which they are familiar (Stewart 1976). As Stewart notes, such individuals may also have significant distrust of physicians and pharmaceuticals. One of Stewart's consultants reported a hierarchy of cures that were used to treat ever more serious conditions, beginning with home remedies, then powwowing, then calling a physician for more serious ailments (convulsions, pneumonia, diphtheria, and so on) and for childbirth.[1] However, Stewart's explanation fails to account for some cases I have collected, in which attempts were made to powwow for pneumonia, diphtheria, kidney infections, and many other serious ailments. Moreover, fewer people today are as familiar with powwowing as they were in 1976, when Stewart conducted her research.

A fourth explanation is that people use powwowing in preference to biomedicine because the former allows the patient to be more of a participant in his or her healing, rather than an object to be acted on by the healer, and that the rituals the patient undergoes are less structured (lacking well-defined ritual periods) than those of biomedicine. It may be objected here that the powwowing patient typically is passive during powwowing healing, and is in fact acted on by the healer. This objection may be answered by reference to the circumstances surrounding powwowing. The powwowing patient, while being physically passive, is not objectified by the healer in the same way the typical biomedical patient is. Restoration is accomplished not by defining the patient's identity in terms of the biomedical paradigm (so that "John Smith," stripped of his clothes and placed in a uniform garment disrespectful of bodily privacy, becomes "the appendectomy in 540") but by acknowledging the patient's identity of "believer," which he or she shares with the powwower. That is, the ritual affirms that powwower and patient are members of the same community of belief.

IS POWWOWING REALLY IN DECLINE?

From the literature it appears that, at the end of the nineteenth century, powwowers like John Rhoads and Peter Bausher often lived in isolated rural areas, which meant that their clients had to undertake journeys to see them or be powwowed remotely. By 1929, powwowers had moved

1. In general, this explanation, suggesting Guttman-scale properties of increasing inclusion and difficulty, is consistent with my field experience (although it was not possible in this study to collect sufficient data relative to this topic to construct a meaningful Guttman scale).

into cities, such as Lancaster and York, and set up shop, sometimes with a prominent shingle, like that used by "Professor" Howard Resh. After the 1960s, powwowing ceased to be practiced much in urban areas, and, at the time of my most intense period of fieldwork (1998–2000), powwowers were difficult to track down. All the traditional powwowers (and most of my other consultants) I interviewed live in rural areas.

This suggests that powwowing may be dying out, as many consultants seem to believe. If this is true, one would expect to see a drop in the number of practicing powwowers throughout the twentieth century. That is an exceedingly difficult proposition to test, however, because one would have to undertake a complete enumeration or collect a random sample of powwowers, a group that tends to be reclusive because of the suspicion that attends the practice. I have tried to give some sense of the extent of powwow activity in each decade of the twentieth century through the case descriptions and the table in Appendix 4. Because of the limitations of the sample, this can only serve as a rough guide. Yet, it is worth noting that if this were a random sample it would not support the notion that powwowing is dying out. Rather, it suggests that, while the number of living powwowers may have diminished (particularly since 1970), the process of replacement has not ceased. Based on initial expectations drawn from scholarly opinion, at the outset of my study my committee at Penn and I defined "success" as locating even one practicing powwower. I have since interviewed six, and know of eight to twelve others whose existence has been reported to me by powwowers who trained them. Powwowing is simply not the relic of the past it has been believed to be.

Indeed, many consultants who expressed the belief that powwowing had vanished or was dying out also expressed the desire that people would "take it up again," suggesting that a need still exists for powwowing treatment. Several "local historians" who know something about powwowing but are not powwowers have complained that their knowledge is a burden, because people approach them asking them to powwow for them and they have to turn them away. I myself have been pressed into service as a "powwow broker" by those who have read of my work. Aaron Boehm's grandson and Daisy Dietrich's granddaughter expressed an interest in powwowing, holding out the possibility that the "art" may continue to be practiced in Pennsylvania Dutch communities. Non–Pennsylvania Dutch persons such as Tom Barone, who have respect for and connections to the culture, have recently been trained in the practice and perform it in a traditional manner. And neo-pagans may be expected to be drawn to powwowing as part of their eclectic magical practice through the work of Wiccan "powwow artist" Silver RavenWolf.

THE FUTURE OF POWWOWING

Today, nine years after I began my study of powwowing, I no longer have any doubt that the practice still exists and most likely will continue to exist in the foreseeable future, if for no other reason because people who are sick will always seek healing wherever it may be found. But there are some concrete reasons to suggest that powwowing will continue to be practiced: the increased cost of biomedical care; the increased acceptance of alternative or New Age therapies; the persistence of belief in hexing; interest exhibited by younger people; and the side effects of research.

The Increased Cost of Biomedical Care

As health insurance premiums rise and employers are cutting back on benefits, more people will seek alternative, low-cost healing methods. Because powwowing today is generally free or offered at a nominal fee, and often appears to cure a variety of ailments, I expect that people will continue to seek powwow treatment, particularly when the illness is minor or the cost of biomedical treatment is high. For instance, Joanna Buck, a retired schoolteacher and horsewoman in central Pennsylvania, asked me to find her a powwower to treat her horse's melanoma. The horse had already been treated successfully by veterinarians, but the cost had been enormous and she could not afford to pay for another course of treatments. She told me that she was "very impressed" with the powwowers I referred her to (who charged her only the cost of the ferry they were obliged to take to reach her) and was hopeful that her horse would get well.

The Increased Acceptance of Alternative or "New Age" Therapies

Plain communities such as the Old Order Amish and Mennonites patronize alternative medical practitioners, particularly chiropractors and reflexologists but also hydrotherapists, therapeutic touch practitioners, and other healers whose work is seen as noninvasive. As sociologist John Hostetler notes, the Amish in particular are wary of "strong medicine" and, while they do not abstain from biomedical treatment, they do take a conservative approach to healing. Powwowing suits this kind of clientele well, although suspicions surrounding the practice can be expected to have a dampening effect.

Religious arguments against the practice of powwowing are irrelevant for a new sort of powwower, the neo-pagan. Thus far, Silver RavenWolf is the only neo-pagan author to publish a how-to book on powwowing, but it is likely that many more neo-pagans have already added powwowing to their "magickal" practices. It is typical of neo-pagans to use an eclectic assortment of magico-religious practices without regard for cultural background, and to instead reinterpret the practices in light of standard neo-pagan beliefs surrounding the "God" and "Goddess" who are manifest in a variety of religious traditions. In the words of one Wiccan high priestess, neo-paganism is a "shopping cart religion," a description that nicely sums up the attitude of accepting and integrating diverse traditions and practices according to the needs of the individual practitioner. Powwowing, then, becomes simply another item placed in the shopping cart. I expect that a good number of future "powwowers" who rely on RavenWolf's interpretation of the practice will be nontraditional, non-Christian, and non–Pennsylvania Dutch.

Can such a radically reinterpreted practice be accurately described as "powwowing"? Practitioners like RavenWolf do indeed use the term "powwow" but refer to themselves as "powwow artists," a term that is unknown to traditional practitioners. It is likely that such neo-pagan or New Age practitioners would use the term "powwow" and, if they lived in the region, would be consulted by the same people who would patronize traditional powwowers. They would therefore serve a similar social function and play a role similar to that of other powwowers. However, their own beliefs would differ radically from those of their clients: such powwowers would see their work not as a channeling of power from the triune Christian God but as the use of a form of white magic ("magick," to use the neo-pagan term) performed by the individual, albeit with the sanction of the neo-pagan goddess. They therefore would not share in the Pennsylvania Dutch cultural model of healing, which is based on the Pennsylvania Dutch worldview. In essence, the difference between traditional and neo-pagan powwowers is the difference between a Catholic priest and a Protestant pastor with respect to the Eucharist—the ritual they perform may be substantially the same, but the meaning of that ritual is different.

Persistence of the Belief in Hexing

Belief in witches and black magic was not uncommon among the Pennsylvania Dutch until after the York Hex Murder Trial. At that point, the idea that hexes could cause illness and misfortune began to decline. During the course of my fieldwork, I came to believe at one point that hexing was virtually extinct; I had collected few cases of hexing since the 1950s. However, Daisy Dietrich is called on about once a year to protect barns or persons from hexes, Sarah was involved in a number of cases involving exorcisms, and most recently I was contacted by Carrie, who claimed that her mother, a witch herself, had hexed her and, following the mother's death, had possessed her and made her desperately ill. She also believes that her biological father was "the biggest warlock in the area." Unless Carrie is a very convincing con artist, her belief in hexing is real and quite disturbing. She claims that there are today many witches plaguing people with hexes and demons in the Reading area. Her only recourse is powwowing or other supernaturally based assistance, and she has begged me to find her a powwower, a request that I was able to honor. So long as a belief in hexing as strong as Carrie's exists, there will be a demand for—and likely a supply of—powwowers.

Interest Exhibited by Younger People

When I discuss my fieldwork with my students, there are always a few who say they would like to learn how to powwow. There is reason to believe that powwowing will be passed on to the next generation. Anita Rahn told me in 1999 that she planned to pass the gift on to her son, then thirty-eight years old. Daisy Dietrich recently trained thirty-seven-year-old Tom Barone as a powwower. The grandchildren of Aaron Boehm and Daisy also expressed an interest in learning to powwow. If powwowing is transmitted through families, it is likely to survive into the indefinite future, and the number of practicing powwowers may even increase as generations perpetuate themselves.

The Side Effects of Research

One phenomenon I noticed in my field research was the way in which my inquiries stirred up memories and made people either ask me to locate a powwower for them or say they wish they had learned to powwow. This was particularly evident at the talks I have given. Following my 2002 J. William Frey lecture at Franklin and Marshall College in Lancaster, which I presented to a standing-room-only crowd, I was approached by a throng of listeners who were eager to share their own powwowing experiences. I was impressed by the collective excitement that the topic generated. It was as if the announcement that powwowing was to be discussed in an official way gave people permission to come forward and recreate events that were highly meaningful to them.

The requests I have received for powwow "referrals"—sometimes by people referred to me by a person I had never met—are indications that people perceive a need for powwowing. Such attitudes, generated in part by publicized books, articles, or speakers, will, I believe, create a demand for powwow treatment where none had existed before, simply because many people did not know that powwowing was still available.

Powwowing today seems to be going in three directions. Traditionalists, who may or may not have ethnolinguistic ties to Pennsylvania Dutch, will likely continue to view the practice as a form of spiritual healing grounded in Christianity and using Christian incantations and symbols in their healing rituals. Ironically, this form of powwowing is an adaptation to modern culture divested of the trappings of white magic. Such individuals, with few exceptions, will likely continue to avoid the use of nonbiblical charm books and material components.

The second direction is a radical departure from the traditional and is articulated by Silver RavenWolf. This innovation moves in a quite different direction, emphasizing the magical nature of powwowing as one magical practice among many, and represents an attempt to present the Christian aspects of the practice as optional. In that, RavenWolf is creating a generic, non-Christocentric form of powwowing that superficially resembles the original practice but is radically different at its core. Christians can feel free to use their own religious terminology in powwow rituals, but so can Wiccans (such as RavenWolf), who would substitute pagan formulae for Christian formulae, so that "Maiden, Mother, Crone" may take the place of "Father, Son, Holy Ghost." Her broad shopping-cart approach is typical of neo-pagan eclecticism in ritual practice and interpretation.

The third direction is a retrenching and reinterpretation of powwowing represented by Tom Barone, who comes from the periphery of the culture but feels drawn to it. Like RavenWolf, Barone is not averse to using his own interpretations and does not look askance at the term "magic," but remains firmly within a Christian belief system. Barone is critical of RavenWolf and her attempts to "paganize" powwowing. Well versed in a number of mystical and esoteric disciplines, he believes that powwowing can be both Christian and magical and that there is no contradiction between the two. He was drawn to powwowing because of his background in other magical practices and also because he feels an affinity with Pennsylvania Dutch culture. In looking back to an earlier time, Barone may be considered a reformer in the world of powwowers.

Previous work has been concerned mainly with collecting stories about powwowing. These stories usually provide a good deal of data, and many of them include material that can be considered cases. My own work is in many ways a continuation of this project. But in order to understand powwowing as more than a cultural artifact, we must take seriously what powwowers, their clients, and those who oppose the practice say. That is, we should take what they say their experiences have been and what their beliefs are and try to understand what shapes the experience and creates the belief.

We can, however, come up with some conclusions based on my study. First, it is clear that powwowing still exists and is probably not declining as rapidly as others have suggested. Indeed, the interest in powwowing shown by younger people suggests that powwowers will continue to be trained in the tradition and will continue to adapt in response to culture changes. It is also clear that people will seek out powwowers for a variety of reasons, from financial to having had no relief with biomedical treatment.

Second, the nature of powwowing has changed over the past century or so, from a form of "white magic," with its reliance on set spells, to a form of "spiritual healing." Powwowers who once used their spells to achieve a variety of results are now almost entirely limited to healing, broadly construed to include spiritual as well as physical illness. The shift in terminology, occasioned by the York Hex Murder Trial and the advent of scientific education, will make powwowing more palatable for religious believers and skeptics alike. There are exceptions, though, such as Tom Barone and Silver RavenWolf, neither of whom avoids the term "magic."

As a healing practice, powwowers treat a range of ailments, from culture-bound syndromes such as livergrown and being hexed, to skin diseases, to the pain caused by cancer. The act of healing involves three general types of rituals, from brief actions, such as rubbing a potato on a wart, to involved procedures employing long incantations, gestures, and manipulations of objects. The more involved the ritual, the more general its applicability. Healing rituals, such as powwowing, can be forms of "identity work," in which patients and powwowers both reinforce or restore their personal and social identities.

Finally, we can say that powwowing is consistent with a model of healing that is shared across Pennsylvania Dutch culture. Within that cultural model, powwowers are channels for the power of God, who does the actual healing. Moreover, this model can accommodate other healing practices, such as biomedicine, and I know of no powwow clients who would refuse biomedical treatment. Yet, critics of powwowing who share the same model can challenge powwowing by depicting powwowers as either receiving power from the devil (who, according to the Pennsylvania Dutch worldview, can act in this world) or otherwise operating beyond the sanction of the church. Critics who do not share the model (for instance, materialists who deny the existence of divine power, or Christians who deny that God uses people as channels for such power) can claim that powwowing does not work at all, because it does not fit into their understanding of the universe.

Much opposition would likely cease if powwowing were to achieve the recognition of other alternative and complementary medical treatments, such as acupuncture and therapeutic touch. It is my hope that this work and others will expose powwowing to the wider public so it can be better understood in its cultural and religious context and adequately assessed by medical researchers. If so, as John George Hohman says in his preface to *The Long Lost Friend*, "all men might have an opportunity of using it to their good."

APPENDIXES

APPENDIX 1: THEORETICAL BACKGROUND

Identity Work

With identity defined as self-image, both social and personal identity may be considered "identity aspects" in anthropologist Anthony F. C. Wallace's terms. Each of these can occupy a number of states, ranging from "ideal" identity (most desirable) to "feared" identity (least desirable). In his earlier work on the "identity struggle" (Wallace and Fogelson, 1965), Wallace divided this range into four segments—ideal, claimed, real, and feared identities—each one being a state. Later, Wallace (1967) reduced this to a three-state model—ideal, indifferent, and feared—with "indifferent" as a category for all intermediate states. The earlier model is more descriptive, but the latter model provides more flexibility and is more amenable to the mathematical manipulations that Wallace uses in the later article. Either model would be suitable for my purposes, but because I have not used Wallace's set theory in my analysis, I prefer the earlier model, where the "real" identity is explicitly not privileged with respect to the other identity states but is every bit as much of a perception by the individual as any other state. The real identity is *believed* by the individual to be an accurate description of himself. A claimed identity is what he wants others to believe is his real identity. The goal of "identity work" by the individual is to keep real identity relatively close to ideal identity (what he wants to be) and relatively far from feared identity (what he does not want to be). Healing constitutes a form of identity work.

Wallace has not explicitly applied these models to social identity. I have done so, with the understanding that it is the individual's self-image as a member of society that is analyzed, not the role as an "objective" element defined with others of its type. The "personal identity" (self-image as individual) and the "social identity" (self-image as player of a culturally defined role) both represent perceptions of a biological, psychological, and spiritual entity who shares a culture with other such entities. I and others have used the term "role" as synonymous with social identity, but that is not quite correct. It is the individual's perception of himself in that role that constitutes what I shall refer to henceforth as "social identity." In fact, "social identity" might be thought of as the point of articulation between personal identity and role. That being the case, understanding both the personal identity and the role of the powwower is crucial to understanding the powwower's social identity.

Schemas and Cultural Models

An individual uses schemas to make sense of events in life and to learn from them. For instance, an individual may have a schema for such things as "mind," "woman," or "schema," which, like scientific theories, may be conceived as a set of interrelated propositions. Both individual schemas and cultural models are reminiscent of Wallace's concept of the "mazeway" in that a mazeway, like a schema, is a set of generalizations built from experience (Wallace 1956, 631).[1] Schemas and cultural models are hierarchical—each may have subschemas to overcome the limits of short-term memory (D'Andrade 1987, 112). All schemas may be portrayed in narrative form, as in the cultural models that Linde identifies as "coherence systems" (Linde 1993, 164).

Claudia Strauss and Naomi Quinn, both cognitive anthropologists, identify two approaches that artificial intelligence researchers have used to conceptualize schemas: the "classical," or "symbolic processing," approach and the "connectionist" approach (Strauss and Quinn 1997, 60–61). The former is depicted using decision trees, the latter by showing inputs (events or objects), outputs (the meanings of events or objects), and hidden processors that take an input and transform it into a relevant output. Connectionism[2] is an approach modeled on neuron activity in the brain, with some inputs excitatory (positive) and some inhibitory (negative). Accordingly, for connectionists a meaning is an "interpretation of a particular situation, while [schemas] are the learned pattern of connections among units, different parts of which will be activated in any given situation" (Strauss and Quinn 1997, 83). "Cultural meaning" refers to the "typical output of the networks of people who have similar histories" (82).

1. In Wallace's terminology, "cognitive residues of perceptions" (Wallace 1970).

2. The connectionist approach has its strengths and weaknesses. It works best when dealing with procedural knowledge (how to do X) rather than declarative knowledge (X is A), and with automatic information-processing (what is 5 times 5?) rather than deliberate conscious control (what is the square root of 62?) (Strauss and Quinn 1997, 57). Symbolic processing is believed to handle the latter types of cognition better. It is also insufficient for a complete theory of cultural meaning (Strauss and Quinn 1997, 51), and it alone is not sufficient to describe cognition, because it does not take into account emotion, motivation, and the world outside the mind (84).

Schemas and cultural models serve as devices for processing experience, so schema theory has implications for any theory of belief. A connectionist model of cognition, for instance, strongly suggests that beliefs are formed from experience, because it postulates few, if any, innate beliefs (Strauss and Quinn 1997, 79). However, it also holds that belief is not created directly from experience, because all inputs are processed through schemas. In other words, belief is a product of interpreted experience. A person possessing a schema for the supernatural might interpret a "natural" event supernaturally, and vice versa. Schema theory holds that even implicit psychological schemas may be brought to consciousness without resistance, and therefore it provides no support for the notion of "unconscious beliefs" proposed by some who seek to explain away reports of supernatural experience (Strauss and Quinn 1997, 259 n.13).

For a study of powwowing, this view suggests that there are schemas for powwowing that are mediated through a larger cultural model of powwowing, which in turn is subordinated to a cultural model of healing existing within the Pennsylvania Dutch worldview.

The difference between (simple) schemas and cultural models is that schemas may be held in short-term memory but cultural models cannot, because of their relative degree of elaboration. If one has a piece of a schema, one can fill in the rest of it with little trouble. Because of their complexity, however, this is not true in cultural models. What also distinguishes cultural models is that they are intersubjectively shared by a group. Examples of cultural models include the cultural model of the mind, the Trukese model of navigation, the Hindu model of reincarnation, and the Pennsylvania Dutch model of healing.

In a conversation with me, anthropologist Melvyn Hammarberg suggested that the next level up is "worldview." This makes sense with respect to sociologist Peter Berger's notion of reality construction, in which our worldview is how we perceive taken-for-granted reality. In my view, the hierarchy of models (schema / cultural model / worldview) exercises a "qualifying" function that specifies what can "count" as legitimate from the top down—that is, worldview (given by culture) qualifies certain cultural models as legitimate, which in turn qualify certain schemas. Experience, as used by David Hufford in his experiential theory, works from the bottom up: experience is had by individuals who come to hold certain beliefs, which then may enter the culture and influence the worldview held by members of that culture.

APPENDIX 2: GLOSSARY OF ILLNESSES

aa-gewachse (*see* livergrown).
abnehme (*see* take-off).
abnemmedes (*see* take-off).
cellulitis: Diffuse and usually subcutaneous or intrapelvic spreading inflammation of connective tissue.
consumption: A progressive wasting away of the body. Also used as a colloquial synonym for tuberculosis.
decline (*see* take-off).
erysipelas (*rote laufa, wildfeier*): This disease, also referred to as "wildfire" or "St. Anthony's fire," is known to biomedicine as an infectious skin inflammation that spreads over the body in a red rash and is caused by the bacterium *Streptococcus erysipelitis* (Estep and Pietchke 1949). It is not limited to any particular region or population and is related to cellulitis. The prescribed biomedical treatment is a course of antibiotics. Prior to antibiotics, to which it responds, physicians had no effective treatment for erysipelas, and powwowing was the treatment of choice. The latest roughly datable case of a powwow cure for erysipelas was from 1952, which suggests that people afflicted with the disease may be seeking biomedical help rather than the services of a powwower. In the 1990s, however, Tom Clemens (Schuylkill County) reports being cured of cellulitis by Daisy Dietrich after biomedical treatment failed.
livergrown (*aa-gewachse, aagewaxe, ah-gewachse*): This ailment, sometimes called "heartspan," (*hartzschparr* in the dialect), appears to be specific to Pennsylvania Dutch culture. According to Brendle and Unger (1935, 193–94), this is an ailment, often found in infants or young children, in which the muscular or fleshy part of the lower chest region contracts, as if stuck to some inner part, leaving the ribs sharply defined and the abdomen protruding. The common reason given for this is that the children were shaken too hard on a carriage or automobile ride (Reimensnyder 1982, 90), an etiology that conforms to the testimony of my consultants. Other symptoms include crying, indicative of abdominal pain. Powwow treatment usually involves either measuring the patient with a red string or passing

him or her around table legs, weaving the patient in and out between the legs. Brendle (cited by Beam 1995, 53) also provides a powwow cure in which the afflicted child lay with his head facing east and the powwower (Mrs. Walck) passed her thumbs down the ribs and around the back to the spine while pronouncing an incantation invoking the Christian Trinity.

opnema (*see* take-off).

quinsy: A sore throat.

rote laufa (*see* erysipelas).

rupture: A hernia.

scurvy: A disease characterized by spongy gums, loose teeth, and a tendency to bleed into the skin and mucous membranes. Caused by a Vitamin C (ascorbic acid) deficiency.

side stitches (*see* stitches).

stitches A local sharp and stabbing pain in the side.

stricture: An abnormal narrowing of a tubular organ, such as the intestines or esophagus. May result from various causes.

sweeny: An atrophy of the shoulder muscles of a horse. May be used to mean any muscular atrophy in a horse.

swinney (*see* sweeny).

take-off (*abnehme*, *abnemes*, *abnemmedes*, *opnema*): A wasting disease, also known as the "decline" or "decay of flesh," in which the victim loses weight. Most common in babies, although one consultant (Mrs. Lenhart) reports that she and her husband suffered from it in adulthood.[1] Dr. Robert Kline, a Lebanon County physician who does not believe in powwowing, characterizes it as "failure to thrive." The prescribed biomedical treatment is vitamins and stimulation (picking up the baby and cuddling it) (Reimensnyder 1982, 70). The powwow treatment usually involved measuring the victim's body with a string or measuring tape. According to an Ohio powwower in 1955, in a healthy person the crown to heel measurement was 7 times that of the length from heel to end of the big toe (Studer 1980, 18).

windgalls: A soft tumor or synovial swelling on a horse's leg in the region of the fetlock joint.

1. Other individuals have said that an adult condition was "like the take-off" (John Blymire [[4.B.4.b]] and Helen Bechtel, the latter referring to Walter Miller [[case 70]]).

APPENDIX 3: AN EXCERPT FROM *ALBERTUS MAGNUS: EGYPTIAN SECRETS*

Below are some representative entries transcribed from *Albertus Magnus: Egyptian Secrets*, a charm book used in powwowing, primarily before the mid-twentieth century. These examples range from simple recipes with no incantation at all to complex spells invoking various supernatural beings. The last of these contains words taken from Greek, Latin, and Hebrew and is strikingly reminiscent of syncretistic Christian magical incantations from Egypt during the Roman period. While this does not prove an actual Egyptian origin for the text, it suggests that some of the spells may have been borrowed from more ancient sources. Its invocation of Satan and demons, though bound by God and his angels, places it on the thin line between white and black magic.

From volume 2, pp. 79–81:

> *If a Horse has Eaten too much and is Swelled*
>
> Take from four to five pounds of fresh milk; mix a few pinches of black snuff tobacco in the milk, or instead of the tobacco some vinegar and ground leaven or yeast. This give to the sick animal, whereupon it should be slowly driven around. The horse will soon have an opening, and is saved in an easy manner from the disease.
>
> *When an Animal is Sprained on the Shoulder Blade or in any other Limb or Member*
>
> In order to dispose of the curdled blood it is necessary to mix and equal part of mutton tallow with turpentine. Grease the limb therewith and rub gently.
>
> *When a Child is Bewitched*
>
> Stand with the child toward the morning sun and speak: Be welcome in God's name and sunshine, from whence didst brightly beam, aid me and my dear child and feign my songs serenely

stream. To God the Father sound my praise, help praise the Holy Ghost that he restore my child to health, I praise the heavenly host. ✝ ✝ ✝

For the Erysipelas

Take a quart of fresh milk, dog's waste stirred therein and strained through a cloth. This is a good internal medicine.

Or make for External Use:

Tormantil wort . . . . .1 drachm
Dragon blood . . . . .2 ounces
Red chalk stone . . . . .1 drachm
Mix together and put in milk.

For Sore Feet

Wounds so good, I stop your smart with God's own blood, that ye never swell, nor fester, till the dear mother of God shall bear another son. ✝ ✝ ✝ Satora robote Netabe ratotta.
S. ✝ ✝ ✝

To Compel a Thief to Return Stolen Property[1]

In the name of the Holy Trinity, I urge and conjure, N.N., thou thief, male or female thief, in the name of God, who knows all, through Aaron the high priest, through whose aid I compel and vanquish all devils, this be imparted to you, Moloch and, Lucifer too will be sent, as also St. Michael, St. Gabriel, St. Raphael with many thousand legions of obedient spirit and holy angels of God, this be thy compulsion, thy obedience, this be thy ransom, this be thy plague, this be thy obligation: Asteroth, God in Gods and of God, the thief who robbed N.N., that thief, be it male or

1. This incantation, which contains divine and demonic names, is meant to mobilize the power of God to compel the devil to, in turn, compel the thief to return stolen property. The implication is that God does not act directly but can compel evil spirits to act on behalf of the petitioner. It is easy to see how a nonpowwower, seeing this spell, might consider it black magic. It illustrates how fine the line between powwowing (*Braucherei*) and black magic (*Hexerei*) could be.

female, bring hither to me in my N.N. house with the articles stolen. Beelzebub be bound, Lucifer be bound, Satan be bound with the rays which emanate from the holy countenance of God; the God who hath given to Moses the commandments, he would aid me N.N., out of trouble, he dishonor you! But I who keep the commandment, love the law, that law be God, a powerful God, a conqueror, a comforter and a savior. Moloch, Lucifer, Asteroth, Pemeoth, Forni gator, Anector, Somiator, sleep ye not, awake the strong hero Holaha, the powerful Eaton, the mighty Tetragramaton; Athe, Alpha et Omega, compel ye that the thief may return the stolen articles into the house of N.N., and that the thief shall have neither rest nor peace through sand and land, through sea or air, on mountain or rock, thou accursed devil, lead the thief back into my house with all the stolen goods.

Behold the mighty God. St. Zaphael be thy prayer, be thy compulsion, the ark of God, the ark of the covenant of the dwelling of the Lord shall aid me to bring the rope for ye devils, and for this be God in God my helper in need and trouble. Jehovah, Saboah, Emanuel, ah Jathos Noio sottis, Ishiros, Kiriel aios Fius Imago Via Veritas Salvator Oberator Tetragramatum Stoch Nahus tribelasus Spenter omnipotens Venus, Sanitus, Trinus, Imenesus, Virtus, Principitatis, Liberator Manus Erobye, Mediator Imbrator Oulus Prillus, teris Judaea arnes humuisien. Psalm 91. Pray: Satan, thou accursed devil, hast thou heard the power of Adonay, our great Lord, then thou must through the power of Jehovah at once compel the thief who has robbed N.N. and force him (or her) that these stolen things be returned into my N.N.'s house.

Immanuel is thy commander, Sada drive thee with the thief into my house. Ishiros force thee, agios Imperator Dominus God Alpha and Omega may send his heavenly power, Cherubim and Seraphim, these mighty princes of heaven. St. Michael, St. Gabriel, St. Sephael, St. Uriel the transparent and penetrating mediator be mediator between thee and me.[2] Hereby I conjure the thief that thou be obedient and tractable like the lightning's flash, obedient to Almighty God; to this end help me, God Father, Son and Holy Spirit.

2. The term "Sephael" is almost certainly a mistranscription of "Raphael."

APPENDIX 4: LIFE DATES OF TWENTIETH-CENTURY POWWOWERS IN THIS STUDY

Table A1 summarizes life dates on powwowers in my study whose name is known or who have been associated with a named consultant. Sometimes these life dates are imprecise and the powwower can be described merely as being "old" at a certain time, therefore providing a clue about their birth date and a limit to their death date. The latter information will take the form "old in 19XX."

I have omitted information that simply notes that a given powwower was alive at a certain time, without clues to the powwower's age. Arrangement of the powwowers is roughly chronological. Information deriving solely from documentary or secondary sources is indicated in italics.

Table A1. Life dates of selected twentieth-century powwowers

Powwower	Life Dates
Andrew Blymire	*1838-1933*
Mrs. Knopt (aka Emma Noll)	*1839-at least 1929*
Katharine George	1845–at least 1930 (deceased by 1938)
Ivan Glick's great-grandmother	Old in 1910
Mary Zetmeyer	c. 1850 to at least 1945
Alice Levengood's great-uncle	Old in 1920
Lovina Arndt	Old in 1920
Nelson D. Rehmeyer	*1869-1929*
Emanuel Blymire	*1870-at least 1929*
"Aunt" Sophia Bailer	*1870-1955*
Mary "Ma" Koenig	1871–at least 1950
Bessie May Weber	1875–1969
Rachel Rahn*	c. 1875–1969
Amanda Farley's* grandmother	Old in 1940s
Marge Lick's grandmother	Old in 1945
Milo Schaeffer	c. 1880 to at least 1930
Barb Reed's grandmother	c. 1880–1971
Old Man Horne	Old in 1955
"Professor" Howard Resh	*1886 to at least 1969*
"Professor" Erwin Emig	*1890 to at least 1967*
Maude Kreisher	*1895 to least 1976*
John Blymire	*1896-1971*
Ida Wagner	1899–1995
Mr. Heebner	c. 1900–1970

Lulu McClure	Old in 1969
Oscar "Doc" Long	Old in 1970
Gertie Guise	Old in 1970s (deceased by 1979)
Ruth Stoner	Old in 1976
Robert Frantz	Old in 1981 (deceased in 1980s)
Preston Zerbe	1907–1993
Helen Bechtel	1910 to at least 1966
Ruth Strickland Frey	1911–1993
Calvin E. Rahn*	1916–1981
Katharine Eberle	1916–
Florida Ross's mother*	1930–
Aaron Boehm*	1931– (still active)
Calvin M. Rahn*	1933–1999
Julius Dietrich*	1938–2005
Anita Rahn*	1939– (still active)
Daisy Dietrich*	1941– (still active)
Leah Stoltzfus*	1942– (still active)
Mrs. May	1945– (still active)
Judy McMullin	1946–
Ivan Fisher	c. 1950–
Jenine Trayer	*1956– (still active)*

* Pseudonym.

APPENDIX 5: CHARACTERISTICS OF TWENTIETH-CENTURY POWWOWERS IN THIS STUDY

The information in Appendix 5 was extracted from my research. Although random sampling was impossible to achieve in this study, making statistical inferences unreliable, the aggregate data do present a more-or-less accurate picture of the practice of powwowing as it existed during the twentieth century.

Sex

Table A2. Sex of powwowers in the twentieth century

Male	46
Female	43
Unknown	1
Total	90

County of Residence

Table A3. County of residence of twentieth-century powwowers noted in this book (total number of responses: 88)

York	21
Berks	14
Lancaster	14
Lebanon	13
Lehigh	8
Schuylkill	5
Montgomery	4
Carbon	3
Adams	2
Bucks	2
Northampton	2

Type of Clientele

Table A4 classifies powwowers according whether they were considered a healing resource by other than relatives, friends, and neighbors. It includes only powwowers about whom there was a clear indication of the type of clientele served.

Table A4. Powwowers' clientele restrictions (total number of responses: 58)

Clientele Restricted to Family, Friends, Neighbors	Clientele Not Restricted
7	51

Size of Clientele

Table A5 classifies powwowers according to the rough size of their clientele, when such information was available.

Table A5. Size of powwowers' clientele (total number of responses: 28)

Size of Clientele	Number of Powwowers
Large clientele	15
Medium clientele	8
Small clientele	5

Payment

Table A.6. Payment options (total number of responses: 42)

Payment Option	Number of Powwowers
Donations accepted	19
No donations accepted	13
Fee specified	10

Range of Ailments Treated

Rarely was any information available on the extent of a powwower's healing power vis-à-vis other powwowers, although often it was assumed that powwowing could treat any ailment. Table A7 is based on explicit indications of the range of ailments treatable by powwowing.

Table A7. Range of ailments treatable by powwowing (total number of responses: 19)

Range of Ailments Treatable	Number of Powwowers
Any	10
Many	4
Few	5

Special Area Used

Some powwowers used special areas of their house set aside for powwowing rituals, or had separate offices for their powwowing practice. Table A8 is based on interview and documentary information on the setting for powwowing ritual.

Table A8. Use of special area for powwowing treatments (total number of responses: 22)

Special Area Used for Powwowing	Number of Powwowers
Yes	16
No	6

Questioning Patient About Belief

Some powwowers and patients indicated that belief in God was required for powwowing healing to be effective. Table A9 provides information on whether the question "Do you believe in God" was asked of patients by powwowers before powwowing treatment. (There is no scaling in these responses; either the powwower always asked this question or never did.)

Table A9. Frequency of questioning patients about belief (total number of responses: 11)

Frequency	Number of Powwowers
Always Asked	7
Never Asked	4

Use of Material Components in Rituals

Table A10 to the use of material components by powwowers. A "yes" response is scored when the use of such components by specific powwowers is attested in the data; a "no" response is scored when the powwower clearly never used such components.

Table A10. Use of material components (total number of responses: 27)

Material Components Used	Number of Powwowers
Yes	25
No	2

Use of Charm Books

Table A11 relates to the use of charm or spell books such as *The Long Lost Friend*. A "yes" response is scored when a powwower clearly used such books, a "no" response is scored when a powwower clearly never used such books (other than the Bible).

Table A11. Use of charm books (total number of responses: 15)

Charm Books Used	Number of Powwowers
Yes	9
No	6

Religious Reputation of Powwower

Table A12 relates to whether the powwower was regarded as religious by others.

Table A12. Public assessment of powwowers' religiosity (total number of responses: 90)

Religiosity	Number of Powwowers
Publicly religious	36
Not publicly religious	54

Age at Which Powwowing Was Learned

Table A13 relates to when in the life-cycle the powwower began his or her practice.

Table A13. Age at training (total number of responses: 16)

Age When Powwowing Learned	Number of Powwowers
Pre-teen	3
Teenager	3
Adult	8
Senior	2

Mode of Transmission

Table A14. Mode of transmission (total number of responses: 21)

Mode of Transmission	Number of Powwowers*
From opposite sex ("crossways")*	10
From same sex	7
From individual of unknown sex	2
Self-taught*	4

*Two of those born with the power ("self-taught") were also taught by members of the opposite sex in order to increase their power.

APPENDIX 6: DATA ON TWENTIETH-CENTURY RITUAL PRACTICE

This information in Appendix 6 derives from the eighty-nine twentieth-century cases Appendix 7, below. Because four of these cases involve me, they receive special consideration. I have decided not to include two of these in the data summaries in this section, the former because I attempted powwowing (apparently with success) myself, the latter because I am uncertain whether what took place (sensing my pain) should be classified as powwowing. I also decided to exclude from the question on belief two other cases in which I was a powwow patient. While my observations of the rituals in which I participated are germane to this study, my own belief or disbelief in the efficacy of those rituals is not.

Source of Cases

Table A15. Source of twentieth-century case data

Interview	65
Documentary research	29
Participant observation	4
Total	98

Purpose of Ritual

Table A16. Purpose of powwowing rituals

Healing	89
Nonhealing	7
Total	96

Success of Ritual

Table A17. Success of powwowing rituals

	Successful	Unsuccessful	Uncertain
Healing	80	8	1
Nonhealing	4	0	3
Total	84	8	4

Kinship Ties Between Powwower and Patient

Table A18. Kin relationship of powwower and patient

Powwower and patient related	21
No kinship relationship	74
Relationship uncertain	1
Total	96

Use of Christian Symbolism in Ritual (signs and utterances)

Data was available on only 75 of the 96 cases examined.

Table A19. Use of Christian symbolism

Definite*	36
Possible**	17
No	22
Total	75

*Prayer, crosses, Bible.
**Use of the number three, the presence of religious icons in the treatment area (for example, pictures of Jesus, crosses mounted on the wall, and so on), religious reputation of powwower.

Payment

Data was available on only 65 of the 96 cases examined.

Table A20. Payment of powwowers from cases

None	42
Donation	18
Specified fee	5
Total	65

Relationship of Belief and Treatment

This question refers to belief in the efficacy of powwowing held by powwowing patients. I excluded data on my own beliefs or disbeliefs following powwowing treatment.

Table A21. Relationship between belief and treatment

Belief preceded treatment	29
Belief followed treatment	16
No belief	10
Uncertain about belief	39
Total	94

Prior Consultation with Physicians

I excluded my own consultations with physicians for arthritis before my powwowing treatments.

Table A22. Prior consultation of physicians

Physician Consulted Prior to Powwowing Treatment	Number of Responses
Yes	18
No	73
Uncertain	3
Total	94

Use of Ritual Components

Below is a summary of the ritual components used in the twentieth-century cases of powwowing healing. My own experiment with powwowing is not included. Components are grouped by type (verbal, somatic, and ritual material).

All verbal components used by powwowers are incantations (whether prayer or other utterance) that are typically inaudible or unintelligible to the patient. Verbal components used by patients are always answers to questions posed by the powwower pertaining the patient's religious beliefs. Somatic components are further broken down into subcomponents (hand movements, laying on of hands, body position). Specific elements of material components are given under that category.

Table A23. Use of ritual components

Component	Used by Powwowers	Used by Patients
Verbal	61	2
Somatic (total)	47	14
Hand movements	28	0
Laying on of hands	16	2
Body position	3	12
Material (total)	47*	4
From powwower	5	0
From patient	4	0
From other human	1	1
From animal	9	0
From plant	4	2
String	8	0
Natural formation	2	0
Other	31	5

*Number of material components is less than the number of elements because one component may use more than one element.

APPENDIX 7: ADDITIONAL POWWOW CASES

The following cases were collected by myself and other researchers, most notably Sara Clark, Norma Gourley, Robert Graham, Arthur Lewis, and Don Yoder. Most of these are briefer than the cases described in Chapter 5, but all share the basic criteria: the event must be roughly datable and include a description of the illness, some details about the treatment procedure, and the result of treatment. These cases do not include a great deal of useful material beyond this basic information, but they nonetheless had an impact on my study.

Because simply picking up where the text left off would create inconsistencies between case number and chronology, I have chosen to number these cases with a unique system, so that the first case would be A1, the second A2, and so forth.

Cases A1–A4 are skeptical and hostile accounts of the practice from the point of view of the Reverend Daniel Weiser (Weiser 1868). He mentions other cases besides the ones listed here, but only in passing. His rhetoric describes believers in powwowing as ignorant, and the practitioners as both ignorant and evil. "Witches hate schoolhouses, as well as water and daylight." He claims that powwowing is in "direct opposition to the Divine Record" (Weiser 1868, 6).

Case A1: Cure for Erysipelas (mid-1800s)

In this case, a woman who was afflicted by erysipelas did not believe in Holy Baptism, because "a few drops of water cannot possibly contain any efficacy," but to placate her husband she had her children baptized. She did, however, believe a story by "some strolling vagabond" that three drops of blood from a big black cat without one white hair would permanently cure the worst case of erysipelas. She canvassed Berks County for such a cat and was unsuccessful in finding one. However, a neighbor woman ("a neighboring hag, equally credulous") assured her that a big black chicken would serve equally well. The blood from the cat was to come from the tip of its tail and contain the same effect as if taken directly from the heart. The chicken's caudal appendage was to serve the same function, but it contained no blood. Apparently some other portion of the chicken provided the blood, the chicken being killed in the process and its body discarded without being eaten. The woman swallowed the three drops of chicken blood and she was cured in three or four days.

At the same time, the couple's family physician had been visiting the house and treating the wife with "medicines and external applications." When the Reverend Weiser suggested that this might have something to do with the cure, the woman responded that the medicines had been worthless, "and besides, don't you know that no doctor can't do nothing with Arry-Siplis?" Weiser feared that by arguing with someone "familiar with the 'black arts' . . . we too might be charmed into their enchanted meshes," so he merely smiled and left. He noted that this woman who believed in the efficacy of "three drops of blood sucked from the head or tail of an out-and-out black cat or dunghill pheasant" did not believe in the "miraculous effects of the blood of Christ as of sufficient efficacy to cleanse of all sin" and that she and "those of her stripe and kidney" had often fallen asleep during his sermons on that topic at church.

Case A2: Cure for Erysipelas (mid-1800s)

A woman in her seventies, who the Reverend Weiser claims was not a churchgoer and who believed that anyone can be "good and sure of heaven, without complying with any such outward forms and ceremonies, in which no possible virtue can be said to reside," taught this philosophy to her children, and they followed in her footsteps. Yet for forty years "that same stubborn crone" traveled as a powwower, claiming to cure erysipelas and all kinds of diseases.

Weiser reports that this woman's cures were performed by blowing, sometimes onto hot coals or embers or from a fire, while speaking "a few talismanic words." He claims to have followed her many times into sick houses, which after her visit smelled "villainously of sulphur and brimstone," indicating that her powers were "not of good angels and the Holy Spirit." Weiser condemns her as "a nasty old sorceress" and states that "any man or woman sound in the faith would rather die or remain a life-long invalid . . . than owe either life or health to a hag, given to such infernal arts."

Weiser recommends that if people believe fire will cure erysipelas (called "wildfire," or "wildfeier" in the dialect), they should "sway the burning coals themselves over the affected parts and neutralize the heat, on the Homeopathic principle that 'like cures like,' without lending their endorsement to such laughable farce." He claims that people are slow to pray in times of affliction and chastisement, despite Jesus' words "If two or more agree concerning one thing, God will give it." This is the most objectionable part of powwowing, that people believe in and practice it in preference to "obedience and worship."

Weiser also opposes the practice of baptism for the purpose of protecting a child's health, claiming that by so doing "the sacramental is sacrificed, while the magical remains."

Case A3: Cure for Diphtheria (unsuccessful) (mid-1800s)

The Reverend Weiser went to a house in which a little boy lay dying of diphtheria, to comfort the parents and intercede for the boy. He waited to be asked to pray and finally had to volunteer. He was permitted to pray for the boy and left. That same night "a dastardly necromancer" was sent for, a man who lived seven miles away from the house. He "tore the soothing applications from the sore and swollen neck and chest of the dying child, and drawing in his vile breath, to swell himself up to the size of a bass drum, he belched a stinking hurricane of effluvia down the sore and ulcerous throat of the dying child." The boy later died, an event explained by Weiser as an act of mercy by Jesus, who "could not permit the barbarian to torture his lamb again."

Case A4: Stopping a Hemorrhage (mid-1800s)

A man's artery was severed, and the blood would not clot. A "famous sanguinary conjuress" was summoned. "She opened her series of signals; waved her sinewy hand back and long, bony fingers, and gyrated up and down, hither and thither, forward and backward, and repeated her wonder-working vocabulary in a frantic way." But the blood would not stop. Finally, his family summoned a physician, who applied a tourniquet and the blood stopped. The Reverend Weiser gleefully recounts how the physician lectured the family and the powwower about blood clots and what will and will not stop bleeding.

Cases A5–A7 concern a powwower called "Mother Weary"[1] in Ashland (Gourley 1936). These accounts were related to Gourley by E. E. Weimer, "an old Pennsylvania German" living in Illinois.

Case A5: Cure for Migraine (mid- to late-1800s)

When E. E. Weimer was a young man, his mother had "severe sick headaches" (from this description, they appear to have been migraines) at least once a week. At times she would "suffer so acutely that the seam in her head would part wide enough to accommodate two fingers" (it is not known to what this might refer). She treated this by filling a beef bladder (cow bladder?) with ice, but if this was ineffective she would "resort to powwowing." She was treated by "old Mother Weary," who went to the house and performed the following procedure:

Mother Weary moistened her fingers, placed them on Weimer's mother's head, drew three crosses, and repeated some Bible verses. Two days later she returned and repeated the same procedure. Shortly thereafter, Weimer's mother's headache was relieved. Weimer stated that his mother believed explicitly in powwowing.

Gourley believes that this procedure derived from *The Long Lost Friend*, which she cites. She then goes on to say that she is positive that this cure "would prove to be very inefficacious in our modern age" (Gourley 1936, 8).

Case A6: Cure for Yellow-Jacket Stings (mid- to late-1800s)

E. E. Weimer was out walking in a field when he was stung on his right instep by two yellow jackets. His father, who was skeptical about powwowing, called in the family physician and another physician for consultation. The two agreed that the foot had to be amputated to save Weimer's life. His father gave consent for this procedure, but his mother

1. Probably originally spelled "Wehry."

called in Mother Weary. Mother Weary came wrapped in an old shawl and, much to the disgust of Weimer's father, examined the leg. She then performed the following procedure:

"She made two crosses on the leg and recited some biblical verses. Then she pulled a string out of her shawl, drew it across the leg, doubled it in the middle, and hung it on the wall with a pin from her clothing. Later she returned, picked the string up, pulled it over his leg three times, repeating the Bible verses and making the two crosses. Soon the swelling started to recede and the leg got better" (Gourley 1936, 6).

Although Weimer denied that he was a believer in powwowing, he believed at the time of the interview with Gourley (many years after the event) that Mother Weary had saved his life.

Case A7: Cure for Toothache (mid- to late-1800s)

The first school that E. E. Weimer attended was directly across the road from Mother Weary's place, and the normal procedure when any pupil had a toothache was to go to see Mother Weary to have it powwowed. Her procedure involved making crosses on the head and on the affected tooth. One day when Weimer had a severe toothache, he went over there, but Mother Weary was not at home. Her husband, who did not know how to powwow, treated the tooth by placing asafetida on it. (Weimer did not know what it was at the time.) The pain subsided.

Case A8: A Spell to Call a Heifer (late 1800s)

When Don Yoder's consultant "Aunt" Sophia Bailer[2] was a young girl, her family moved from Berks County to Schuylkill County. Her brother John had a boarder there and also owned a few pigs and a cow (he was raising all the animals for slaughter). One morning they found the heifer gone. The boarder rose from a card table (presumably in the parlor), took a pack of cards, and laid them on the table and asked John to go out and get him three hairs from where the heifer was lying, promising that the animal would (otherwise) be dead in half an hour.

2. From Bailer's "Witches I Have Known" (1952a).

John brought the hairs, and the man took them and went into the open field. Aunt Sophia believes he said or did something, but no one was present with him. The heifer soon came running, jumped over the fence, came up to the man, and bleated.

Case A9: Cure for Burns (1900s)

My great-grandparents, Howard and Bessie May (Weber) Kriebel, had a hot stove in front of their house. One of the neighbor children touched it and burned his hand. My great-grandmother (who said she could "powwow") and great-grandfather healed the burn by laying on of hands. Bessie May also claimed to be able to either find water or cause it to rain (my consultant, my father James, was not clear on this point). There is also a legend that she put a "curse" on anyone who would ever try to harm any member of our family, but when I asked if that was a hex, my father denied it.

Case A10: Removal of a Sty in the Eye (1910)

Ivan Glick of Lancaster reports that his Old Order Amish father had a sty in his eye when he was a boy that was removed by Ivan's great-grandmother (also Amish) through powwowing. Her procedure was to remove a coal shovel from hot coals and recite a charm. The sty was gone after that.

Case A11: Cure for Rupture (about 1910)

Abe Roan repeated the account of a man from Rittersville (Lehigh County) who said his father could "powwow for rupture." His method was to go with his patient to the county line in a place near a willow tree. He would straddle the line, take a pen knife, and cut three hairs from the patient's head. Then he would go to the willow tree, make a slash in the trunk, and insert the hairs into the slash. When the slash in the tree's bark healed, the patient's rupture would heal.

Case A12: Spell to Calm a Mad Dog[3] (1912)

Arthur H. Lewis (1969, 23–24) cites Amos King's account of how John Blymire (later one of the defendants in the York Hex Murder Trial) stopped a mad collie in its tracks. Frothing at the mouth and howling, the dog was running toward King and some other men leaving work at a cigar factory. Suddenly Blymire, then seventeen, stepped out in front of the dog, and the animal stopped, although it was still howling and frothing at the mouth. Blymire looked the dog in the eye and whispered something to it, and everyone, including the dog, became quiet; the only sound audible was the dog's panting. Then Blymire made the sign of the cross over the collie's head. It stopped frothing at the mouth and Blymire petted it. The dog started licking Blymire's hand. Then Blymire walked away, and the dog followed him, wagging its tail.

Case A13: Cure for the Take-Off (1912–14)

Eugene Smith was taken as a young boy to see a Mrs. Koenig in Lancaster (almost certainly Mary "Ma" Koenig; see cases A52 and A53 for later cases involving her) to be cured of the *abnehme*, or the "take-off." Both Smith's family and Mrs. Koenig lived in the Cabbage Hill area of the city, a clannish neighborhood that was home to many Lutheran and Roman Catholic German immigrant families (their motto was "the Hill against the world"). The procedure took about thirty minutes, including the exchange of pleasantries. Smith recalls that Mrs. Koenig had him sit in a chair, then prayed over him and moved a red string over his body, working from head to toe. He reports that his mother was satisfied that the ritual had cured him of the ailment, although Smith himself had no idea anything was wrong with him in the first place.

Cases A14–A17 relate to Abram Huber, who practiced until his death in 1918. They all derive from Robert Graham's interview with Huber's grandson, Graybill Huber (Graham 1951). Abram's cures were witnessed by Graybill, who related them to Graham. Graham wrote them down,

3. From the description, the dog was probably afflicted with rabies.

then checked his work by showing what he had written to Graybill, who concurred.

Case A14: Two Cures for Warts (1910s)

Abram Huber had two cures for warts:

1. He would tell his patient to go out and find a whip. When the patient had done this, he would bring it to Abram, who would cut three notches in the handle. He would then tell the patient to go to the nearest crossroads and leave it there. The first person who came along and picked up the whip would get the wart the patient had had.
2. He would take a plate and hold it over the patient's face. He would then rub the plate three times while quoting a passage from the Bible.

Case A15: Cure for Bee Sting (1910s)

Abram Huber would take a salt solution and rub over the area where the patient had been stung. The patient was then to go straight home and talk to no one along the way. By the time the patient arrived home, the sting and stinger would be gone.

Case A16: Cure for Erysipelas (1910s)

Abram Huber has a cure for erysipelas, but he did not like to use it, because if the patient was cured, there was a great chance that he might catch it himself and be unable to get rid of it.

Case A17: Cure for Rupture (1910s)

Abram Huber sent the patient to get an egg from the nest of a black hen and told him not to speak to anyone on the entire trip. When the patient brought the egg back to Abram's office, Abram would rub the egg across the ruptured area three times and then put the egg in an oven and close the door. When the white and yolk had completely evaporated, the rupture would be gone.

Case A18: Stopping Bleeding in a Steer (1919)

Elizabeth "Tilly" (Burkman) (Mock) Noll reports that once when a steer on her parents' farm was dehorned the animal bled profusely, prompting her parents to call a veterinarian. The veterinarian could do nothing, so they sent word to a powwower requesting his help. The man did not come to the farm but powwowed remotely, without even a telephone (because he had none). The steer's bleeding stopped immediately afterward.

Case A19: Wart Removal (1923 or 1924)

John Hickernell of Schaefferstown (Lebanon County) remembers that his neighbor, Eliza Hartmann, removed a painful wart on his hand using a penny. She instructed him to put a penny (probably provided by her) on top of the wart and rub it, telling him not to look at the date on the penny. Then she said, "I bought the wart for a penny." The wart vanished within a week.

Case A20: Cure for Erysipelas (1923 or 1924)

Eugene "Genie" Young, who lived near Smithville (Lehigh County), powwowed my consultant Mary Weaver's sister for erysipelas. He used "scripture," touched her on the arm, and said something. She was healed of the disease after that.

Case A21: Cure for Erysipelas (early 1920s)

John Hickernell's brother-in-law Henry Ruth used to "powwow" and was especially good in curing erysipelas (he had a 90 percent cure rate). However, he always got the erysipelas himself, although it would disappear in a couple of days. Another powwower said he got the disease because his faith wasn't strong enough.

Case A23: Locating an Individual (early 1920s)

My consultant Mrs. Levengood of Schaefferstown (Lebanon County) recalls that her maternal great-uncle believed that he was responsible for bringing a young man from the area, then in a Virginia jail, home. She asked how he did it, and all he said was, "The Seven Books of Moses." She did not recall whether this was actually "The Sixth and Seventh Books of Moses" but notes, "You'd be surprised how many people had those books in their homes many years ago."

Case A24: Cure for "Rote Laufa" (Erysipelas) (1920s)

When Harry Adam of Hamburg (Berks County) was vaccinated, he developed *rote laufa*, one of the dialect terms for erysipelas. His great-grandmother Katharine George put her hand over the affected area, and Harry could see her lips move but could hear nothing. She told him it was a Bible verse.

Cure A25: Cure for Side Stitches (1920s)

When Harry Adam was a boy, he would get "side stitches," a kind of cramping in the side. He and his wife Erma believed that people never talked about side stitches anymore, although I recall as a child (1960s and 1970s) my older relatives warning me I'd get a "stitch" from running around too much. His great-grandmother, grandmother, and father "did for that" by spitting on a stone and throwing it over Harry's head.

Case A26: Cure for Bloating in Cattle (1920s)

Harry Adam's family had twenty head of cattle on their farm, which was considered "quite a herd" at that time. Sometimes the cattle ate clover, which would kill them if not treated. One time, the whole herd had eaten clover and all the cattle were bloated. Harry recalls the incident: "My great-grandmother said, 'Let me at them.' She went and brought the cattle in. The idea was to make them run and deflate them. So she went from cow to cow. She was repeating certain verses in the Bible. None of them died. She couldn't go too well, but the cattle wasn't frisky, so she could follow."

Case A27: Wart Removal (1920s)

Mary Louise Gingrich, the Lebanon reporter who covered the story of Mrs. May's arrest, had a great-grandmother who powwowed (Lehigh and Monroe counties). When her mother was a young girl, her great-grandmother removed a wart from the child by tying a string around her head while "praying or mumbling something." Then she buried the string. When the string rotted, the wart disappeared.

Mary Louise said that people feared her great-grandmother, but when I asked whether she put hexes on people, she replied that she did not think so. However, she did use *The Sixth and Seventh Books of Moses* (Mary Louise's mother called it "The Fifth Book of Moses," but she admitted that her mother might have been mistaken about that, because the fifth book of Moses is the biblical Book of Deuteronomy). Many Pennsylvania Dutch who know about that book associate it with black magic, because it contains formulae for conjuring demons.

Case A28: Healing a Foot Injury (1925 to 1928)

When Harriet Miller was a young girl (ten to thirteen years of age) she was hired out by her father to work on a farm in Berks County. During this time, she lived with her grandmother, who was a powwower. While she was working, Harriet stepped on a fishbone and cut her foot badly. The physician (Doctor Fritsch) wanted her to go to the hospital, but Harriet called for her grandmother, Rosina Arndt, who told her to walk around the pasture barefoot and step in cow dung. This procedure actually healed the injury.

Case A29: Cure for Whooping Cough (late 1920s)

When Alton Stein (born 1921) was "a little kid," he had a terrible case of whooping cough. A physician made the diagnosis but did not cure him of the cough. As Alton describes it, "I was coughing my silly head off. It hurt real bad, but I couldn't keep from coughing."

His parents took him to a powwower, an old man who lived on a farm, but Alton does not remember its location. He does, however, remember the old touring car in which they rode, and how cold it was that winter day with only the window curtains for protection.

They took Alton into the man's kitchen, and the man sat the boy in a kitchen chair. Alton recalls that the man said "verses of the Bible," although he does not remember the exact incantation. He does not recall any hand gestures on the part of the powwower. Immediately after the powwow ritual was finished, his coughing stopped and never recurred.

Case A30: Cure for Erysipelas (1929)

When Elizabeth "Tilly" (Burkman) (Mock) Noll (Lebanon County) was pregnant with her first child, she developed erysipelas, which made her hands red and itchy. The physicians she consulted did not know what to do, so she went to see an elderly woman in Kleinfeltersville. The woman ran her hands over the affected area (without touching the skin) and her mouth moved, but Tilly could not make out what she was saying. She began to experience relief a quarter of a mile after leaving the powwower's. The next day the redness and itching were gone.

Case A31: Finding a Lost Relative (early 1930s)

This case concerns the same "*brau* doctor" mentioned in Case 6 in Chapter 5. Mrs. Schultz's family was attempting to find a lost uncle, whom she characterized as a "tramp."

> I had an uncle who left his family of three children, and he just disappeared. Of course, they didn't know if he had been killed or he was dead, and different things, and they would go to this guy [the "*brau* doctor"] and he would, I think, pray for him [the uncle]. They said they were going to powwow for him, and he would tell them—oh, no, he's alive, and I don't know if he would know what he was saying, but he said, he's far away, and he did

come back after about a year. He had been in California. He was just a tramp, and he came home like a bum.

Case A32: Hex Removal (1936)

Around 1936 in Berks County, a boy was hexed by a witch so that he would become very sick and die (Shaner 1961). His grandmother insisted that his parents take him to a "*brauch* doctor" in Emmaus, Lehigh County. When they arrived, the *brauch* doctor told the parents why they came to him and what the nature of the boy's sickness was, without the parents having spoken a word. He told them that the child was hexed by someone in that locality and how to break the spell while at the same time exacting revenge on the witch. He told them to do the following:

1. Make a wood figure of the witch.
2. Drive a nail into the figure—but not the heart, or the witch would die.
3. Bury the figure in the ground.

The father did all this after he arrived home. Within three days the child showed improvement, and one of their neighbors, a woman, received a broken leg. The leg that was broken was on the same side as the wood figure's leg, into which the father had driven a nail. Thus, the boy lived and the "witch" suffered a broken leg for her meanness.

Case A33: Cure for St. Vitus Dance (1938)

Tilly Noll took her nine-year-old daughter to a male powwower from Terre Hill (Lancaster County). The man's office was lined with books. His hands moved over the girl and he whispered, but she could not hear what she was saying. She thinks that he was speaking out of the Bible (Ezekiel 9). The treatment took nine weeks, during which time the daughter was to follow Tilly all the time. They went to see the powwower once a week, on Sundays. At the end of that time, the symptoms started to disappear. Tilly noted that the condition came on slowly and went away slowly. The man received a weekly payment "in the two- or three-dollar range."

Case A34: Cure for Kidney Infection (1938–39)

Hazel Sauer reports that Rachel Rahn cured her daughter of a kidney infection when the girl was an infant and the Sauers shared a house with Mrs. Rahn and her children. Mrs. Rahn's procedure was to hold the infant on her lap, running her hands up and down her and speaking words under her breath. The girl recovered.

Hazel believes powwowing can cure nearly any ailment. She specifically named kidney problems, gallstones, eczema, psoriasis, bleeding, upset stomach, goiter, and infected teeth.

Case A35: Cure for Psoriasis (late 1930s)

Hazel Sauer reports that Mrs. Rahn cured psoriasis using an egg and string when she roomed with Hazel's family in Glenville. "She took a string around the egg, and whatever she did, she put it in a cook stove and burned it." The stove used wood and coal for fuel. The phrase "whatever she did" refers to some kind of incantation that Hazel could not hear.

Case A36: Cure for Eczema (late 1930s)

Hazel said that Mrs. Rahn cured a child of eczema by passing a red silk string over the child's body while "mumbling."

Case A37: Cure for Bedwetting (late 1930s)

Tilly Noll took her son, Clifford, and youngest child, Erma, to the same Terre Hill powwower to cure their bedwetting. He and the children would sit on kitchen chairs, facing each other. "He sat in front of you and talked," Clifford said. "He moved his hands in front of you." Both Clifford and Tilly agreed that it worked.

Case A38: Wart Removal (1940)

According to an article in the *Philadelphia Inquirer* (Schreiber 1976), Maude Kreisher was tending her husband's general store in Reading when a child came in with warts on his hand. She "prayed" for them to go away, and they did. The child was astounded and spread the news. It was the beginning of her powwow practice.

Case A39: Wart Removal (1940)

Harry Heebner,[4] a Schwenkfelder and prominent Republican politician in Center Point (Montgomery County), reports that his father could "powwow" warts. In this case, a man who worked for a farm co-op met his father near Center Point, and his father noticed that the man had warts all over his hands. His father offered to remove them. He wet his tongue, touch his fingers to it, and then rub the spittle all over the man's hands. When they met later, his father asked the man whether he still had warts. The man replied yes, but then looked at his hands and saw that the warts were all gone.

Harry believes in powwowing and wishes that his father had passed the ability to his sisters, but they were not interested in learning. He would have learned it himself, except that one male cannot teach another male.

Cases A40–A44 are from Susan Stewart's 1976 study of powwowing in rural York County.

Case A40: Cure for Livergrown and Pneumonia (1940s)

In rural York County in the 1940s, members of one poor family who lived on a tenant farm often asked the son of the farmer to take them to a local "powwow doctor" to be cured (Stewart 1976). The children often suffered from a malady called "taking off" or "livergrown."[5] The powwow doctor attempted to cure the sick child by putting him through a horse collar or making the child crawl around a table leg. If the child had pneu-

4. Pseudonym.

5. As I understand it, the "take-off" (*abnehme, abnehmes, abnehmedes*) is not the same as "livergrown" (*aa-gewachse, ahgewachse*). The "take-off" is a wasting disease, and "livergrown" is supposed to cause abdominal pain.

monia, the powwow doctor would throw an egg into the stove while speaking a charm.

Case A41: Cure for Stomach Fever (1940s)

In the community where her family lived, Mrs. X's father was well known as someone who could powwow for stomach fever, or, in children, "livergrown" (Stewart 1976, 14). Mrs. X defined "livergrown" as not growing properly, causing stomach upset. In adults she described it as a "cramp in your stomach." Stomach fever and livergrown both involved nausea—"You can't keep nothing down."

Her father cured stomach fever as follows. He took a fresh chicken egg and wrapped a "cord string" around it "not lengthwise, but the round way" (I take this to mean the circular cross-section of an egg). While he wrapped the egg in string, he said things, but he could not tell Mrs. X what it was because she was a relative (he could confide in strangers, though). After he had wrapped the egg, he put it in the fire. "If the egg busted, why, you had stomach fever and it would be cured. If it didn't bust, you didn't have stomach fever, and then you'd have to seek for something else for a cure. I guess you went to a regular doctor—I don't know."

Mrs. X did not know how her father learned to powwow, but she believed it had to have been a friend because it could not be passed from one family member to another.

Mrs. X believed that physicians used watered-down powwow cures to keep patients coming back.

Case A42: Powwowing for "Sore Mouth" (1940s)

For illnesses that her father could not cure, Mrs. X's family went to the local powwow doctor, who lived on the next farm (Stewart 1976, 15). When Mrs. X's brother was young, he had "an awful sore mouth," and the family got a Mrs. H to powwow for him. She took straw from the barn, from the cow's stable, and placed the straw in the boy's mouth. She spoke as she moved the straw in the boy's mouth, but no one could hear what she said. This was common, Mrs. X indicated. "The person being cured usually can't hear what the powwower says."

Case A43: Taking the Fire out of Burns (1940s)

Another time, a baby cousin of the Mrs. X spilled a cup of hot coffee on himself. A woman powwow doctor came every day and "took the fire out" of the burns with her cures.

Case A44: Countering a Hex (1940s)

Mrs. X's other brother had a fever at age six, and the family suspected he had been hexed by an old woman who was a neighbor, whom they had always blamed for various community misfortunes. They took the boy to a powwow doctor (apparently another neighbor), who took a lock of the boy's hair, bored a hole in the doorway that the boy passed through, right at the boy's height, and drove the lock of hair into the hole with a wooden peg. The boy immediately got better.

Mrs. X's mother had blamed the same woman, whom they called a "witch," for the death of a previous child, who had died in a diphtheria epidemic. (It is interesting that witchcraft was invoked even when a natural cause [the epidemic]was sufficient to explain the event.) Mrs. X's family also believed that the witch had killed her own son because he joined the army, telling him, "You'll never get any farther than camp." Mrs. X claimed that in the book of World War I casualties one would find his name with the legend "Died in camp—cause unknown."

Case A45: Wart Removal (1940s)

Amanda Farley's grandmother, who was a York County powwower, removed a wart from Amanda's finger by tying a string around it and burying it in the soil of a house plant. She was supposed to bury it in the backyard, but they didn't have a backyard so they used the potted plant, and the wart went away in a couple of days. Amanda believes that the ability to powwow can be passed from mother to daughter but never from mother to son. This view contradicts the orthodox belief that the skill must be passed on through cross-gender transmission.

Case A46: Placing a Hex (1940s)

Deborah Meck,[6] a reflexologist in Lebanon, recalls that when she was a young girl she stayed overnight at the house of a friend, whose family shared it with a "little skinny woman in her nineties" named Mary Zetmeyer. This woman always wanted Deborah to come to the house and stay overnight. Deborah remembers that after they went to bed the old woman took a juice glass, filled it with water, covered the glass with a piece of rolling paper, and placed a toothpick on top of the paper. She placed the glass in front of her friend's bedroom door. Deborah woke up in the middle of the night, hearing the old woman talking to her friend, saying "Lay straight, lay straight" over and over again. In the morning, her friend complained that the old woman had hexed her.

Case A47: Cure for Migraines (1945)

Mary Glick in Bethlehem (Northampton County) was powwowed by her grandmother over the telephone for migraine headaches when she was eight years old. Because it was by telephone, she was unable to observe any gestures, but it did seem to cure her migraines. Mary is a believer in powwow and would use it now.

Case A48: Removal of a Sty from the Eye (mid-late 1940s)

A woman in her late fifties or early sixties who worked at the Hess station in Schaefferstown (Lebanon County) reports that her grandmother "powwowed" to remove a sty from her eye when she was six or seven years old. Her procedure was to place a wedding ring over the eye in such a way that the ring encircled the eye. After the sty was gone, she asked her grandmother what she had done, and her grandmother said, "I couldn't

6. Pseudonym.

tell you if I did remember." The woman reported that anytime there was a health problem in the family, her grandmother would say "I'll powwow for it."

Case A49: Cure for a Wasting Disease, Possibly Tapeworm (1948–50)

Elaine Madeira was taken by her parents to Mrs. A to be cured of a wasting disease that apparently involved passing worms. This was when Elaine was between six and eight years of age. "Dr. Brunner couldn't even cure it. We went to this woman, and she worked on me. We went about four to five times because I was seriously, really, ill. I had a problem keeping food down."

When they arrived at Mrs. A's one-room shack in the mountains, Elaine said, "Everything was ready. Like the first time my parents came in and she asked why they were bringing me back, and they told her what was wrong with me. She said, 'Okay, you have to leave. I'll take care of her.'"

She had Elaine close her eyes, then began her ritual by moving her hands over Elaine's body.

David: When she ran her hands over you, did she run it over your entire body or just the parts that seemed to be affected?
Elaine: I could feel her rub my stomach.
David: When you opened your eyes and looked at her, where was she moving her hands?
Elaine: She was finished. I peeked one time and seen her moving her hands over my whole body, and she was mumbling something. It seemed that all the things she was saying were the same.
David: Was she whispering?
Elaine: She wasn't loud.
David: She was speaking in another language, not Dutch?
Elaine: If it was Dutch, I could have understood it.

The cure worked after about the fourth visit (when Elaine was eight), and they did not return to Mrs. A: "I had only about three or four sessions.[7] Then I started getting my appetite back. They found out I was very active. My metabolism was very high, and I wasn't gaining or losing weight. I stayed at a weight level. So they didn't bother taking me back, because she said I would be okay."

Case A50: Powwow Against a Witch (late 1940s)

A few years before 1952 a man came to see Sophia Bailer at Tremont, asking her to powwow for his wife (Bailer 1952b). When she asked what was wrong, he said (in Sophia's words, word breaks preserved, punctuation amended), "Someone comes at night and torments her, sits on me ⟦her⟧, and all most kills me ⟦her⟧, taking my ⟦her⟧ breath." Sophia said it sounded like a witch was doing it.

She told the husband to go to the drugstore, buy a new bottle that had never been used, and get a pack of new pins and a pack of new needles. She instructed him to place nine of the new needles and nine of the new pins in the bottle, points up. (It is not clear whether this step was before or after the next one, because she added it later in the conversation as an afterthought. It is also not clear how this operation was to be accomplished, unless the pins and needles had flat bases.) The husband was then to defecate ("void") in the bottle before sunrise, talking to no one and allowing no one to talk to him, and then to lock the bottle in a wooden box, chest, or trunk (which Sophia supplied) and putty the keyhole shut. The person who locked the box was not to be the one who carried the key (Sophia performed the latter function). Finally, the couple was not to loan anything in or out of the house and not leave anything standing in or out of the house, not even the laundry on the clothesline.

The husband did all this. He said "some thing" came at night and rattled the box so much that it was impossible to sleep. He saw it (the thing) was a young girl who begged "her" (probably a reference to the wife) to open the box because she could get no rest. This young girl told the couple: "You went to Tremont to a woman, and she told you what to do. I took a bucket of water and I seen her picture in the water and I made her good and sick." Sophia became sick with stomach trouble but

7. A slight discrepancy, probably due to the vagaries of remembering an event that took place more than fifty years ago. Essentially, Elaine was at Mrs. A's about four times, possibly with a fifth scheduled but proving to be unnecessary.

didn't know what was wrong. Sophia then says (apparently quoting the witch; the lack of punctuation in the original makes it difficult to follow), "If I would have known it right away, she would be under the ground."

After this event, Sophia "called a blessing" on the wife to stop the witch.

The man (and presumably his wife) moved to Allentown. Sophia believed they moved to avoid the witch.[8]

Case A51: Cure for "Anything" (late 1940s-1971)

Barb Reed (born in 1941) reports that her grandmother (Lehigh County), who was known as a healer, used to powwow her for "anything" from childhood to age thirty. Her procedure remained the same: she moved her hand back and forth and said "In the name of the Father, Son, and Holy Ghost," inserting the patient's name at the end. Barb believes in the efficacy of powwowing. She is now a born-again Christian and encounters some opposition from her church concerning her belief in powwowing and her grandmother's activities.

Case A52: Cure for a Skin Disease, Possibly Erysipelas (1949)

This account concerns a man who went to Mary Koenig to be healed. A man who had been working in a pretzel factory developed an external cancer of the lip. "He was, of course, fired from his job immediately," the article notes, and as the cancer got worse he was unable to find work. The sore was open and festering and, according to Ma Koenig, emitted a "lecherous" smell. He tried a number of physicians, without any result. Either they could not help him or they refused to take his case because he had no money. Finally, one of them jokingly suggested that he try Ma Koenig, which he did. The first thing she did was cover the wound and begin her prayer treatment. Within two weeks he was completely cured. He passed a medical examination and returned to his job in the pretzel factory.

8. The phenomenon described resembles the "Old Hag" or "Mara" experiences documented by Hufford (1982). The cure is similar to that of Mrs. K's encounter with a witch.

Case A53: Cure for Wart (unsuccessful) (1950)

After Mary Koenig was finished treating Graham for sleeplessness (see Case 11 in Chapter 5), she called his friend with the wart over (Graham 1951). The ritual was much briefer in his case. "She only held his wart with one finger and mumbled her saying." She then told him his wart would be gone some morning when he awakened. Two weeks later, the friend still had the wart but remained hopeful it would go away.

At the end, Graham and his friend offered to pay her, but she told them she never charged firemen, policemen, or college students. Both students found the experience interesting.

Cases A54–A55 are from Don Yoder's consultant "Aunt" Sophia Bailer, based on letters to Yoder and interviews conducted by him that were published in *The Pennsylvania Dutchman* in the summer of 1952. In each of these cases, the relevant section is reproduced verbatim but with errors of punctuation, capitalization, and spelling corrected (the original is run together without any punctuation or capitalization).

Case A54: Powwow for Livergrown (1952)

"Aunt" Sophia Bailer tells in her own words her method for curing livergrown:

> Now I am going to tell you how to cure any person that is livergrown and heart span as I was taught. You take lard in a saucer, put a little camphorated oil in. Put about a half teaspoon in the lard. Melt it over the fire. Grease the person over the chest and the back and go down the chest and back with your two hands and say:
>
> Livergrown heart span
> Move out of this body
> Like Jesus Christ moved out of the Manger!
> God the Father God the Son and God the Holy Ghost
> Help to this amen!

I done this to some people that were grown ups. A doctor in our town wants me to do it. He even tells them (presumably his patients) to get me.

Case A55: Stopping a Hemorrhage (1952)

"Aunt" Sophia Bailer tells how to stop bleeding:

> I have stopped some people that were bleeding out of the nose by calling on God for his help, some that were bleeding by being hurt in the mines that the doctor said he would die.
>
> They phoned his name to me and I stopped it by calling on God.
> This is another one I am going to tell you. When one is bleeding, you say
> Jesus Christ Dearest blood
> That stoppest the blood
> In this help [NN]
> (mention the name as he is christianed)
> God the Father God the Son God the Holy Ghost amen!
> Help to this!
>
> You must walk while you do it. Then when you are finished, say the Lord's Prayer.

Case A56: Cure for Bad Nerves (1952)

Joyce Doxtater reports that when she was a child she would take a relative who was a powwower to treat another relative for "bad nerves." She does not recall any details of the treatment, but the fact that it occurred regularly for an indeterminate time, rather than for a set series of sessions, makes it notable.

> And then, my first experience with powwow was back in early 1952, I'd say. A distant relative of mine, we actually picked up this man in Lebanon, Charles Allwein. He was a powwow doctor

> and we'd take him to this relative who lived, probably about forty miles away. And all I knew at that time—I was just a kid—that this relative had nerve problems, "bad nerves" they were called at that time. And he'd powwow her, I think it was every other Wednesday night, and that supposedly kept her from being sent to a mental hospital. Now that's what I was told.

Case A57: Wart Removal (early 1950s)

Clifford Mock, Tilly Noll's son, developed warts all over his hands as he worked. Charlie Hartman said he'd buy them for a penny. He gave Clifford a penny and all the warts went away. "That made me a believer," Clifford said.

Case A58: Hex Removal (1950s)

Joyce Doxtater's mother said Joyce's two younger brothers were hexed by a woman who made a sign at them and said that they were bad and that she was putting a hex on them. As a result of the hex, the boys could not sleep at night. Her mother believes the woman had "taken their rest." Joyce's mother broke the spell by placing a Bible under the boys' pillows and making the sign of the cross on their beds.

Cases A59–A60 are from Sam Kriebel, a distant cousin of mine who lives on a two-hundred-year-old family farm outside Souderton (Montgomery County). Sam believed that some practitioners were good and some were evil: "Some was of the Lord, some was demon powers. I know to whom was a powwow." Sam was originally Reformed but is now a Mennonite, a sect that usually condemns all powwowing as from the devil. He also mentioned that there used to be many powwowers in the Souderton area: "'*Brauch doktor*' was mentioned many times around Souderton."

Case A59: Healing Severe Leg Pain (1950s)

Sam Kriebel's mother was powwowed by a man who lived three or four miles from his farm. His mother could not walk because her legs hurt.

"The man told her, 'Edna, you're going to get more pain. Come in two days.'" Sam's mother's legs hurt terribly and were swollen, but two days later, she got up, went to the man's house, and walked in. The man never charged for what he had done.

Case A60: Birthmark Removal (probably 1950s)

Sam Kriebel's third child was born with a birthmark on the top of his head, bigger than a silver dollar. Sam's uncle came up and brushed it a little bit, then said something over it and blew on it. He said, "That should take care of it." A few months later, the birthmark was gone.

Case A61: Wart Removal (1955)

Karen, a young Pennsylvania Dutch woman who works for the York County government, reports (June 1999) that her father (since deceased) was "powwowed" at age thirteen to remove a wart from his foot. The powwower took half a potato and rubbed it on his foot at the site of the wart, then buried the potato so that it faced east or west (Karen could not remember which). The wart subsequently vanished. The younger people pooh-poohed it, but her father believed in powwowing. His sister was also powwowed as a child in order to gain weight—now she's six feet tall and jokes that her parents should never have had it done.

Cases A62–A63 are from Tom Clemens, a farmer in southern Schuylkill County. Both take place in 1955 and deal with pneumonia.

Case A62: Cure for Pneumonia (1955)

Tom Clemens's first experience with powwowing was when his mother got pneumonia in March 1955, following the death of his father:

> I took her to a doctor in Stroudsburg. He said there was nothing he could do. He said she was going to die. Her fever was 105 or 106 degrees. She was really sick. On the way home I said to my

> wife, "There must be something you can do." So I thought of this guy over next—Old Man Horne. I told him the room number of the hospital in Stroudsburg and the next day we came out, Mom was sitting in bed smiling. The doctor said he didn't know what happened, and I never told him. Then I started believing in powwowing.

Case A63: Cure for pneumonia (1955)

Later that year, Tom Clemens's brother in South Dakota also got pneumonia. His nephew called him and said, "Can you get a powwow for Dad? He's in the hospital with pneumonia." Tom reports, "At ten o'clock at night he said, 'I knew you had powwowed for me.'" His brother recovered from pneumonia, but the fact that he was in the hospital renders the success of the powwowing problematic.

Cases A64–A65 are reported by Sara Maynard Clark (1956) and have to do with her experiences with a powwower in Bucks County.

Case A64: Cure for Headache (1955)

Sara Clark had a terrible headache and learned of a "powwow doctor" living less than ten miles from Doylestown, from a man who had his dog powwowed. Aspirin and newer medications were ineffective, so she went to see him and took a friend.

The powwow doctor lived in a small stone house and was elderly, although "smooth shaven, strictly modern," in appearance. He had been powwowing for more than forty years (since before 1915). Sara was ushered into a tiny room off the parlor where she told the powwow doctor about her headache.

The powwow doctor stood behind her—Sara does not say whether she was sitting or standing—and passed his hands over her head, "flicking them away as though brushing away the pain," speaking inaudibly. He repeated this three times. Sara characterized the experience as "quick and businesslike." She indicated that powwow doctors never charge but will usually accept "any folding money the patient is inclined to give."

The symptoms remained after the treatment, but several days later Sara realized that the pain in her head had "vanished." She was undecided about whether the powwowing was the cause of her relief or not.

Case A65: Powwow for Good Luck Talisman (1956)

(Note: Sara Clark uses the word "charm" interchangeably with "talisman." Both descriptors here are equivalent to what I call an "amulet.")

A friend of Sara Clark went to see the same powwow doctor for a talisman that she could wear. The powwow doctor told her he could not make up the charm while she waited, because a number of factors had to be considered, such as the phase of the moon, "especially in connection with her birth date." When he finished the charm, it was to be sewn up in a small, white sack (similar to the "gigger"; see Chapter 5, case 6) that the client must never open.

The same client informed Sara that the powwow doctor had questioned her about her various ailments and symptoms and after ten minutes gave her the same diagnosis that physicians had arrived at after two years of tests and examinations. Clark suggests telepathy as a possible reason for this, noting that the powwow doctor was "a firm believer in mental telepathy."

Case A66: Hex Removal to Cure Disease (late 1950s)

When Tina, a woman from north of Lebanon, was a young girl, her sister was sick and her grandmother believed it was due to a hex. She went to a "powwow lady" down the street who agreed to heal the child. The powwower took an egg and had the sick child urinate on it. Then she stuck a needle into the egg and buried it. Within three days a woman came to the house and said she had not been able to "go to the bathroom" since that time. She demanded to know where the egg was buried, but no one would tell her. Soon after she went away, the child recovered from the disease—the hex had come off.

After this, I asked Tina if she believed in "powwowing." She said no, but she did not believe there was anything wrong with it. I asked her why, and she replied simply, "I just don't." I suspect that she may not want to be associated with belief in powwowing, possibly for the same reason that she declined to be recorded on tape: "I sound very Dutchified," she explained.

Case A67: Wart Removal (about 1959)

A waitress in Lebanon County recalls that she was powwowed for warts in Reading (Berks County) by a man who was part-Amerindian and part–Pennsylvania Dutch. She did not remember the event well, but when I asked whether he had moved his hands over her and muttered something, she said yes. She was more certain about the hand movements than the muttering. She attributed his power to his Amerindian ethnicity.

Cases A68–A69 were experienced by Abe Roan, a local historian in Montgomery County.

Case A68: Cure for Warts (1959)

Abe Roan was powwowed by a young woman in Kutztown (Berks County) in order to remove warts. He was "not much of a believer" at the time. She laid his hand on her lap and stroked it three times and repeated some words in Pennsylvania Dutch (which he did not understand well) three times. The wart went away in three months.

Case A69: Curing a Wart (1962)

Abe Roan was working on an Amish farm and developed a wart. Ivan Fisher, a young Amish boy working with him, offered to take care of it. Fisher rubbed Abe's hand once and said in Pennsylvania Dutch:

> Warts geh weh in namen Vater
> Warts geh weh in namen Sohn
> Warts geh weh in namen Heilige Geist

In English:

> Warts go away in the name of the Father
> Warts go away in the name of the Son
> Warts go away in the name of the Holy Spirit

The wart went away overnight.

Case A70: Curing Livergrown (early 1960s)

Florida Ross[9] (Lehigh County) reports that her mother, who lived in Northampton County, had her sister "pollywagged" for an illness that fits the description of livergrown. The procedure involved the customary treatment of passing the child around a table:

Florida: My mother lived in Steel City, and her mother lived in Selingsburg. So to take her to her mother's house is about a mile down the road. It was a real rough road then, and the strollers had maybe two bumpy wheels in the back and one in the front. Maybe it was the kind that turned around. They had four wheels—I don't know.

It was a real rough ride, and my sister was a cranky child, and they put that together and figured it was because of the rough ride in the stroller that she was cranky, so they had to undo this so they pollywagged her around the kitchen table. So they literally put her around the kitchen table three or four times, and she was suppose to have gotten better.

David: How did they move her round the table?

Florida: From what I understand, they just took her head and took her around the table.

David: Three times?

Florida: Yeah. Three or four times. You should talk to my mother. She's the one that did it.

Unfortunately, due to time constraints, I was not able to interview Florida's mother at that time to get more information.

9. Pseudonym.

Case A71: Curing Livergrown (early 1960s)

Joyce Doxtater's eldest daughter had livergrown as an infant. Lizzie Kreider, a Plain woman (Brethren), powwowed for it by running her hands over her chest and stomach. The process took a few minutes.

Case A72: Curing Livergrown (early 1960s)

Elaine Madeira's eldest daughter was diagnosed with livergrown by her father, Mr. Sunday, who powwowed for it by passing her around table legs. Elaine describes the process:

Elaine: My oldest daughter, when she was born she was colicky, and them children, they cried all the time mostly and would get really severe stomachaches. So my father would come up and we'd pass her around the table leg. Nobody could be in the room but my father and I. Daddy and I used to do that. We'd pass her around one way, then pass her around the other way, and then he would say something. I couldn't remember what it was.

David: Was he speaking in Dutch?

Elaine: Yes. He'd say something. He believed when children were small like that and they were colicky from riding home in the car, they'd get livergrown.

David: When you passed her around the table leg, how did you hold her?

Elaine: Like that (*demonstrated holding the infant*).

David:

Would you crawl around the table with her?

Elaine: No. We weren't allowed to get underneath the table. If Daddy was going around one side, I'd have to reach under and he'd pass her to me on her back, and then we'd go to the next table leg and I'd pass her through, and he would take her. And that's the way we did it around the whole table.

David: How many legs did the table have?

Elaine: Four.

David: Do you know if the number four was special, or was it just however many legs it happened to be?

Elaine: I think it was just how many legs it happened to be.

David: If there were six, they'd do six?
Elaine: Yes. It was like a weaving thing though. It wasn't like pass her through and catch her on one side then take her to the other side.
David: You would make one circle of the table. He would say something. Would he lay hands on her?
Elaine: He would put his hands on her stomach and say something.

After this treatment, the daughter got well and ceased being colicky. Elaine would not hesitate to go to a powwower today.

Case A73: Curing Burns (mid-late 1960s)

This account concerns powwower Calvin E. Rahn (Lewis 1969, 183), who reported that a man was rushed in to see him with third-degree burns of the arm. "I 'blowed' his fire, and by night he was cured."

Case A74: Healing Swollen Ankles (late 1960s)

Helen Bechtel, one of the few Roman Catholic powwowers (Carbon County), performed this healing ritual in the presence of Arthur Lewis (1969, 205) at the request of the patient, Mrs. Dougherty, who was present at the interview. Mrs. Bechtel had Mrs. Dougherty remove her shoes and carefully examined the patient's ankles. She then went into the kitchen to get a bottle filled with what she called "holy water." Mrs. Bechtel splashed the patient's ankles liberally with the holy water, then touched both ankles lightly with her hands. Slowly she moved her hands up over the patient's legs and body, stopping at the top of her head, where Mrs. Bechtel rested her fingers for a few minutes.

Mrs. Bechtel then bent down on her knees in front of the patient and whispered softly for at least ten minutes. Then she made the sign of the cross, rose, sprinkled the patient with holy water again, tossed some at Lewis, then stoppered the bottle. She promised the patient that she would be better soon and advised her to throw away her orthopedic shoes.

Lewis had the chance to speak with Mrs. Bechtel, who was a retired nurse, after they left the house. Mrs. Dougherty reported that she had a "very strange feeling": "While Helen was touching my ankles and working her fingers up to my head, it was almost as though she was drawing the pain from my feet and moving it through my body and out through the top. Actually, my feet do feel a lot better now. Best they've felt in years." Mrs. Dougherty had known Mrs. Bechtel for a long time, knew of her remarkable cures, and believed she was absolutely sincere.

Case A75: Healing a Sore (late 1960s)

Rick Shaw reports that his family powwower, Mrs. McClure, would rub her finger on the sore and speak a verse from the Bible to remove that sore. However, as was her practice, she spoke in such a way that he could not understand what she was saying.

Case A76: Wart Removal (1960s)

An anonymous consultant in York County informed me (in June 1999) that her ex-husband had a "mole" removed by a female "powwow" in York County when he was a boy. The powwower rubbed a potato (when asked, the man's ex-wife believed it was half a potato) on his hand at the site of the mole and buried it in his backyard. The mole subsequently went away. Because this is a common procedure for wart removal, I believe either that the "mole" was actually a wart and that my consultant had misremembered the details, or that the term "wart" used in the literature to describe problems treated this way actually refers to an entire class of skin eruptions that resemble warts but that can also include moles.

Case A77: Cure for Teething ("Cutting the Teeth") (late 1960s–early 1970s)

My consultant Sarah reports that her powwower, Gertie Guise (Adams County), helped with the teething pain of Sarah's children. Sarah again does not name her in this account.

> There's some good in powwow, but if you do wrong, that's not good. That's like with everything.
>
> I used the powwow [Mrs. Guise] for the cutting of the teeth

in my children. What they did there was take an egg—I'm assuming it was a hardboiled egg. I don't know for sure—and they would put it in the little children's mouth. Then you were to take that egg with you when you left and put it at the highest point in your house. So my thing was in the attic in the eaves. I don't live in the same house, and I don't know what happened to the egg, to be truthful. It was to relieve the pain and for the teeth.

Case A78: Preventive Measures (1971)

Joyce Doxtater went to be "powwowed" for bad nerves at the urging of Nora Gearhart, her husband's grandmother. She went to Nora's powwower, Frank Frederick, who lived between Lititz and Rossville. The bad nerves derived from a car accident in which Joyce was injured: "Every time I'd hear a car screeching or something . . . kind of shake you up. So I went with her."[10]

He had her sit in a straight-back chair while he ran his hands over her arms, upper back, and lower back, touching her as he moved. She thinks he "mumbled something" as he worked. "He went kind of over me and said I was going to have inward problems, but now I won't. Now, at that time, I had been having some gall bladder problems and never—my doctor never pursued that I should go get gall bladder tests or anything, so I don't know if that's what I was gonna have, but to this day I haven't had any . . . inward problems."

She and Nora (who was also powwowed that day for an ailment Joyce does not remember) each left two or three dollars on the table as they left.

Case A79: Healing a Burn (1973)

According to an article on powwowing in the *Philadelphia Inquirer* (1976), Judy McMullin's son burned himself badly on a motorcycle exhaust pipe. Blisters rose on his leg. She "held his hand and prayed, not really expecting it to help." Suddenly the boy stopped crying and said, "Mommy, it doesn't hurt anymore."

10. This appears to be post-traumatic stress disorder.

Case A80: Cure for Eczema (probably 1970s)

Ruth Strickland (later Frey) powwowed Harriet Miller to cure her eczema. The cure required eight sessions, each lasting two and a half hours. During that time, Mrs. Strickland urged her not to take her medication for eczema. Harriet consulted with her physician, a Seventh-Day Adventist, and he said it was okay to cut back. She began the process on Good Friday and the eczema was gone by Memorial Day.

Case A81: Curing a nervous condition (1970s)

Sarah recounts how Gertie Guise (and Preston Zerbe) would cure nerves: "Mrs. Guise . . . would hold your hand and mumble something. But you couldn't hear. She would press her hands on the forehead. She would be in the back of me. Her arms were out here [gesturing in front of her face]. That had something to do with the nerves."

Case A82: Healing a Burst Gall Bladder (1981)

Ruth Frey (Lehigh County) powwowed for Harriet Miller's gall bladder when it "burst." Harriet said Mrs. Frey "de-toxicated" her. She had Harriet sit in a chair and hold the Bible, then ran her hands over her. Harriet had one treatment every week for four weeks. At the end of that time, the gall bladder was better.

Case A83: Healing Burns (1981)

Before Daisy and Julius Dietrich learned powwowing, their granddaughter was terribly burned by a curling iron. They took her to see their neighbor Robert Frantz, who healed the burn "right away." Daisy describes seeing "the heat rising" as he worked. After the treatment, "it didn't bother her whatsoever," Daisy said, and continued, "She stopped crying. It actually had blisters already. That's how bad it was." The treatment even removed the blisters: "The blisters was gone. But by the time they left for home, you could just bite that upper portion of that shin right off, and it didn't bother that child. Because all that inflammation had left. To this day, there never was a scar there."

Case A84: Healing an Injured Foot (1980s)

After the death of Gertie Guise, Sarah became a client of Preston Zerbe, whom Mrs. Guise had instructed. Her son, who worked in a foundry, hurt his foot on the job. Zerbe told Sarah how to release the pain and stop the bleeding by using two scripture verses.

> Also, I had the blood—a cut. In this case my son worked at a foundry, and he was in a kiln. Some foundry stuff fell on his foot and cooked his toes. I was immediately in contact with Preston Zerbe to relieve the pain. However, he did not ever see him—was through me. All I did was call up and say the problem. These are two scriptures from the Bible, but I don't know them, and I think they [Preston Zerbe and Mrs. Guise] probably used those scriptures.

Case A85: Curing a Nervous Condition (early 1990s)

Sarah indicated that Preston Zerbe practiced Gertie Guise's method of healing nerves. Sarah did not have this done to her personally, but learned it as part of her beginning powwow training. As a nontraditional healer herself, she recommends that her patients see a "powwow" for this if she believes they need to have this done.

Case A86: Cure for Cellulitis (early 1990s)

Tom Clemens, a farmer and Army veteran in Schuylkill County, believes he got cellulitis after injuring a toenail. He visited Daisy Dietrich after seeking biomedical treatment.

I had an injured toenail, and I used to cut it out myself. But every few weeks it would come back again. Then I went to the foot doctor [presumably a podiatrist⟧, and he said he could fix it. Then I got this ⟦cellulitis⟧. I was out delivering hay, and it was a dirty place and maybe I picked up something up there. I had Daisy[11] work on it three times. You have to wait so many weeks. Then I went back again.

I don't think powwowing is that hard to learn. Of course, you have to remember how to do it. She does it in German and English.[12]

Tom is now a vocal advocate of Daisy's ability.

Case A87: Cure for Cancer (unsuccessful) (probably 1990s)

Mr. F, of northwestern Lehigh County, had a friend who sought a cure for cancer and followed procedures that sound like powwowing. The following account is incomplete because it is from someone who did not witness much of the actual procedures used. It is told from the point of view of a disbeliever who actively opposes the practice of powwowing.

David: Do you think people around here ⟦Allentown⟧ still believe in hexes, or do you think they pretty much don't? Do you believe in them?

F: No. I had an old friend. She had cancer and the doctors told her to go home. She reverted back to the powwowing phase, homeopathic medicine, and she truly believed that certain things she said, certain things that she did, certain things that she ate in certain sequences would prolong her life. But that wasn't so. I respected her because she was a fine woman.

David: It didn't help her? Was she a powwow? Did she see a powwow doctor?

F: No, but I think she was very versed in it because she said certain things that resembled what I would consider powwowing. She said certain verses even though she was a Christian, and she went to church every Sunday. Her husband tried to discourage some of these things, but he respected her wishes.

11. Tom also had Daisy use powwow to help his brother stop smoking after his brother moved back to the area (Allentown).

12. I am unsure how Tom learned this fact because I have been treated by Daisy and found her to be virtually inaudible. Perhaps they were discussing it and she told him.

David: She used books? Did she use the Bible or *Long Lost Friend*?

F: I don't know where she got the verses, but I know they were kind of strange. I mean I wouldn't say certain things like that. Of course, she did read her Bible. I don't know if she took anything out of there or not. But some of the things she said did not make sense, but they were composed and she seemed to memorize them.

David: Do you know what the lady's name was?

F: I don't want to degrade the family. She was such a wonderful person. To say something against the family is not very Christian. Your neighbors are supposed to be as loyal to you as you are to them.

Cases A88–A89 deal with my consultant Leah Stoltzfus, an Old Order Amish woman in Lancaster County. Both derive from an article on powwowing in a midwestern newspaper, although I was able to interview Leah personally about case A88.

Case A88: Cure for Brain Problems (unsuccessful) (mid-1990s)

An Amish woman who was dissatisfied with Leah Stoltzfus's treatments told the newspaper reporter that her teenage nephew visited Leah for an unspecified cerebral problem that eventually led to brain surgery. "Leah put her hands on him, and that was supposed to help. But she didn't cure him." The account was confirmed by the boy's father.

I asked Leah about this case, and she claims that the account of the boy's aunt is biased because the aunt prefers biomedical treatment: "We [[presumably Leah was assisted by her husband]] did relieve him a lot, but he finally did get surgery after all. But [[the aunt]] was a doctor person. Some people want to run to a doctor."

Case A89: Cure for Skin Spots (unsuccessful) (mid-1990s)

The same Amish woman complained that Leah Stoltzfus was unsuccessful in removing some unwanted spots from her skin. She also thought Leah's treatment was odd: "With me, she held her hand over me and her mouth did this strange yapping. Then I ended up buying some of her vitamins for these spots I've been getting on my skin."

The vitamins seemed to have no effect on the woman's skin. The "yapping" she is referring to is almost certainly Leah's response to sensing pain. When I witnessed it, she made a popping sound.

BIBLIOGRAPHY

Albertus Magnus. c. 1900. *Albertus Magnus, Being the approved, verified, sympathetic and natural Egyptian secrets; or, White and black art for man and beast.* Hackensack, N.J.: Wehman Brothers.

Astin, John, Elaine Harkness, and Edzard Ernst. 2000. "The Efficacy of 'Distant Healing': A Systematic Review of Randomized Trials." *Annals of Internal Medicine* 132, no. 11: 903–10.

Aurand, Ammon Monroe. 1929. *The "Pow-Wow" Book*. Harrisburg: Aurand.

———. 1942. *The Realness of Witchcraft in America: Witch-Doctors, Pow-Wows, Hexerei, Angels, Devils, Hex, Sex: Witches or No Witches, You Should Read This Account*. Harrisburg, Pa.: Aurand.

———. 1979. *Popular Home Remedies and Superstitions of the Pennsylvania-Germans*. Lancaster, Pa.: Aurand.

Bailer, Aunt Sophia. 1952a. "Witches . . . I Have Known." *The Pennsylvania Dutchman*, May: 8.

———. 1952b. "How to Stop a Witch." *The Pennsylvania Dutchman*, May: 8–9.

———. 1952c. "How I Learned Powwowing." *The Pennsylvania Dutchman*, June: 8.

———. 1952d. "How I Pow Vow [*sic*] for *Rote Laufa*." *The Pennsylvania Dutchman*, July: 5.

Barney, Sandra Lee. 2000. *Authorized to Heal: Gender, Class, and the Transformation of Medicine in Appalachia, 1880-1930*. Chapel Hill: University of North Carolina Press.

Barrick, Mac E. 1987. *German-American Folklore*. Little Rock, Ark.: August House.

Beam, C. Richard, ed. 1995. *The Thomas R. Brendle Collection of Pennsylvania Dutch Folklore*. Lancaster, Pa.: Historic Schaefferstown.

Beissel, James D. 1998. *Powwow Power*. Willow Street, Pa.: Crystal Education Counselors.

Benson, Herbert. 1997. *Timeless Healing: The Power and Biology of Belief*. New York: Simon & Schuster.

Berger, Peter L. 1969. *The Sacred Canopy: Elements of a Sociological Theory of Religion*. Garden City, N.Y.: Anchor Books.

———. 1971. *A Rumour of Angels: Modern Society and the Rediscovery of the Supernatural*. London: Penguin.

Boyer, Dennis. *Once Upon a Hex*. Oregon, Wisc.: Badger Books, 2004.

Brendle, Thomas R., and Claude Unger. 1935. *Folk Medicine of the Pennsylvania Dutch: The Non-Occult Cures*. Proceedings of the Pennsylvania Dutch Society 45. Norristown, Pa.

Burch, Edith White. 1938. "Barricke Mariche: Mountain Mary". *Historical Review of Berks County* 4, no. 1: 6–10.

Canon, Scott. 1996. "Amish 'Voodoo' Implies Belief in Healing Power." *Kansas City (Missouri) Star*. October 21.

Cassedy, James H. 1991. *Medicine in America: A Short History*. Baltimore: Johns Hopkins University Press.

Chambers, Reuben. 1842. *The Thomsonian Practice of Medicine*. Bethania, Pa.

Chevalier, Jean, and Alain Gheerbrant 1996. *The Penguin Dictionary of Symbols*. Translated by John Buchanan-Brown. London: Penguin.

Circlot, S.E. 1983. *A Dictionary of Symbols*. Translated by Jack Sage. New York: Philosophical Library.

Clark, Sara Maynard. 1956. "White Magic." *Bucks County Traveler* 8, no. 1 (October).

Commonwealth v. John Blymire. 1929. Transcript. York County Courts of Oyer and Terminer, no. 1.

Cowen, David L. 1987. "The Folk Medicine of the Pennsylvania Dutch." In *Folklore and Folk Medicines*, ed. John Scarborough. Madison, Wisc.: American Institute of the History of Pharmacy.

Csordas, Thomas J. 1994. *The Sacred Self: A Cultural Phenomenology of Charismatic Healing*. Berkeley and Los Angeles: University of California Press.

———. 1996. "Imaginal Performance and Memory in Ritual Healing." In *The Performance of Healing*, ed. Carol Laderman and Marina Roseman. London: Routledge.

D'Andrade, Roy. 1987 "A Folk Model of the Mind." In *Cultural Models in Language and Thought*, ed. Dorothy Holland and Naomi Quinn, 112–48. Cambridge: Cambridge University Press.

Dieffenbach, Victor C. 1975–76. "Powwowing Among the Pennsylvania Dutch." *Pennsylvania Folklife* 25, no. 2: 29–46.

Dluge, Robert L., Jr. 1972. "My Interview with a Powwower." *Pennsylvania Folklife* 21 (Summer): 39–42.

Dossey, Larry. 1993. *Healing Words: The Power of Prayer and the Practice of Medicine*. San Francisco: HarperSanFrancisco.

Douglas, Mary. 1996. *Natural Symbols: Explorations in Cosmology*. New York: Routledge.

Estep, Glenn, and William Pietchke. 1949. "A Study of Certain Aspects of Spiritualism and Pow-Wow in Regard to the Folklore of Lancaster County." *The Pennsylvania Dutchman* (volume and page unknown).

Finkler, Kaja. 1998. "Sacred Healing and Biomedicine Compared." In *Understanding and Applying Medical Anthropology*, ed. Peter J. Brown, 118–28. New York: Mayfield.

Firth, Raymond. 1973. *Symbols, Public and Private*. Symbol, Myth, and Ritual Series, ed. Victor Turner. Ithaca: Cornell University Press.

Fogel, Edwin. 1915. "Beliefs and Superstition of The Pennsylvania Germans." Publications of The Pennsylvania German Folklore Society, 18.

Foster, George M. 1998. "Disease Etiologies in Non-Western Medical Systems." In *Understanding and Applying Medical Anthropology*, ed. Peter J. Brown, 110–17. New York: Mayfield.

Foster, George M., and Barbara G. Anderson. 1978. *Medical Anthropology*. New York: Wiley & Sons.

Frazer, Sir James. 1922. *The Golden Baugh: A Study in Magic and Religion*. New York: Macmillan.

Frese, Pamela, ed. 1993. *Celebrations of Identity: Multiple Voices in American Ritual Performance*. Westport, Conn.: Bergin & Garvey.

Good, Byron. 1994. *Medicine, Rationality, and Experience: An Anthropological Perspective*. Cambridge: Cambridge University Press.

Goodenough, Ward H. 1965. "Rethinking 'Status' and 'Role': Toward a General Model of the Cultural Organization of Social Relationships." In *The Relevance of Models for Social Anthropology*, ed. Michael Banton. London: Tavistock.

———. 1971. "Culture, Language, and Society." *Current Topics in Anthropology: Theory, Methods, and Content*, vol. 2, module 7. Reading, Mass.: Addison-Wesley.

Gourley, Norma Mae. 1936. "Some Phases of Witchcraft Among the Pennsylvania Dutch." M.A. thesis. University of Illinois. Reprinted in *The Pennsylvania Dutchman* 5, no. 14: 7–8.

Graham, Robert L. 1951. "The Pow-Wow Doctor." *The Pennsylvania Dutchman*, April: 2.

Hahn, Robert A. 1995. *Sickness and Healing: An Anthropological Perspective*. New Haven: Yale University Press.

Hand, Wayland D. 1980. *Magical Medicine*. Berkeley and Los Angeles: University of California Press.

———, ed. 1976. American Folk Medicine: A Symposium. Berkeley and Los Angeles: University of California.

Heindel, Ned D. 2005. *Hexenkopf: History, Healing, and Hexerei*.

Herr, Karl. 2002. *Hex and Spellwork: The Magical Practices of the Pennsylvania Dutch*. York Beach, Maine: Weiser.

Hochstetler, Dean. 1978. Letter to Gerald Studer, July 1. Studer Collection, Mennonite Heritage Center, Harleysville, Pa.

Hohman, John George. 1971 (1820). *Pow-wows, or The Long Lost Friend*. Pomeroy, Wash.: Health Research.

Holland, Dorothy, and Naomi Quinn, eds. 1987. *Cultural Models in Language and Thought*. Cambridge: Cambridge University Press.

Hostetler, John A. 1976. "Folk Medicine and Sympathy Healing Among the Amish." In *American Folk Medicine: A Symposium*, ed. Wayland D. Hand, 249–58. Berkeley and Los Angeles: University of California Press.

———. 1983. *Mennonite Life*. Scottdale, Pa.: Herald.

———, ed. 1992. *Amish Roots: A Treasury of History, Wisdom, and Lore*. Baltimore: Johns Hopkins University Press.

———. *Amish Society*. 1993. Baltimore: Johns Hopkins University Press.

Hufford, David J. 1982. *The Terror That Comes in the Night: An Experience-Centered Study of Supernatural Assault Traditions*. Philadelphia: University of Pennsylvania Press, 1982.

———. 1992. "Folk Medicine in Contemporary America." In *Herbal and Magical Medicine: Traditional Healing Today*, ed. James Kirkland, Holly F. Matthews, C. W. Sullivan III, and Karen Baldwin, 14–31. Durham, N.C.: Duke University Press.

———. 1995. "Beings Without Bodies: An Experience-Centered Theory of the Belief in Spirits." In *Out of the Ordinary: Folklore and the Supernatural*, ed. Barbara Walker, 11–45. Logan: Utah State University Press.

———. 1998. "Beings Without Bodies." Unpublished manuscript. ms.

Jordan, Mildred. 1978. *The Distelfink Country of the Pennsylvania Dutch*. New York: Crown.

Kemp, Phyllis. 1935. *Healing Ritual: Studies in the Technique and Tradition of the Southern Slavs*. London: Faber & Faber.

Kett, Joseph F. 1968. *The Formation of the American Medical Profession: The Role of Institutions, 1780–1860*. New Haven: Yale University Press.

King, Francis. 1975. *Magic: The Western Tradition*. London: Thames & Hudson.

King, Lester S. 1991. *Transformations in American Medicine: From Benjamin Rush to William Osler*. Baltimore: Johns Hopkins University Press.

Kirkland, James, Holly F. Mathews, C. W. Sullivan III, and Karen Baldwin, eds. 1992. *Herbal and Magical Medicine: Traditional Healing Today*. Durham, N.C.: Duke University Press.

Klees, Fredric. 1950. *The Pennsylvania Dutch*. New York: Macmillan.

Kleinman, Arthur. 1980. *Patients and Healers in the Context of Culture*. London: University of California Press.

Knauss, James O. 1952. Letter. *The Pennsylvania Dutchman* 4, no. 6 (October).

Kriebel, David W. 2000. "Belief, Power, and Identity in Pennsylvania Dutch *Brauche*, or Powwowing." Ph.D. dissertation. Ann Arbor, Mich.: UMI.

Kuhn, Thomas S. 1962. *The Structure of Scientific Revolutions*. Chicago: University of Chicago Press.

Kulp, Clarence, Jr. 1978. Interview by Gerald Studer, September 12. Studer Collection, Mennonite Heritage Center, Harleysville, Pa.

Laderman, Carol, and Marina Roseman. 1996. "Introduction." In *The Performance of Healing*, ed. Carol Laderman and Marina Roseman. London: Routledge.

Landes, Simon M. 1853. *The American Improved Family Physician or Home Doctor*. Lancaster, Pa.: Independent-Whig.

Lewis, Arthur H. 1969. *Hex*. New York: Pocket Books.

Linde, Charlotte. 1993. *Life Stories: The Creation of Coherence*. New York: Oxford University Press.

Luhrmann, T. M. 1989. *Persuasions of the Witch's Craft: Ritual Magic in Contemporary England*. Cambridge: Harvard University Press.

"Magic Healing Among Berks County Rocks: Pow-wower Rhoads and His Big Family—Stone and Sticks—An Odd Habitation." 1895–99. *Reading Eagle* article. In Brown Scrap Book, 1895–99, Historical Society of Berks County, Reading, Pa.

Malinowski, Bronislaw. 1954. *Magic, Science, and Religion and Other Essays by Bronislaw Malinowski*. Garden City, N.Y.: Doubleday Anchor Books.

McClenon, James. 1995. "Supernatural Experience, Folk Belief, and Spiritual Healing." In *Out of the Ordinary: Folklore and the Supernatural*, ed. Barbara Walker, 107–21. Logan: Utah State University Press.

McGuire, Meredith B., and Debra Kantor. 1988. *Ritual Healing in Suburban America*. New Brunswick, N.J.: Rutgers University Press.

Miller, Levi. 1981. The Role of a Braucher-Chiropractor in an Amish Community." *Mennonite Quarterly Review* 55:157–71.

Millspaw, Yvonne J. 1978. "Witchcraft Belief in a Pennsylvania Dutch Family." *Pennsylvania Folklife* 27, no. 4: 14–24.

Morley, Peter, and Roy Wallis, eds. 1978. *Culture and Curing: Anthropological Perspectives on Traditional Medical Beliefs and Practices*. London: Peter Owen.

Newall, Venetia. 1971. *An Egg at Easter: A Folklore Study*. Bloomington: Indiana University Press.

Nyce, James M. 1987. "Convention, Power, and the Self in German Mennonite Magic." Ph.D. dissertation. Ann Arbor, Mich.: UMI, 1996. 8715542.

Orion, Loretta. 1995. *Never Again the Burning Times: Paganism Revived*. Prospect Heights, Ill.: Waveland.

"Peter Bausher—Powwower." 1953. *The Pennsylvania Dutchman* 4, no. 13 (March 1): 11, 15. Reprinted from an 1895 *New York Sun* article.

Pinch, Geraldine. 1994. *Magic in Ancient Egypt*. Austin: University of Texas Press.

RavenWolf, Silver. 1997. *HexCraft: Dutch Country Magick*. St. Paul: Llewellyn.

Reimensnyder, Barbara L. 1982. *Powwowing in Union County: A Study of Pennsylvania Dutch Folk Medicine in Context*. New York: AMS.

Rossi, Ernest Lawrence. 1993. *The Psychobiology of Mind-Body Healing*. New York: Norton.

Rubel, Arthur J., and Michael R. Hass. 1996. "Ethnomedicine." *Handbook of Medical Anthropology*. Westport, Conn.: Greenwood Press.

Scarborough, John, ed. 1987. *Folklore and Folk Medicines*. Madison, Wisc.: American Institute of the History of Pharmacy.

Schlabach, Erv. 1978. Letter to Gerald Studer, September 5. Studer Collection, Mennonite Heritage Center, Harleysville, Pa.

Schreiber, Karen. 1976. "The Strange Art of Pow-Wow Healing." In *Today: The Inquirer Magazine*. in *Philadelphia Inquirer*, February 22 (n.p.).

Shaner, Richard. 1951. "The Pow-Wow Doctor." *The Pennsylvania Dutchman*, April 1: 2.

———. 1961. "Powwow Doctors." *Pennsylvania Folklife* 12, no. 2 (Summer): 72.

Shapiro, Arthur K., and Elaine Shapiro. 1997. *The Powerful Placebo: From Ancient Priest to Modern Physician*. Baltimore: Johns Hopkins University Press.

Shoemaker, William P. 1951. "A Hex and a Head of Cabbage." *The Pennsylvania Dutchman*, January: 2.

Shore, Bradd. 1996. *Culture in Mind: Cognition, Culture, and the Problem of Meaning*. New York: Oxford University Press.

Siegel, Sidney, and N. John Castellan. 1988. *Nonparametric Statistics for the Behavioral Sciences*. Second ed. New York: McGraw-Hill.

Snellenburg, Betty. 1969. "Four Interviews with Powwowers." *Pennsylvania Folklife* 18, no. 4: 40–45.

Snow, Loudell F. 1977. "The Religious Component in Southern Folk Medicine." In *Traditional Healing: New Science or New Colonialism?* Ed. Philip Singer. New York: Conch Magazine.

Stein, Howard F. 1990. *American Medicine as Culture*. San Francisco: Westview.

Stewart, Susan. 1976. "Rational Powwowing: An Examination of Choice among Medical Alternatives in Rural York County, Pennsylvania." *Pennsylvania Folklife* 26, no. 1: 12–17.

Strauss, Claudia, and Naomi Quinn. 1997. *A Cognitive Theory of Cultural Meaning*. Cambridge: Cambridge University Press.

Studer, Gerald C. 1980. "Powwowing: Folk Medicine or White Magic?" *Pennsylvania Mennonite Heritage*, July: 17–23.

Turner, Edith. 1992. *Experiencing Ritual*. Philadelphia: University of Pennsylvania Press.

———. 1993. "American Eskimos Celebrate the Whale: Structural Dichotomies and Spirit Identities Among the Inupiat of Alaska." In *Celebrations of Identity: Multiple Voices in American Ritual Performance*, ed. Pamela R. Freese, 15–34. Westport, Conn.: Bergin & Garvey.

———. 1996. *The Hands Feel It: Healing and Spirit Presence Among a Northern Alaska People*. Dekalb, Ill.: Northern Illinois University Press.

Turner, Victor. 1967. *The Forest of Symbols*. Ithaca: Cornell University Press.

———. 1982. *The Ritual Process: Structure and Anti-Structure*. Ithaca: Cornell University Press.

———. 1988. *The Anthropology of Performance*. New York: PAJ Publications.

Walker, Barbara, ed. 1995. *Out of the Ordinary*. Ogden: Utah State University Press.

Wallace, Anthony F. C. 1956. "Mazeway Resynthesis: A Biocultural Theory of Religious Inspiration." *Transactions of the New York Academy of Sciences* 18:626–38.

———. 1966. *Religion: An Anthropological Approach*. New York: Random House.

———. 1967. "Identity Processes in Personality and in Culture." In *Cognition, Personality, and Clinical Psychology*, ed. Richard Jessor and Seymour Feshback, 62–89. San Francisco: Jossey-Bass.

———. 1970. *Culture and Personality*. Second edition. New York: Random House.

Wallace, Anthony F. C., and Raymond Fogelson. 1965. "The Identity Struggle." In *Intensive Family Therapy*, ed. Ivan Boszormenyi-Nagy and James Framo, 365–406. New York: Harper & Row.

Weiser, Daniel. 1868, "*Braucherei*" (originally published in "The Guardian," a Lutheran or Reformed periodical in the Dutch country (presumably Berks County, due to local references) in 1868. Reprinted by *The Pennsylvania Dutchman* 5, no. 14: 5–6.

Weiss, Gregory L., and Lynne E. Lonnquist. 2000. *The Sociology of Health, Healing, and Illness*. Upper Saddle River, N.J.: Prentice-Hall.

West, Edward N. 1989. *Outward Signs: The Language of Christian Symbolism*. New York: Walker.

Westkott, Marcia. 1969–70. "Powwowing in Berks County." *Pennsylvania Folklife* 19, no. 2: 2–9.

Yoder, Don. 1951. "Aunt Sophia Bailer: Saint of the Coal Regions." *Pennsylvania Dutchman* 3, no. 3 (June 1): 1.

———. 1952. Letter from Aunt Sophia Bailer of Tremont, Pa. *The Pennsylvania Dutchman* 4, no. 3 (July): 5.

———. 1967. "Twenty Questions on Powwowing." *Pennsylvania Folklife* 17, no. 4: 38–40.

———. 1976. "Hohman and Romanus: Origins and Diffusion of the Pennsylvania Dutch Powwow Manual." In *American Folk Medicine: A Symposium*, ed. Wayland D. Hand, 235–48. Berkeley and Los Angeles: University of California Press.

———. 1990. "Discovering American Folklife: Studies in Ethnic, Religious, and Regional Culture." Ann Arbor: University of Michigan.

INDEX

Page numbers in *italics* indicate tables, photographs, and graphs.

Pennsylvania German History and Culture Series,
Number 8

Publications of the Pennsylvania German Society,

Volume 41

Previous titles in the series

Margaret Reynolds, *Plain Women: Gender and Ritual in the Old Order River Brethren*, edited by Simon J. Bronner

Steven M. Nolt, *Foreigners in Their Own Land:*

Pennsylvania Germans in the Early Republic

Jeff Bach, *Voices of the Turtledoves: The Sacred World of Ephrata*

Corinne and Russell Earnest, *To the Latest Posterity: Pennsylvania-German Family Registers in the Fraktur Tradition*

David L. Weaver-Zercher, editor, *Writing the Amish: The Worlds of John A. Hostetler*

Don Yoder, *The Pennsylvania German Broadside: A History and Guide*

Donald B. Kraybill and James P. Hurd, *Horse-and-Buggy Mennonites: Hoofbeats of Humility in a Postmodern World*

The Pennsylvania German Society

The Pennsylvania German Society is a non-profit, educational and literary organization. Its purpose is to preserve, disseminate, and advance knowledge of the history and culture of the Pennsylvania German people and their 300-year history in America, including their contributions to the development of American society. To accomplish these purposes, the Society promotes scholarly research, publishes in print and other media, and offers educational programs of interest to the membership and the general public.

www.pgs.org